# LAW IN AN ERA OF "SMART" TECHNOLOGY

# LAW IN AN ERA OF "SMART" TECHNOLOGY

By
Susan W. Brenner

OXFORD
UNIVERSITY PRESS

# OXFORD
## UNIVERSITY PRESS

*Oxford University Press, Inc., publishes works that further Oxford University's objective of excellence in research, scholarship, and education.*

Copyright © 2007 by Oxford University Press, Inc.
Published by Oxford University Press, Inc.
198 Madison Avenue, New York, New York 10016

Oxford is a registered trademark of Oxford University Press
Oceana is a registered trademark of Oxford University Press, Inc.

Library of Congress Cataloging-in-Publication Data

Brenner, Susan W., 1947-
  Law in an era of "smart" technology / By Susan W. Brenner.
    p. cm.
  Includes bibliographical references and index.
  ISBN 978-0-19-533348-0 (clothbound : alk. paper)   1.   Technology and law. 2.     Justice, Administration of—Technological innovations.
3.    Technological innovations—Law and legislation.   4.     Computers—Law and legislation   5.     High technology industries—Law and legislation. I. Title.
  K487.T4B74 2007
  344′.095—dc22                                                        2007023638

**Note to Readers:**

This publication is designed to provide accurate and authoritative information in regard to the subject matter covered. It is based upon sources believed to be accurate and reliable and is intended to be current as of the time it was written. It is sold with the understanding that the publisher is not engaged in rendering legal, accounting, or other professional services. If legal advice or other expert assistance is required, the services of a competent professional person should be sought. Also, to confirm that the information has not been affected or changed by recent developments, traditional legal research techniques should be used, including checking primary sources where appropriate.

*(Based on the Declaration of Principles jointly adopted by a Committee of the American Bar Association and a Committee of Publishers and Associations.)*

# Contents

# CHAPTER 1

# Introduction

In the twenty-first century the technology revolution will move into the everyday, the small and the invisible. The impact of technology will increase ten-fold as it is imbedded in the fabric of everyday life.[1]

## Phase Shift

Somewhen, in the not-too-distant future, Anne comes home from work. As she turns into the driveway of the family home, the garage door opens automatically, the home having anticipated her arrival. She gets out of the car and walks through a door that has been unlocked for her and into the kitchen. As she enters, she calls out, "any messages"? The communication system that is an integral part of intelligent technology installed in the home responds: "Richard will be at least half an hour late, and Jennie is having dinner at her friend Sharon's house." Anne goes upstairs, to the bedroom she shares with her husband (Richard). The house has turned on lights so she can see her way, and has a hot shower waiting for her in the bathroom she and Richard share. She showers, dresses and comes down to set the table for the dinner she and Richard will share. The house has cooked the main dish—a casserole she left before she went to work. As Ann sets the table, the house reminds her that she and Richard are expected at a dinner party the following evening.

Another somewhen, in the same not-too-distant future: Richard leaves home and drives to his office. As he nears the parking garage, the gate opens for him to enter; his assigned parking place is empty and as he walks toward the elevator he will take to his office, it arrives, ready to take him to his floor. Like the home he shares with Anne, the parking garage is equipped with embedded, intelligent technology

---

1    Alexandru Tugui, "Calm Technologies in a Multimedia World," *Ubiquity* (March 23, 2004): 5, http://www.acm.org/ubiquity/views/v5i4_tugui.html (quoting Mark Weiser).

that anticipates his arrival based on signals from sensors embedded in his vehicle. Intelligent technology in his office receives those signals and advises the co-workers with whom Richard will be meeting that he has arrived and will be in his office within a few minutes.

Same somewhen: Richard walks into his office and has a conversation with its intelligent technology. He asks about the meeting, and is told everyone is present and will be assembling in the meeting room in fifteen minutes. The communication system in his office tells him he has received four voicemails and twenty-five emails; in response to Richard's asking for details, it tells him whom each message is from and summarizes the content. Richard instructs the system to send a customized response to each message, telling each person he will respond in detail later. He also asks about, and is updated on, the status of several pending matters.

A different somewhen, in the rather-more-distant future: Anne leaves home on her way to work. She gets into her automated motor vehicle and instructs it to take her to an office building on the far side of town, where she has an early meeting. As the vehicle complies, Anne uses the interactive technology installed in the vehicle to check her voicemails and emails and to communicate with her own, artificially intelligent office. By the time the vehicle drops her off at the front of the building where her meeting will be held, she has dealt with several work-related matters, spoken to her daughter's teacher and made the final arrangements for a vacation she, Richard and their daughter will take the following month.

An even more different somewhen, in the probably-fairly-distant future: Richard gets up, breakfasts, interacts with the home technology on several domestic matters, showers, and dresses in comfortable clothes, after which he goes into the room he and Anne use as a home office. They each have a physical office in a remote building they can use if their actual presence is required there, for some reason. For the most part, though, Anne and Richard, like most people whose work does not involve interacting with the physical environment, use their home office if, indeed, that term is appropriate.

In this somewhen, Anne and Richard, like most everyone, have a computer interface embedded in their brains.[2] This interface allows them to communicate

---

[2]   For a detailed description of what this might involve, see Ramez Naam, *More Than Human* (New York: Broadway Books, 2005), 202–207.

directly with anyone who has a similar implant; those with implants can communicate verbally, using words, and they can also transmit images, sounds, emotions, and even abstract ideas to each other.[3] Their neural interfaces also allow them to communicate directly with computer systems that facilitate their interactions with other human beings by providing data, capturing the essence of what is communicated, and storing that information for future reference. The interfaces eliminate the need for face-to-face meetings, for the most part. Richard can sit in his home office and interact with anyone, anywhere in the world, as long as they have a compatible interface. Indeed, Richard could sit anywhere he liked and do this, but he tends to prefer using a dedicated space that lets him concentrate on the business matters at hand. Anne feels the same way.

A very, very different somewhen, in the presumably much-moredistant future: Humans have, in varying degrees, become cyborgs—a fusion of human biology and machine technology.[4] The "Enhanced," which is what those who have taken this route call themselves,[5] are stronger, smarter and more attractive (in an evolved way) than the few, stubborn "Naturals" who refuse machine enhancements.[6] The Enhanced are also functionally immortal.[7] They, though, are not the only intelligent citizens of this alien future; these fundamentally biological intelligences share this world with pure machine intelligences, conscious, self-aware nonbiological entities that are, for all intents and purposes, the equal of Enhanced humans in intelligence, creativity and emotional capacity.[8] The Singularity—the point at which technology irreversibly alters human life—has arrived.[9]

We can reasonably assume that some variants of these not-too-distant and rather-more-distant futures will come to pass based on technologies already in existence and those in development. No one knows if, or when, the Singularity will arrive; no one knows what the future of machine intelligence, and our relationship with it, will be.

---

[3]   See *id.*

[4]   See Joel Garreau, *Radical Evolution* (New York: Doubleday, 2004), 63. "Cyborg" is a human body that has been "altered and augmented" with machine technology.

[5]   See *id.* at 7–8.

[6]   See *id.* at 7–8.

[7]   See Ray Kurzweil, *The Singularity Is Near* (New York: Viking, 2005), 324–325.

[8]   See *id.* at 316–317, 376–380.

[9]   See Garreau, *Radical Evolution*, at 7.

I am not a futurist and I lay no claim to being able to predict what the future has in store for us. For that, I rely on the insights of many talented people who are futurists and/or who understand where technology seems to be taking us. My goal is not to write about technology as such, but to explore how technology has, and will, affect law.

## The Book

"Law and technology" is a common phrase, and many books (and articles) have been written on the topic. You might wonder, then, why we need another book dealing with "law and technology."

This is not, exactly, a book about "law and technology." It *is* about law, and it *is* about technology, so in that sense it *is* a book about "law and technology." This book, however, is not concerned with parsing details of the relationship that has so far existed between the two concepts. It does examine that relationship as it has evolved over the last several millennia, but this examination is merely a preface, an empirical foundation for the issue with which we are really concerned.

That issue is how the traditional relationship between law and technology must evolve to accommodate a fundamental shift in the nature of technology, one that has already begun. This shift will transform how we "use" technology; more precisely, it will change our relationship with technology from "using" technology to "interacting" with technology. As Chapter 6 explains, the shift will be the product of evolving ambient, or "smart," technologies.

Our history to date with technology has been one of "use"—an active, intelligent human being "uses" passive, "dumb" technology (a simple tool or mechanical device). Though many of these technologies are functionally complex, they operate only at the will of a human being; cars do not drive themselves, iPods do not entertain themselves, and Roombas do not decide when floors need cleaning. Some of these "dumb" technologies are able to carry out a level of activity on their own, but they all ultimately depend on us for their implementation . . . and their purpose. Unless we give these technologies "life" and goals by intentionally "using" them, they are nothing. Our laws assume this dynamic because it is all there has ever been.

Thanks to evolving computer technology, we are on the threshold of developing a new dynamic—one that will involve "interaction" rather than "use." This dynamic is the product of new, "smart" technologies: "things that think," as one expert put it.[10] Like their "dumb" predecessors, these "smart" technologies will exist to help us, to serve us, to make our lives easier and more interesting. (Assuming, of course, that the *Terminator* and other Franken-technology scenarios are indeed fantasy, not prophecy.)

Unlike their "dumb" predecessors, which exist for essentially the same reasons, these "smart" technologies will play a much more active role in our mutual endeavors. Instead of my office being the passive context in which I "use" twentieth-century-style "dumb" technology (a computer and a telephone, say), it becomes my partner: My new, "smart" office manages my calendar, vets my incoming voice and email communications, arranges my travel, handles research, creates presentations for me, and otherwise plays an active, essential role in my professional life.[11] This is only one example of how "smart" technology can, and will, be integrated into our lives; it will definitely not be reserved for our professional lives. As Chapter 6 explains, "smart" technologies will permeate our homes, our vehicles, our public buildings, and our public spaces.

The dynamic we will have with these "smart" technologies will be much more "egalitarian" than the dynamic we have always had with "dumb" technologies. The dynamic shifts from deliberate physical manipulation to an unconscious, presumed symbiosis. Some theorists who work in the area of ambient technology cite electricity as an analogue of "smart" technology; their goal is to make these "smart" technologies as ubiquitous, and as invisible, as electricity is to us. I am sitting in my study writing this on my laptop. I am aware that I am "using" the laptop, but until I began this topic, I was quite unaware that I am also "using" electricity. My awareness will be fleeting; electricity has come to my consciousness for the moment, but in a few seconds it will recede into the background and I will forget it, again.

My goal, to this point, is simply to illustrate how the "smart" technologies that are being developed (and deployed) differ from the technologies we have known so far. As the example given above and the scenarios with which this chapter began

---

[10]    Neil Gershenfeld, *When Things Start to Think* (New York: Owl Books, 2000), 11.
[11]    For more "smart" technology scenarios, see Chapter 6.

demonstrate, "smart" technologies differ from traditional "dumb" technologies in two important respects: One is that thanks to artificial intelligence, "smart" technologies are capable of acting on their own. They can therefore work with us by anticipating our needs and fulfilling them; they can also replace us by taking over certain tasks, such as operating motor vehicles. The second difference is that "smart" technologies are meant to be, and will be, unobtrusive; as noted above, they will fade into the background and disappear from our awareness. This is why they are commonly referred to as "ambient" technologies.

As the next four chapters explain, our law assumes "dumb" technology and the consequent "user" dynamic. This foundational assumption is actually an aggregate of accreted assumptions that have evolved over the centuries as "dumb" technologies became more complex and took on more functions. That the disconnect between this foundational assumption and the role modern technologies play in our lives and in our societies is accelerating is increasingly apparent—at least to those of us who work with law. Our emerging awareness of this disconnect has prompted some to call for remedial measures such as "updating our tech statutes," "adopting new tech laws," or "wiping the slate clean and starting over" with our statutory frameworks. None of these measures has been implemented, none of them is likely to be, and none is likely to be effective if it is implemented. These are traditional fixes for a nontraditional problem. We need to rethink—reconceptualize—the relationship that should exist between our law and our technology, a necessary but daunting undertaking, quite beyond the scope and ambitions of this book. My goal in this book is to explain *why* we need to reconceptualize this relationship and to offer some suggestions as to *how* we might best go about doing this.

Throughout most of this book, I assume a stark differentiation between "dumb" and "smart" technologies; I also assume that once "smart" technologies populate our environments, they will dominate to the point that "dumb" technologies will recede into insignificance, if not oblivion. Both assumptions are to some extent artificial; for at least a good part of the foreseeable future, we will certainly see a blending of the two types of technology. And I, at least, assume "dumb" technologies will always be with us. What, after all, would replace a hammer? (Perhaps I should ask, instead, if we really need a "smart" hammer.) I make these exaggerated assumptions because I believe they will make it easier to follow my exposition of how the relationship that currently exists between law and technology evolved and also my argument as to why the relationship must evolve if it is to continue to achieve its intended purposes.

# CHAPTER 2

# Law and Technology: An Overview

Since this book is about "law" and "technology," we should probably begin by defining those terms. We do that in this chapter; we also survey the general contours of the historic relationship that evolved between law and "dumb" technologies.

## Definitions

*Black's Law Dictionary* defines "law" as the "regime that orders human activities and relations through systematic application of the force of politically organized society, or through social pressure, backed by force, in such a society."[1] *Black's* also notes that the term denotes the "aggregate of legislation, judicial precedents, and accepted legal principles . . . courts . . . apply in deciding controversies brought before them."[2]

As most of us know, "law" is divided into "civil law" and "criminal law."[3] Criminal law differs from civil law in two very important respects: One is that a criminal case is brought by the sovereign (a state or federal government in the United States), while a civil case is brought by a private person.[4] This distinction is relevant for several reasons, one of which is that the victim of a crime—the person

---

[1]   *Black's Law Dictionary*, 8th ed. (St. Paul, Minn.: Thomson/West, 2004).

[2]   *Id.*

[3]   See IV William Blackstone, *Commentaries on the Laws of England*, reprint (Boston: Beacon Press, 1962), 5.

[4]   See *id.*, 4–6: "[P]rivate wrongs, or civil injuries, are an infringement . . . of the civil rights which belong to individuals, considered merely as individuals; public wrongs, or crimes . . . , are a breach . . . of the public rights and duties due to the whole community."

actually "injured" by the crime—has no control over the case.[5] The sovereign can, and will, prosecute even if a victim does not want the case to proceed. In criminal law, the victim functions as a source of evidence, a witness. In a civil case, on the other hand, the plaintiff—the party who claims to have been "injured"—controls the litigation and decides whether to sue, whether to settle, and so forth.

The other difference lies in the sanction imposed. A defendant who loses a civil suit can be forced to pay money (damages), or to do certain things, or stop doing certain things (injunction). The purpose of civil sanctions is to make the plaintiff whole by paying her money or having the defendant do, or stop doing, something that is damaging the plaintiff or her interests. The sovereign "punishes" defendants who are convicted in criminal cases.[6] Punishment is not about making the victim whole. (To obtain redress, crime victims can sue those whom they believe have committed crimes, as in the O.J. Simpson civil case). Punishment is about controlling behavior.[7] Punishment is intended to control crime by discouraging (a) one who has been convicted of a crime from committing future crimes and (b) others from following his example by committing the same or similar crimes.[8] In the United States, and in most countries, we punish people by locking them up and/or by fining them. (Unlike civil damages, fines do not go to the victim; they go to the sovereign because their purpose is punitive, not remedial.) In the United States we also execute people on occasion, though this measure is reserved for homicide; the Supreme Court said several decades ago that capital punishment is so severe that it has to be limited to this most serious of crimes.[9]

Definitions of "technology" are many, some broad, some narrow. *The Chambers Dictionary*, for example, defines it as "the practice of any or all of the applied sciences that have practical value and/or industrial use."[10] The *Oxford English Dictionary* defines "technology" as "the application of scientific knowledge for practical purposes,"[11] while *Wikipedia* says it is the "state of our knowledge of how

---

[5] See, *e.g.*, C. Quince Hopkins, et al., "Applying Restorative Justice to Ongoing Intimate Violence," *St. Louis Public Law Review 23* (2004): 289, 290.

[6] See, *e.g.*, Blackstone, *Commentaries*, 8–10.

[7] See Susan W. Brenner, "Toward a Criminal Law for Cyberspace: Distributed Security," *Boston University Journal of Science & Technology Law 10* (2004): 1, 65–76.

[8] *Id.*

[9] See *Furman v. Georgia*, 408 U.S. 238 (1972) (per curiam).

[10] *The Chambers Dictionary*, 9th ed. (Edinburgh: Chambers Harrap, 2003), 1556.

[11] *Concise Oxford English Dictionary*, 10th ed., rev. (New York: Oxford, 2002), 1471.

to combine resources to produce desired products, to solve problems, fulfill needs, or satisfy wants."[12] I like the definition I found in a book by Ron Westrum, who defines "technology" as the "objects, techniques, and knowledge that allow human beings to transform and control the inanimate world."[13] I like his definition because it imports a more expansive conception of knowledge. Many definitions of "technology" are purely instrumental formulations of the concept;[14] as such, they focus only on technology-as-applied-science. For the purposes of this discussion, I prefer to conceptualize "technology" as encompassing not only scientific ("pure" as well as "applied") but also cultural knowledge. As one scholar noted, technology has "an epistemological dimension that is crucial" to the analysis "of technology-related issues."[15]

## Transition

Having defined these basic terms, we need to address one final prefatory issue before we begin to trace the historical evolution of the relationship between technology and law. This issue goes to a cultural aspect of technology; as the next section explains, "dumb" technologies have historically functioned only within a specific cultural context. This will not be true of the twenty-first-century technologies with which this book is concerned: The functioning of the "smart" technologies we examine in Chapter 6 will not be limited to a particular cultural context. Their functions will be networked and consequently distributed across contexts; unlike their historical antecedents, these technologies will be pervasive throughout society.

## Context

As the next three chapters demonstrate, the technologies we have encountered so far have been compartmentalized technologies; each affected society in very specific ways. The legal strategy we developed to deal with the various consequences attendant upon implementing these context-specific technologies relied upon

---

12    "Technology," *Wikipedia*, http://en.wikipedia.org/wiki/Technology.

13    Ron Westrum, *Technologies & Society: The Shaping of People and Things* (Belmont, Calif.: Wadsworth, 1990), 7.

14    See, *e.g.*, James B. McOmber, "Technological Autonomy and Three Definitions of Technology," *Journal of Communication* 48 (1999): 137, 141–143.

15    Joseph C. Pitt, *Thinking About Technology* (New York: Seven Bridges, 2000), 1.

rules that were also compartmentalized, that is, were designed to address the precise, segmented issues raised by each technology.

Rail transportation, for example, created issues that led to the adoption of rules setting rates, establishing safety requirements, and addressing other matters, all of which were specific to the operation of railroads. These context-specific rules targeted those who engaged in this context-specific, specialized activity. Twenty-first-century "smart" technology is the antithesis of context-specific technologies such as rail transportation; the goal and practice of this "smart," pervasive technology is to integrate sophisticated interactive technologies into the fabric of our everyday lives. As Chapter 6 explains, to do this, "smart" technologies must communicate . . . with each other, as well as with us. Therefore, instead of being an externality—something we consciously use for a specific purpose in a particular technical context—pervasive technology disappears into the background and becomes an integral part of our lives.[16]

In discussing the pervasiveness of technologies, differentiating between the pervasive *effects* of a technology and the pervasiveness of a *technology* is essential. In both instances, we are speaking of the extent to which something (effect or technology) diffuses throughout a society. As the next three chapters demonstrate, for most of our history, technologies were pervasive only in their effects; the introduction of such a technology influences us as members of that society, but we, personally, do not implement that technology. The effects of a technology ripple through a society, altering the course of daily life in subtle or dramatic ways, but the technologies themselves are in the hands of specialists, people who have been specifically trained to implement them. Technologies that are

---

[16] See, *e.g.*, "Pervasive computing," SearchNetworking.com, http://searchnetworking.techtarget.com/sDefinition/0,,sid7_gci759337,00.html. See also Joe Luedtke, "RFID Tags: Computing in Your Pocket, on Your Key Chain and in Your Car," *DM Review* (July 17, 2003), http://www.dmreview.com/article_sub.cfm?articleId=7096:

[S]omething that is truly pervasive becomes almost invisible to the end user. That . . . "something" becomes so widely adopted, so ubiquitous within its environment that it is readily taken for granted and given very little thought. Electricity is an excellent example of a pervasive technology. If you need a light, just flip on the light switch. If you need to plug in your laptop, just look around the room, there will undoubtedly be a few electrical outlets.

The phenomenon is also known as "ubiquitous computing," "ubiquitous technology," or "ambient intelligence." See, *e.g.*, Mahesh S. Raisinghani, et al., "Ambient Intelligence: Changing Forms of Human-Computer Interaction and their Social Implications," *Digital Information* (August 2004): 5J, http://jodi.tamu.edu/Articles/v05/i04/Raisinghani/.

pervasive only in their effects are context specific; that is, they have a specific function and are used within a discrete societal context.

Commercial air transportation is a good example of context-specific technologies: Its effects are societally (indeed, globally) pervasive; by vastly increasing our mobility, commercial air travel has altered our lives and cultures.[17] But while the effects of the technologies that give us commercial air transportation are pervasive,[18] the technologies themselves are not; we "civilians" can enjoy the benefits of commercial air transportation, but its implementation remains in the hands of a cadre of interlinked specialists. And like other technologies that are pervasive only in their effects, the technologies that sustain commercial air transportation are context specific: The discrete technologies involved in aircraft design and operation have but one purpose and are applied in but one context: the process of moving people and objects from one place to another. We experience commercial air transportation solely in this distinct context; this is true both for those who travel by air and for the specialists who implement commercial air transportation.

"Smart," pervasive technology is a very different phenomenon; here, the *technologies* permeate a society. They diffuse because their implementation is not reserved for specialists (though specialists will create and support these technologies). Indeed, the opposite is true; these technologies are intended to be democratic, that is, to be used by everyone. Like the antecedent context-specific technologies, these technologies are also pervasive in their effects; but because the technologies themselves are pervasive, their effects are not compartmentalized. Ultimately, "smart," pervasive technologies will affect every aspect of our lives.

As the next three chapters demonstrate, for centuries our technologies were purely context specific. The "use" of specialized artifacts and techniques that comprised a "technology" was reserved exclusively for a cadre of specialists, just as commercial air transportation is today reserved for a cadre of specialists. As Chapters 4 and 5 explain, toward the end of the nineteenth century, a few technologies emerged that were pervasive in themselves as well as in their effects; this trend

---

17      See Robert E. Skinner, Jr., "Transportation in the Twenty-First Century," *Public Roads 42* (September 1, 2000): 2.

18      Unlike many of the technologies discussed in the next three chapters, commercial air transportation is not "a" technology. It is instead the focus of aggregated technologies (flight, navigation, weather) that have a single purpose—the transport of individuals and objects. See, *e.g.*, Alexander T. Wells and Clarence C. Rodrigues, *Commercial Aviation Safety* (New York: McGraw-Hill, 2004), 220–263.

accelerated with the rise of a new type of technology—consumer technology—in the twentieth century. For various reasons, the most important being their very limited potential for misuse, law was able to adapt the strategy it used for truly context-specific technologies—the use of compartmentalized rules—to accommodate these modestly pervasive technologies.

Because it is not context specific, "smart," pervasive technology creates new challenges for law. We cannot, as Chapter 7 explains, rely on the traditional strategy—using compartmentalized rules—to address the social and behavioral consequences of implementing twenty-first-century "smart" technologies. We cannot continue with the *ad hoc* strategy we long ago developed for simpler, antecedent technologies. We must devise a new strategy, one that is at once flexible and parsimonious. Chapter 7 explains why such a strategy is essential at this point in history and suggests how we can adapt law to the dynamic social landscape that will be a constant for many years to come.

## Scope

Before we proceed, I need to clarify an aspect of the analysis that follows: Though it has a more general application, the analysis I present here focuses almost exclusively on criminal law for several reasons.

One is the matter of scale; the general issue we are dealing with encompasses a myriad of varied and complex subissues. As I noted earlier, very different rules and policies come into play when one deals with civil versus criminal law; therefore, analyzing both in a work of this limited scope is not practical. If I attempted to deal with criminal *and* civil law, I would do justice to neither. To postulate and dissect a new "tech-law" strategy within the confines of one domain of law, criminal law, is consequently more productive than to attempt a comprehensive treatment of such a strategy's applicability to the entire corpus of American law.

(I should also note that although the analysis is predicated on American law, it is not limited to the law of any particular jurisdiction. This discussion assumes American law because I am an American lawyer and that is what I know. The principles we will be dealing with, however, are not that parochial and should therefore be equally applicable in any jurisdiction.)

Another reason the analysis focuses on criminal law is that criminal law tends to be law's "canary in the coal mine:"[19] Because lawbreakers are usually among the first to adopt new technologies,[20] criminal law is often the first area of law that has to deal with the consequences of implementing these technologies; this situation has certainly been true for computer technology.[21]

Finally, the focus on criminal law is appropriate because our analysis is ultimately concerned with human behavior—with how we can adapt legal rules to channel human behavior into socially acceptable, socially adaptive paths without sacrificing the rights and liberties we cherish. This tension between rights and social order is an integral feature of criminal law, our oldest and in many ways most primitive form of law.[22]

---

[19]    Until relatively recently, canaries were used to detect carbon monoxide in mines. See, *e.g.,* "Coal Mine Canaries Made Redundant," *BBC News* (December 30, 1986), http://news.bbc.co.uk/onthisday/hi/dates/stories/december/30/newsid_2547000/2547587.stm.

[20]    See David Ronfeldt and John Arquilla, "What Next for Networks and Netwar?" in *Networks and Netwars: The Future of Terror, Crime and Militancy,* ed. John Arquilla and David Ronfeldt, 311, 313 (Santa Monica, Calif.: RAND, 2001); available at http:// www.rand.org/publications/MR/MR1382.

[21]    See Brenner, *Toward a Criminal Law for Cyberspace,* 65–76.

[22]    *Id.*

# CHAPTER 3

# Law and Tool Technology

This chapter is concerned with "tools," while Chapter 4 is concerned with "machines." We will therefore begin this discussion by differentiating the two.

"Tool" has been defined often, and variously.[1] We will use the following definition because it captures the essence of what a "tool" is without unnecessarily complicating matters: "A tool is a detached object that is controlled by the user to perform work (in the mechanical sense of transferring energy), usually as an extension of the user's anatomy."[2]

In 1876, Franz Reuleaux formulated what has become the classic definition of "machine:" "A machine is a combination of resistant bodies so arranged that by their means the mechanical forces of nature can be compelled to do work accompanied by certain determinant motions."[3] Lewis Mumford explained how a "tool" differs from a "machine":

> The essential distinction between a machine and a tool lies in the degree of independence in the operation from the skill and motive power of the operator; the tool lends itself to manipulation, the machine to automatic

---

[1] See, *e.g.*, Edward O. Wilson, *Sociobiology* (Cambridge, MA: Harvard University Press, 2000), 172 (defining tool use as "the manipulation of an inanimate object, not manufactured internally by the organism, which is used in a way that improves the organism's efficiency in altering the position or form of some other object"). See also Terry L. Hunt, Carl P. Lipo, and Sarah L. Sterling, *Posing Questions for a Scientific Archaeology* (Westport, CT: Bergen and Garvey, 2001), 75, defining tool as "the maximal set of co-occurring functional attributes associated within the boundaries of an individual object"; "Tool," Dictionary.com, http://dictionary.reference.com/search?q=tool; tool is a "device, such as a saw, used to perform or facilitate manual or mechanical work. For a discussion of varieties of tool use, see Wilson, *Sociobiology*, 172–175.

[2] Thomas Wynn, "Tools and Tool Behavior," in *Companion Encyclopedia of Anthropology*, ed. Tim Ingold, 133–134 (New York: Routledge, 1994). See also supra note 1.

[3] Lewis Mumford, *Technics and Civilization* (New York: Harcourt Brace, 1963), 9 (quoting Franz Reuleaux, *The Kinematics of Machinery: Outlines of a Theory of Machines* [London: Macmillan, 1876]).

action. . . . The difference between tools and machines lies primarily in the degree of automatism they have reached.[4]

We further develop this distinction and address machines as a distinct type of technology in the next chapter. For now, our concern is with tools.

## Tools

Humans have been using tools for millions of years.[5] For most of that time, the tools were simple devices we employed to perform the basic tasks required for survival.[6] And tool-fabrication was a "democratic" process, one that involved no occupational differentiation or specialization.[7]

Our tools became more sophisticated around 10,000 years ago when we began moving from hunting and gathering to farming.[8] As part of that shift, humans developed specialized techniques—technologies—for cultivating and irrigating crops.[9] The settled lifestyle and greater population densities associated with agriculture prompted further innovation; we therefore developed technology in other areas, such as engineering, textiles, metallurgy, and shipbuilding.[10]

---

[4]   *Id.*, 10. See, *e.g.*, James Essinger, *Jacquard's Web* (New York: Oxford University Press, 2004), 16 (early looms were not machines but tools).

[5]   See, *e.g.*, Ravi Korisettar and Michael D. Petraglia, *Early Human Behavior in Global Context* (New York: Routledge, 1998), 1–10.

[6]   See Brian P. Kooyman, *Understanding Stone Tools and Archaeological Sites* (Alberta, Canada University of Calgary, 2000), 69–76. See also T. K. Derry and Trevor I. Williams, *A Short History of Technology from the Earliest Times to A.D. 1900* (New York: Oxford University Press, 1961), 3–44.

[7]   See James E. McClellan III and Harold Dorn, *Science and Technology in World History* (Baltimore, MD: Johns Hopkins University Press, 1999), 17–23; Michael Rice, *The Archaeology of the Arabian Gulf, C. 5000–323 B.C.* (New York: Routledge, 1994), 7–8.

[8]   See Wilson, *Sociobiology*, 569. See also Peter Raven, "A Time of Catastrophic Extinction," *The Futurist 38* (September–October 1995): 29, agriculture was "invented independently in eastern Asia, the eastern Mediterranean, Mexico, and Peru some 8,000 to 11,000 years ago."

[9]   See, *e.g.*, Arnold Pacey, *Technology in World Civilization* (Cambridge, MA: MIT Press, 2001), 6–19; T. K. Derry & Trevor I. Williams, *A Short History of Technology from the Earliest Times to A.D. 1900* (New York: Oxford University Press, 1961), 48–62.

[10]  See Pacey, *Technology in World Civilization*, 20–33; Wilson, *Sociobiology*, 569; Derry and Williams, *A Short History of Technology*. See also John W. Humphrey and John P. Oleson, *Greek and Roman Technology* (New York: Routledge, 1998), 75–380; R. J. Forbes, *Man, the Maker: A History of Technology and Engineering* (New York: Abelard-Schuman, 1958), 19–88; Georges Contenau, *Everyday Life in Babylon and Assyria* (New York: St. Martin's Press, 1954), 94–100.

During the same era, we developed writing, our first communications technology; it was, among other things, used to record laws.[11]

The techniques humans developed during this era were still tool technologies; that is, they were more or less complex implements/processes an individual used to carry out a physical task, such as planting crops or weaving cloth. As such, these technologies were merely extensions and extrapolations of the earlier, more primitive tools that were once used to carry out simpler versions of the same tasks. The effects of these evolved tool technologies were pervasive in that they improved nutrition and other aspects of life,[12] but the technologies themselves were not.[13]

Artisans who understood the arcane processes involved in, say, making glass or pottery, mastered and controlled the evolved tool technologies.[14] A tool technology was therefore specific to a particular context; a discrete segment of a society, not by the populace as a whole, implemented each.[15]

---

[11]  See Robert Mcc..Adams, *Paths of Fire: An Anthropologist's Inquiry into Western Technology* (Princeton, NJ: Princeton University Press, 1996), 38–40; Michael Rice, *The Archaeology of the Arabian Gulf, C. 5000–323 B.C.* (New York: Routledge, 1994), 7–8. See also Derry and Williams, *A Short History of Technology*, 3–23; Alfred Burns, *The Power of the Written Word: The Role of Literacy in the History of Western Civilization* (New York: Peter Lang, 1989), 6–13. Writing was used to record laws at least by 1900 B.C., a century before Hammurabi issued his law code. See, *e.g.*, Stephanie Dalley, et al., *The Legacy of Mesopotamia* (New York: Oxford University Press, 1998), 69; Rice, *The Archaeology of the Arabian Gulf*, 110.

[12]  See McClellan and Dorn, *Science and Technology*, 22; Forbes, *Man, the Maker*, 17–59. See also Pacey, *Technology in World Civilization*, 31.

[13]  This is an inevitable consequence of implementing specialized technologies. As is explained later in the text, tool technologies produced specialists—individuals who were skilled in the use of a particular tool technology. This, in turn, produced a division of labor between (a) specialists and nonspecialists and (b) specialists of varying types. See, *e.g.*, McClellan and Dorn, *Science and Technology*, 22:

> In the early Neolithic, little or no occupational specialization differentiated individuals. . . . This . . . changed by the later Neolithic, as greater food surpluses and increased exchange led to more complex . . . settlements with full-time potters, weavers, masons, toolmakers, priests and chiefs.

See also Mcc..Adams, *Paths of Fire*, 41: "at around the end of the third millennium B.C., cuneiform texts permit us to recognize handicraft production with a complex division of labor." The division of labor that began in the Neolithic era continued for millennia and accelerated as technologies became more sophisticated in the eighteenth and nineteenth centuries, id., 46.

[14]  See John Hunter and Ian Ralston, *The Archaeology of Britain: An Introduction from the Upper Palaeolithic to the Industrial Revolution* (New York: Routledge, 1999), 129; John McHugh and Roland De Vaux, *Ancient Israel: Its Life and Institutions* (New York: McGraw-Hill, 1961), 76–77.

[15]  See Rudi Volti, *Society and Technological Change*, 4th ed. (New York: Worth Publishers, 2001), 137–138; Rice, *The Archaeology of the Arabian Gulf*, 79. See also Steven A. Epstein, *Wage & Labor Guilds in Medieval Europe* (Chapel Hill, NC: University of North Carolina Press, 1991), 21–25.

This, in turn, structured how law dealt with evolved tool technologies. The societal need for rules that addressed certain consequences of the implementation of a tool technology resulted from several factors, the most important of which was that evolved tool technologies created specialists.[16] Instead of making my own pottery or building my own ship, I could buy what I needed from a potter or a shipbuilder.[17] This created a perceived need to regulate specialists: to ensure that they dealt fairly with those who bought their goods or hired their services and vice versa.[18]

## Laws

Though technology regulation was not as pervasive in the ancient and medieval worlds as it is today, evolved tool technologies did produce rules—laws—that defined standards of conduct for the specialists who controlled particular technologies.[19] These laws were context specific because the technology-based

---

[16] See Rice, *The Archaeology of the Arabian Gulf*, 79. Other reasons for the emergence of legal rules targeting tool technologies were, e.g., to ensure the efficient resolution of specialist-client disputes and to set standards for controlling access to specialist professions.

[17] *Id.*; Derry and Williams, *A Short History of Technology*, 3–23.

[18] See "Code of Hammurabi," The Avalon Project at Yale, http://www.yale.edu/lawweb/avalon/medieval/hamframe.htm:

> 233. If a builder build a house for some one, even though he has not yet completed it; if then the walls seem toppling, the builder must make the walls solid from his own means. . . .

> 235. If a shipbuilder build a boat for some one, and do not make it tight, . . . the shipbuilder shall take the boat apart and put it together tight at his own expense. . . .

See also Gary Beckman, et al., *A History of Near Eastern Law*, vol. 1 (Leiden: Brill, 2003), 624, 642; Hittite code defined "artisan" and set fees for training apprentices as carpenters, smiths, weavers, or fullers.

In addition to regulating the work of specialists, these laws also specified fair payment for their work. See, *e.g.*, "The Code of the Nesilim, c. 1650–1500 BCE," *Internet Ancient History Sourcebook*, http://www.fordham.edu/halsall/ancient/1650nesilim.html; "If a smith make a copper box, his wages are one hundred pecks of barley. He who makes a copper dish of two-pound weight, his wages are one peck of emmer." See also Beckman, *A History of Near Eastern Law*, 218, Sumerian law set wages for weavers.

[19] "Law" is defined in Chapter 2. A "rule" is "a compulsory principle that governs action and inaction; [it] specifies which actions are allowable and which are not." Susan W. Brenner, "Toward a Criminal Law for Cyberspace: Distributed Security," *Boston University Journal of Science & Technology Law 10* (2004): 1, 6.

A common model in the ancient world and in preindustrialized societies was to organize the artisans who controlled tool technologies into guilds, which then set rules governing matters such as product/service quality, pricing, and entry into the profession. See Morris Silver, *Economic Structures of Antiquity* (Westport, CT: Greenwood Press, 1995), 6, 147; Steven A. Epstein, *Wage & Labor Guilds in Medieval Europe* (Chapel Hill, NC: University of North Carolina Press, 1991), 21–25. See also Mercia MacDermott, *A History of Bulgaria 1393–1885* (London: Allen & Unwin, 1962), 75–76; John Burgess Stewart, *The Guilds of Peking* (New York: Columbia University Press, 1928), 191–200.

activity was context specific; that is, a discrete occupational group within a distinct sector of society carried it out. Laws governing potters only applied to potters, laws governing carpenters only applied to carpenters, and so on. These laws focused on the application or misapplication of a specific technology and on the consequences each had for those who controlled that technology.[20] The laws tended to be simple in structure because the transactions they addressed were relatively simple in structure.

Before we examine "machines"—the implementation of which involved dramatic innovations in both law and technology—we should note two distinctive aspects of the laws that regulated these evolved tool technologies. One is that there was a one-to-one correlation between a tool technology and a "law." These laws were specifically, and solely, concerned with the implementation of a particular technology. More precisely, they were concerned with ensuring a baseline of quality in the implementation of tool technologies; the laws therefore set performance standards for the specialists who implemented these technologies and specified the remedy that was available when a specialist defaulted on his duty to abide by these standards.[21] These prescriptive laws were therefore "civil" laws; they were the means societies used to redress the injury inflicted on someone who had relied to her detriment on a defaulting specialist.[22]

Prescriptive laws "specify conduct that is . . . required within the context of a given institution or practice."[23] They are characterized as "positive" law because they impose an affirmative obligation to act in a particular way; the laws that set performance standards for the specialists who implemented evolved tool technologies are an example of this type of law. The counterpart—the antonym—of prescriptive law is proscriptive law. Proscriptive laws are characterized as "negative" law because they require "people to refrain from behavior" that threatens the social order, in greater or lesser degrees.[24]

---

[20]  The rules also affected "civilians" who deal with specialists by, among other things, setting acceptable standards of performance and providing a means of redress when a specialist's performance was inadequate, but their primary concern was with the specialists.

[21]  See supra note 16.

[22]  The function of "civil" law is explained in Chapter 2.

[23]  Richard B. Stewart, "Reconstitutive Law," *Maryland Law Review 46* (1986): 86, 89.

[24]  Karene M. Boos and Eric J. Boos, "At the Intersection of Law and Morality," *Journal of Law in Society 5* (2004): 457, 484.

Societies use both prescriptive and proscriptive laws to create and sustain order. Prescriptive laws create "the structure of a society by defining relationships among those who comprise that society; they also allocate essential tasks among the members of the society and ensure that the tasks are performed."[25] Because humans are intelligent entities who can violate laws, societies cannot rely only on proscriptive laws to maintain social order. They therefore implement a second set of proscriptive laws—"criminal laws"—to target law-violators. These laws impose criminal liability and sanctions on those who do not obey prescriptive laws.

As Chapter 2 explained, criminal laws have a very different function than civil laws; civil laws redress injuries, while criminal laws inflict punishment. Societies assume that sanctioning law violators maintains order by preventing violations. This basic assumption incorporates two subordinate assumptions: (a) sanctions deter violations by presenting us with a simple choice—obey laws or suffer the consequences; and (b) law violators will be identified, apprehended and sanctioned.[26] Because our concern is with the relationship that exists between law and technology, rather than the efficacy of particular laws, we will accept these assumptions, at least for the purpose of analysis.

This brings us to the other distinctive aspect of the laws that regulated evolved tool technologies: Because they were prescriptive, regulatory laws, these laws were "use" laws. They were, as noted above, concerned with ensuring that the evolved tool technologies were implemented correctly, effectively—which brings us to an issue we have not yet addressed.

The correct, effective implementation of technology is a matter of no moment to the law; law becomes concerned with the implementation of technology only when that implementation somehow goes awry.[27] This state of affairs prevails because law—and society in general—generally assumes that the implementation of technology is a "good" thing, that is, that it benefits society in general and individuals in particular. This is an issue to which we will return in a later chapter. Law—and society in general—also assumes that it is a "bad" thing when the

---

[25]  Susan W. Brenner and Anthony C. Crescenzi, "State-Sponsored Crime: The Futility of the Economic Espionage Act," *Houston Journal of International Law, 28* (2006): 389, 441.

[26]  See Brenner, *Toward a Criminal Law for Cyberspace*, 65–76.

[27]  We are, and will be, concerned only with the process of implementing a technology—of putting it to work, as it were. Our focus is on laws that address this process, not with antecedent laws that govern the process of establishing ownership of the scientific or mechanical principles that underlie a particular technology.

implementation of technology goes awry because this produces some level of "harm," to particular persons and/or to society.

The implementation of a technology can go awry in either of two ways. One technique is by "defective" implementation. Defective implementation occurs when a technology is not implemented with the technical precision necessary to avoid negative effects, the "harm" noted above. Defective implementation is a failure of "use," a default in the application of technology-specific principles. It is the product of inadvertence, not intent, an error, not a misdeed. Defective implementation is therefore appropriately addressed with the civil, "use" laws described previously. Because the failure of "use" is *not* contumacious, the focus is on redressing the injury—the "harm"—resulting from the failure.

"Improper" implementation is the other way in which implementation can go awry. Improper implementation occurs when someone deliberately exploits a technology to achieve negative effects, to cause "harm" to someone other than the person employing the technology. Improper implementation is "misuse"—the purposeful abuse of a technology. It is the product of intent, not inadvertence, and is a misdeed, not an error.

Improper implementation—or "misuse"—is a contumacious effort to disrupt basic principles of social order. Since the "misuse" *is* contumacious, it cannot be adequately addressed only with the civil "use" laws described above; the intent, the *mens rea*, responsible for the "misuse" removes it from the category of inadvertent "civil" wrong and transforms it into something much more serious as far as the maintenance of social order is concerned. As we will see, societies developed "misuse" laws—technologically specific *criminal* laws—to deal with the abuse of particular technologies.

It is important to note that "misuse" laws are inherently "about" a technology. Like other criminal laws, they are concerned with discouraging the infliction of particular "harms," the incidence of which threatens to erode social order. Unlike other criminal laws, such as, say, assault, theft, and murder laws, "misuse" laws are concerned not with a generic category of "harm" but with a specific, technologically vectored "harm." The "misuse" of the technology is consequently an essential element of these prohibitions.

To understand this aspect of "misuse" laws, it is helpful to consider a hypothetical example. Assume that John Doe, who is angry with Richard Roe for whatever reason, decides to kill Roe. They both live in the same apartment building, Roe on the third floor and Doe in a second-floor apartment that overlooks the entrance to the building. Doe knows Roe will leave the apartment building at 8:00 AM the next morning, on his way to work. Doe decides to make Roe's death look like an accident, so he removes the air-conditioning unit that has been in a window of his apartment overlooking the entrance to the building. The next morning, Doe "accidentally" drops the air-conditioning unit on Roe, killing him; Doe claims he was reinstalling the unit after repairing it.

The Roe killing is in a literal sense a "misuse" of technology because the air-conditioning unit is "technology" and because it was utilized to inflict a socially intolerable "harm"—Roe's death. The Roe killing is not, however, an instance of "misuse" in the sense in which I am using that term. In this hypothetical, the air-conditioning unit's status as technology is functionally irrelevant to its infliction of a proscribed "harm"; Doe could have achieved the same result by using a boulder, a large safe, a television set, a suitcase packed with cement, and so on. The air conditioner's status as technology was minimally relevant to his infliction of "harm" in that it gave him a perhaps more credible basis for claiming the death was the product of accident, rather than malice, but that circumstance is too tangential to qualify this as a "misuse" of air-conditioning technology (assuming such a thing is possible). "Misuse" occurs only when someone exploits the unique characteristics of a technology to inflict "harm" in a way that would otherwise not be possible. As I noted above, it is the abuse of a technology—a distortion of its intended purpose.[28]

"Misuse" laws did not appear for the evolved tool technologies. This is inferentially attributable to two factors: One is that specialists monopolized the evolved tool technologies; as we shall see, the specialists who implement technologies are generally much less likely to "misuse" them than are "civilians."

The second factor derives from the relative simplicity of the evolved tool technologies: The capacity for "misusing" a pot or a brick, or the process used to manufacture either, is very limited; the end product (pot or brick) can be "misused" to damage ("harm") a person or a thing, but the type and level of damage is functionally indistinguishable from that which can be inflicted by other means.

---

[28]  For more on this issue, see the discussion of bicycle "misuse" in Chapter 4.

What this means is that traditional criminal, proscriptive law can adequately address the underlying conduct; criminal law is probably the oldest type of law and, as such, long ago formulated laws that encompass the use of one's body or simple implements to "harm" another person or another's property.[29] At this stage in the evolution of the relationship between "law" and "technology," there was therefore no need for "misuse" laws because the misuse of evolved tool technology subsumed itself into existing principles of criminal law.

This, as we will see in the next chapter, changes with the rise of "machine" technologies.

---

[29]  See "Code of Hammurabi," The Avalon Project at Yale, http://www.yale.edu/lawweb/avalon/medieval/ hamframe.htm (Laws 196–206). See also Brenner, *Toward a Criminal Law for Cyberspace*, 65–75.

# CHAPTER 4

# Law and Machine Technology

We noted a basic difference between "tools" and "machines" at the beginning of the last chapter. We need to elaborate a bit on that difference before we examine how law responded to the rise of machine technology and the consequent need to control its defective and improper implementation.

In Chapter 3, we noted that the basic difference between a "tool" and a "machine" lies in the need for human effort. The more significant difference between the two is that a "machine" *replaces* human effort:

> [A] tool is passive in the worker's hands; his muscular strength, his . . . skill . . . determine production. . . . The machine . . . render[s] his hands unnecessary. . . . Instead of being a tool in the workman's hand, it is itself an artificial hand. It differs from a tool not so much by the automatic force which keeps it in motion as by the movements it can perform, the mechanism planned by the engineer's art enabling it to replace the processes, habits and skill of the hand. A spinning wheel is hardly a machine, because even though it spins, the thread has to be drawn out by hand. . . . We can thus define a machine as . . . a mechanism which, worked by any motive power, executes the elaborate movements of a technical operation, which it had previously taken . . . several men to do.[1]

Machines are not new; ancient inventors produced complex mechanisms and understood a great deal about the physical forces underlying mechanical technology.[2] What is new is the way we approach technology: In many ancient

---

[1]    Paul Mantoux, *The Industrial Revolution in the Eighteenth Century: An Outline of the Beginnings of the Modern Factory System in England* (New York: Macmillan, 1961), 189–190.

[2]    See Derek J. De Solla Price, *Science Since Babylon* (New Haven, CT: Yale University Press, 1961), 38–44. See also "The Antikythera Mechanism: The Clockwork Computer," *The Economist* (Sept. 19, 2002),

cultures, machines were regarded as curiosities and remained little more than toys.[3] This tendency to ignore or resist new technologies, which was the product of various social and cultural forces, persisted for centuries.[4]

This changed—at least in Europe—several centuries ago. The mid-eighteenth century saw the emergence of the "Machine Age"—the rise of industrialization and mechanized travel.[5] As machine technologies continued to evolve during the nineteenth century, other applications emerged.[6] By 1900, these technologies had already had a profound impact upon society.[7]

---

http://www.economist.com/displaystory.cfm?story_id=1337165 (early computer); "Ancient Greek Scientists: Hero of Alexandria," *Technology Museum of Thessaloniki*, http://www.tmth.edu.gr/en/aet/5/55.html (steam engine invented in first century B.C.).

[3] See, *e.g.*, A. Wolf, *A History of Science, Technology and Philosophy in the 16th and 17th Centuries* (London: MacMillan, 1935), 543. See also "The Subcommittee on Technology to the National Resources Committee," *Technological Trends and National Policy* (Washington, DC: U.S. Government Printing Office, 1937), 51.

[4] See *Id.*, 39–66. See also John W. Humphrey, John P. Oleson, and Andrew N. Sherwood, *Greek and Roman Technology* (New York: Routledge, 1998), 579–595.

[5] "The latter half of the eighteenth century inaugurated a period which the historians . . . have called the Industrial Revolution. It was characterized by the emergence of . . . machinery and engineering, and was accompanied by far-reaching changes and upheavals in the social, economic, and political institutions of the civilized world." R. J. Forbes, *Man, the Maker: A History of Technology and Engineering* (New York: Abelard-Schuman, 1958), 172. See also Peter N. Stearns, *The Industrial Revolution in World History*, 2nd ed. (Boulder, CO: Westview Press, 1998), 33–56; K. Derry and Trevor I. Williams, *A Short History of Technology from the Earliest Times to A.D. 1900* (New York: Oxford University Press, 1961), 273–310. For the spread of the industrial revolution to other parts of the world, see Stearns, *The Industrial Revolution in World History*, 73–85.

[6] See Forbes, Man, the Maker, 172–213. See also Elting E. Morison, *From Know-How to Nowhere: The Development of American Technology* (New York: Basic Books, 1974), 114–146; John W. Oliver, *History of American Technology* (New York: Ronald Press, 1956), 206–220, 433–448, 346–361. The nineteenth century also saw dramatic advances in other areas, such as building technology, metallurgy, chemistry, mining and agriculture. See Oliver, 314–345, 362–390, 401–414. See also Subcommittee on Technology, 97–388.

[7] See Derry and Williams, *A Short History of Technology*, 275–310. See also Oliver, *History of American Technology*, 295:

[M]achine technology triumphed. The machine . . . harvested . . . crops that helped to feed . . . the world. The . . . meat packing industry, with assembly-line methods and the introduction of artificial refrigeration, provided . . . fresh meats the year round.

The machine held sway in giant steel mills and in textile mills where production surpluses sought an outlet beyond our borders. The manufacture of steel rails laid the foundation for a new era in railroad expansion. . . . American steel made possible the skyscraper. . . .

The harnessing and utilization of electricity gave man his greatest mechanical servant. The incandescent light arrived. . . . The . . . typewriter, the mimeograph, the multigraph, the developments in photography, and the improvements in high-speed printing brought major changes in the . . . rapid communication.

Because technological innovation is an incremental process,[8] it can be difficult to assign discrete technologies to a particular era—to cast one as a nineteenth-century technology and another as a twentieth-century technology.[9] We are concerned, though, not with technologies, as such, but with their influence on society, with the extent to which particular technologies are pervasive in their effects or in themselves.[10] With that focus, we can legitimately distinguish between the pre- and post-1900 eras.

Like tool technologies, the machine and other technologies that had emerged by 1900 were pervasive only in their effects.[11] In analyzing that phenomenon, it is useful to divide the pre-1900 technologies into four categories: (a) industrial technologies, (b) transportation technologies, (c) communication technologies, and (d) electricity.[12]

Before we proceed, I should note caveats that apply to two of the technologies examined below. Although communications technologies involve the use of "machines," these technologies themselves do not really fit within the definition of "machine" quoted above. Instead of using mechanical devices to replace human activity, communications technologies use them to let humans do what they could not do before, for example, broadcast news over the airwaves or over the Internet.

Something similar is true of electricity. While electrically powered devices can, and do, fit within the definition of "machine," electricity itself is not a "machine": It is a power source for machines; it is also a product of machinery.[13] Electricity is

---

See also Oliver, *History of American Technology*, 389, 395–398; Yaffa Claire Draznin, *Victorian London's Middle-Class Housewife* (Westport, CT: Greenwood Press, 2001), 71; Sally Mitchell, *Daily Life in Victorian England* (Westport, CT: Greenwood Press, 1996), 6–12.

8    See Ron Westrum, *Technologies & Society: The Shaping of People and Things* (Belmont, CA: Wadsworth, 1990), 92–93.

9    See William F. Ogburn, "National Policy and Technology" in The Subcommittee on Technology, 4.

10   For the source and import of this distinction, see Chapter 3.

11   For a comprehensive survey of nineteenth century technologies, see K. Derry & Trevor Williams, *A Short History of Technology*, 275–699. See also Oliver, *History of American Technology*, 157–448.

12   Certain of these technologies anticipate the consumer technologies examined in the next chapter. Before 1900, though, there really were no consumer technologies. See Trevor I. Williams, *A Short History of Twentieth-Century Technology* (New York: Clarendon Press, 1982), 387–395. See also Draznin, *Victorian London's Middle-Class Housewife*, 47–69; Mitchell, *Daily Life in Victorian England*, 117–122.

13   The precise nature of electricity was a matter of some uncertainty when the technology was new. See David E. Nye, *Electrifying America: Social Meanings of a New Technology* (Cambridge,

associated with, but distinct from, "machines." And like the communications technologies it makes possible, electricity's uses are not limited to replacing human effort; electricity also lets us do what we could not do before, for example, broadcast news, maintain websites, and listen to music on our iPods while jogging. We address these issues later in this chapter.

## Industrial Technologies

This category encompasses machine technologies that are used in commercial enterprises.[14] These are the technologies we tend to associate with the "Machine Age," the Industrial Revolution. We are all familiar with the Industrial Revolution, but it is still helpful to note the distinct characteristics of the phenomenon that fundamentally altered work, commerce, and society:

> In the eighteenth century, a series of inventions transformed the manufacture of cotton in England and gave rise to a new mode of production—the factory system. . . . [O]ther branches of industry effected comparable advances, and all these together, mutually reinforcing one another, made possible further gains on an ever-widening front. The . . . innovations . . . may be subsumed under three principles: the substitution of machines— rapid, regular, precise, tireless—for human skill and effort; the substitution of inanimate sources of power. . . ; the use of new and far more abundant raw materials.[15]

The new industrial technologies included machine-tools, metallurgy, mining, chemicals, textiles, food-processing, building construction, and agriculture.[16]

---

MA: MIT Press, 1997), 138:

> The public encountered electrification in many guises. . . . Yet despite its ubiquity, electricity seemed to defy definition and remained a mystery to the citizenry who saw it every day in the street. As Charles W. Eliot wrote for inscription on the Union Depot in Washington, D.C., "Electricity: carrier of light and power, devourer of time and space; bearer of human speech over land and sea; greatest servant of man—yet itself unknown."

Electricity was, as Nye observes, "ubiquitous yet inscrutable," 138. Over the years, electricity has become invisible to us, so we no longer speculate about its precise nature.

[14]  See Theodore E. Burton, *Financial Crises and Periods of Industrial and Commercial Depression* (New York: Appleton & Co., 1902), 15–16. See also James E. McClellan III and Harold Dorn, *Science and Technology in World History* (Baltimore, MD: Johns Hopkins University Press, 1999), 277–287.

[15]  David Landes, *The Unbound Prometheus* (Cambridge, England: Cambridge, 1969), 41.

[16]  See Derry and Williams, *A Short History of Technology*, 343–599. Prior to 1900, the technologies in this category were a mix of tool technologies and machine technologies, 311–599. That is, while many tasks were automated, some industries still relied heavily on human labor augmented by the use of tools.

The technologies in this category are all extensions of tool technologies:[17] The activity (e.g., mining, textiles) is not new; what is new is that in the conduct of the activity mechanized devices replace human labor and simple tools. This change produced a corresponding change in the nature of specialization; the automation of endeavors that were the province of specialized artisans in the era of tool technologies resulted in the decline, or disappearance, of those specialties as occupations.[18] The operation of industrial technologies absorbed the skills that artisans had once mastered, as well as the artisans themselves.[19] This did not, though, spell the end of occupational specialization; the implementation of industrial technologies required the assistance of new specialists, individuals who were trained "to carry out complex industrial processes".[20]

Like the tool technologies that preceded them, industrial technologies are context specific.[21] Each has distinct functions and is implemented in a specific societal context by, as I noted above, a dedicated occupational sector—a cadre of specialists.[22] Like tool technologies, therefore, industrial technologies are pervasive in their effects but not in themselves;[23] the effects of their implementation

---

[17]   See Stearns, *The Industrial Revolution in World History*, 56.

[18]   See, *e.g.*, Mantoux, *The Industrial Revolution in the Eighteenth Century*, 68–74.

[19]   See, *e.g.*, Leonard R. Berlanstein, *The Industrial Revolution and Work in Nineteenth Century Europe* (New York: Routledge, 1992), 27: "mechanical ingenuity took the place of handicraft skill." See also Mantoux, *The Industrial Revolution in the Eighteenth Century*, 68–74.

[20]   Robert B. Gordon and Patrick M. Malone, *The Texture of Industry* (Oxford 1994), 39. The authors use "puddling iron (the principal nineteenth century method of converting pig iron to wrought iron)" as an example of how factory workers had to be trained to carry out specialized processes: "decisions had to be made about the temperatures to be used, the rate of charging the pig iron into the furnace, the type and amount of fettling (oxidizing agent), and the amount of slag to be drawn off." *Id.* They explain that while some factory jobs "are routine and undemanding", others "challenge the intellect and manual dexterity of even the most skilled . . . employees." *Id.* at 347. These authors also point out that even relatively undemanding industrial jobs are part of an intricate, complex process requiring coordination among many workers. See *id.* at 347–352.

Essentially, these authors argue that implementation of industrial technologies resulted in replacing artisans—or craftsmen—who were "responsible for the production of an entire object" with skilled workers who were trained to carry out specific tasks that culminated in the production of an object, or service. See *id.* at 6–7.

[21]   See Chapter 3. The context specificity of industrial technologies derives from the phenomenon noted earlier, i.e., the increasing division of labor that accompanies the introduction of specialized technologies.

[22]   See Derry and Williams, *A Short History of Technology*, 343–599.

[23]   For the substance and import of this distinction, see Chapter 2.

---

ripple through society, improving daily life in more or less significant ways, but the technologies remain in the hands of specialists.[24]

Like tool technologies, industrial technologies became the focus of context-specific laws.[25] This occurred because, as with tool technologies, law's concern was with preventing the defective implementation of a technology.[26] It was also a function of simple logic; laws addressing concerns such as safety and product quality must reflect the societal context and technical intricacies that are unique to a technology.[27] Laws devised for chemical processing are not appropriate for food-processing or mining.[28] The practice of utilizing context-specific laws arose with tool technologies consequently carried over to their direct successors, the industrial technologies that evolved in the nineteenth century.

## Transportation Technologies

The practice of using context-specific laws also carried over to the pre-1900 transportation technologies. Until 1900, the dominant transportation technologies

---

[24]    See Oliver, *History of American Technology*, 391:

> Before the close of the nineteenth century, the time had passed when the coarse jeans and the imported broadcloths differentiated the farmer from the "gentleman." Machine production had made it possible for the farmer and the small town merchant to dress as well as the city banker. His suit was made of material of the same pattern, and was cut in the same style, and only the closest scrutiny could reveal the difference in texture or in the refinements of tailoring.

See also 389, 395–393; Draznin, *Victorian London's Middle-Class Housewife*, 71; Mitchell, *Daily Life in Victorian England*, 6–12.

[25]    See, *e.g.,* Mark C. Christie, "Economic Regulation in the United States: The Constitutional Framework," *U. Rich. L. Rev. 40* (2006): 949, 973. For context-specific tool technology laws, see Chapter 3.

"[I]n the nineteenth century . . . many state governments were heavily involved in regulating industry." Aaron L. Friedberg, *In the Shadow of the Garrison State: America's Anti-Statism and Its Cold War Grand Strategy*, ed. Jack L. Snyder, et al. (Princeton, NJ: Princeton University Press, 2000), 13–14. See General Mining Act of 1872, ch. 152, 17 Stat. 91; *Daniels v. Hilgard*, 77 Ill. 640 (Ill. 1875). See also Derry and Williams, *A Short History of Technology*, 548, the British Explosives Act of 1875 set standards for manufacture of explosives); Mitchell, *Daily Life in Victorian England*, 125, laws directed at food quality.

[26]    For a discussion of "defective implementation" as a legal and technical construct, see Chapter 3.

[27]    See Ehsan H. Feroz, Stephen Haag, and Raymond Raab, "An Income Efficiency Model Approach to the Economic Consequences of OSHA Cotton Dust Regulation," *Australian Journal of Management 26* (2001): 26, cotton dust standards are "an epic example of contemporary industry specific regulation."

[28]    See Public Law 101–549, Title III, § 304, November 15, 1990, 104 Stat. 2576 (chemicals); 21 U.S. Code §§ 342 & 342 (food); 30 U.S. Code §§ 801–818 (mine safety).

were railroads, ships, and bicycles.[29] Railroads and ships were pervasive in their effects, both directly and indirectly.[30]

## Railroads and ships

People experienced the effects of these technologies directly when they traveled by ship or by rail.[31] They experienced their effects indirectly when they enjoyed the increased variety of food and goods that were available because of rail and/or ship transport.[32] As one author explained, the

> transformation brought by rail travel was truly astonishing. In the late 1820s, many people laughed at the idea of railways. Twenty-five years later, railways had completely altered many aspects of daily life. Before the railways, most people never traveled more than ten or twenty miles from home; all their work, shopping, and recreation were done within walking distance. Rail travel was dependable, fast, and cheap. . . . Passenger service was remarkably frequent; in 1888 . . . there were twenty-nine express trains daily between London and Manchester. . . . Townspeople and country dwellers went into the city for a day's shopping; middle-class urbanites could spend weekends in the countryside. Servants and factory workers made quick visits home to see their relatives and took day trips to the seashore on holidays. Even the most ordinary aspects of daily life were changed: fresh milk, for example, could be brought daily from the country to city doorsteps; and fresh fish, quickly transported inland, made fish and chips the most popular fast food in working-class neighborhoods.[33]

The development of mechanized rail and ship travel made transportation technology more context specific and less generally accessible than it had ever been. Until the nineteenth century, transportation technology consisted of walking,

---

[29]   See Derry and Williams, *A Short History of Technology*, 364–392; Oliver, *History of American Technology*, 415–431. There were other modes of transportation, such as horse-cars. See Mitchell, *Daily Life in Victorian England*, 75–76. But since the use of animals as a means of transport dates back into antiquity and did not involve the use of machine technologies, it does not qualify as a "technology" as the term is used in this article.

[30]   For the substance and import of this distinction, see Chapter 3.

[31]   See Oliver, *History of American Technology*, 420–426. See also Mitchell, *Daily Life in Victorian England*, 73–75.

[32]   See *id.*, 74.

[33]   *Id.*

animal transport, or nonmechanized water transport (rowing or sailing).[34] In fact, the last two may not have been universally available to everyone in a society, but this was a function of resources, not of specialized technology. Though the implementation of animal transport and nonmechanized water transport both require some skill, neither involves the specialized technical expertise associated with mechanized rail and ship transportation.

The effects of mechanized rail and ship technologies profoundly influenced daily life in the nineteenth century. But neither was a pervasive technology; like the other technologies discussed so far, both were context specific.[35] The implementation of rail and ship travel was (and is) consigned exclusively to specialists trained in the intricacies of one of these technologies.[36] The logic that governed the industrial technologies (and tool technologies before them) was consequently applied to these new transportation technologies, as well; they, too, became the focus of context-specific laws that set operating and safety standards.[37]

Congress' first foray into regulation of transportation technologies was prompted by the unsafe conditions on steamboats, which arose after early nineteenth-century entrepreneurs quickly moved to put

> advances in boiler construction to . . . turning a profit. The new technology was far from perfect, and the . . . operators of it were sometimes less than competent. The result was death . . . among passengers and crews of riverboats where most of the boiler explosions occurred. . . . In 1838 . . . 496 lives were lost as a result of steamboat explosions, a number that

---

[34]  See Derry and Williams, *A Short History of Technology*, 190–213.

[35]  See *Id.*

[36]  See, *e.g.*, Joel Seidman, *Brotherhood of Railroad Trainmen: The Internal Political Life of a National Union* (New York: Wiley, 1962), 6–9; Helen M. Gibbs and Carl E. McDowell, *Ocean Transportation* (New York: McGraw-Hill, 1956), 213–214. See also "History of the United States Merchant Marine Academy," U.S. Merchant Marine Academy, http://www.usmma.edu/about/History.htm.

[37]  See Steven W. Usselman, *Regulating Railroad Innovation: Business, Technology and Politics in America, 1840–1920* (Cambridge, England: Cambridge University Press, 2002), 276–277 (nineteenth century federal railroad safety legislation); John F. Stover, *American Railroads*, 2nd ed. (Chicago, IL: University of Chicago Press, 1997), 54–68, 118–135 (nineteenth century federal and state railroad legislation). For a detailed review of American railroad legislation, see Paul Stephen Dempsey, "Transportation: A Legal History," *Transportation Law Journal 30* (2003): 235, 261–269. For an overview of some of the current statutes that are intended to ensure the safety of rail travel, see, *e.g.*, 49 U.S. Code §§ 20131–20153. For similar laws directed at ensuring maritime safety, see, *e.g.*, 46 U.S. Code §§ 3302–3318, 3501–3506, 8104(h). See also "Guidelines on Surveys and Inspections under the Protocol of 1978 Relating to the SOLAS and MARPOL Conventions," IMO Resolution A.413 (XI), November 15, 1979.

exceeded . . . losses in . . . England and France where government regulated the new technology. . . .

Congress in 1852 passed the nation's first major regulatory act. It governed the operation of steamboats, set standards for boiler construction, and established boards to inspect, license, and investigate steamboat operators. It also contributed to a dramatic decline in steamboat accidents.[38]

According to one scholar, the 1852 legislation was particularly noteworthy in requiring that steamboat engineers be trained, licensed professionals.[39] From our perspective, this aspect of that legislation is a perfect example of context-specific law adopted to regulate the implementation of an industrial technology. In another context, Congress adopted similar legislation designed to enhance the safety of maritime travel.[40]

---

[38]    Kermit L. Hall, *The Magic Mirror: Law in American History* (New York: Oxford University Press, 1989), 93 (notes omitted). For more on the empirical context that produced this legislation, see Stephen P. Rice, *Minding the Machine: Languages of Class in Early Industrial America* (Berkeley, CA: University of California, 2004), 139–142.

[39]    See *id.*,141–142:

> Congress passed a new regulatory law in August 1852 requiring the examination and licensing of engineers aboard passenger steamboats. . . . "Whenever any person claiming to be qualified to perform the duty of engineer upon steamers carrying passengers, shall apply for a certificate," the law read, the area board of inspectors must `examine the applicant in order to evaluate his " . . . knowledge, and experience in the duties of an engineer." If satisfied, they could then issue him a license for one year. While this was only one of a number of provisions of the new law, it did the most to address the concern that accidents frequently were due to incompetent engineers who failed to properly "manage" their engines. The idea of licensing engineers had been around a long time but had never been enacted into law. . . .

[40]    For general maritime regulation, see J. Michael Lennon, Note, "The Law of Collision and the United States Navy," *Buffalo Law Review 50* (2002): 981, 987–988:

> [T]he British began adopting collision regulations in the mid-nineteenth century. The success of these regulations . . . led the British Board of Trade to . . . promulgate a complete set of collision regulations. . . . In 1863, the French agreed . . . to follow the British regulations, and "by 1868, 33 other nations . . . had notified the United Kingdom that their vessels would be bound by the rules, even when outside British waters."

> Eventually, the United States Congress decided to make its presence felt as well, enacting legislation relating to navigational lights in 1838 and 1849, and, in 1851, directing the U.S. Navy to enforce a regulation requiring "all U.S. steam vessels to display a white masthead light and red and green side lights." . . . Congress . . . in 1864, enacted a set of high seas rules nearly identical to those of their British counterparts. . . .

> (quoting Nicholas J. Healy and Joseph C. Sweeney, "Basic Principles of the Law of Collision," *Journal of Maritime Law and Commerce 22* (1991): 359, 363–364. See also *United States v. Standard Oil Co.*, 384 U.S. 224, 226–227 (1966) (reviewing nineteenth century statutes regulating discharge of marine ballast).

## Bicycles

The bicycle differed markedly from the technologies examined above in at least one notable respect: It was pervasive both in its effects and in itself.[41] The nineteenth-century bicycle was concededly not as pervasive a technology as the twentieth-century consumer technologies we will examine in Chapter 5,[42] nor did its pervasiveness begin to approach that of the twenty-first century technologies we will examine in Chapter 6. But the bicycle was definitely not a context-specific technology. Its implementation was democratic rather than being reserved for a class of specialists:

> The period from the early 1880's until the advent of the automobile is known as the "era of the bicycle craze." The two-wheeled, rubber-tired bicycle took America by storm. Everyone who could afford it bought a bicycle—professional men, lawyers, bankers, clerks, clergymen, college professors, and the ladies. For women, the bicycle and the typewriter . . . served to emancipate them from the age-old restricted home life.[43]

A historian who studied the evolution of "cyclomania" explained that while there is "no way" to know precisely how many bicycles there were in the United States in 1890, two years after the modern bicycle was introduced,[44] we do know that

---

[41] The discussion above uses the terms "bicycle" and "bicycle technology" to encompass not only the standard, more modern bicycle but also variants such as tricycles, which were also popular in the nineteenth century. See *Toedtemeier v. Clackamas County*, 34 Or. 66, 68, 54 P. 954, 955 (Or. 1898) (Act of November 25, 1885 was intended "to regulate the passage of bicycles, tricycles [and] velocipedes . . . on the public highways or streets"); *Rowland v. Wanamaker*, 20 Pa.C.C. 621, 7 Pa. D. 249, 1898 WL 3637 *1 (Pa.Com.Pl. 1898) (Act of April 23, 1889 declared that "bicycles, tricycles and all vehicles propelled by hand or foot" were "entitled to the same rights and subject to the same restrictions" as "persons using carriages drawn by horses").

[42] The bicycle was the precursor of the automobile; like the automobile it changed American culture, as well as transportation. For the automobile's influence on law and culture, see Chapter 5.

[43] Oliver, *History of American Technology*, 427. See also Derry and Williams, *A Short History of Technology*, 390, "the bicycle, which brought new life to the roads, romance to the young, and emancipation to the weaker sex, was a technological development which . . . did much to transform the leisure hours of civilized man"; Mitchell, *Daily Life in Victorian England*, 224, "Bicycling blossomed into an enormous fad in the mid- 1890s"; *Lee v. City of Port Huron*, 128 Mich, 533, 535 87 N.W.637, 637 (Mich. 1901) ("The bicycle has become almost a necessity for the use of workmen, clerks, and others in going to and from their places of work").

[44] The bicycle traces its origins at least to the seventeenth century. See Robert A. Smith, *A Social History of The Bicycle* (American Heritage Press, 1972), 2–4. But it was in the early eighteenth century that the first version of the modern bicycle—the "highwheeler"—appeared. See *id.* at 6–8. The high-wheeler was difficult to operate safely because of the great disproportion between the size of its wheels and because of the distance the rider was from the ground. See *id.* It was not until the mid-1880s that a viable version

"twenty-seven American cycle manufacturers were hard at work trying to meet the demand, even at the high prices they were charging for the new machines."[45] Over the next few years, prices went down and "the demand for bicycles grew in spite of the financial panic that had struck the country."[46] As one scholar noted, "for a time all America was divided into two classes of people—those who rode the bicycle and those who did not."[47]

The implementation of bicycle technology was not reserved for a class of specialists because it was a much simpler technology than the technologies involved in, say, rail and ship transport. Rail and ship technologies were collective transportation technologies; each involved the design, manufacture, and operation of equipment that transported many people and quantities of goods, simultaneously, often at relatively high rates of speed. The bicycle, on the other hand, was for the most part an individual transportation technology: A bicycle generally (though not always) transported only one person, and its motive power was the "muscular strength" of that person. The bicycle is, in this respect anyway, more analogous to the tool technologies discussed earlier than it is to the other complex machine technologies that emerged in the nineteenth century.

Because it was a pervasive technology, the bicycle, like the other technologies we have so far considered, produced laws that were intended to prevent its defective implementation.[48] These laws were designed to control the implementation of this new technology and avoid, insofar as possible, "harm" resulting from its use.[49]

---

of the modern "safety" bicycle appeared, with its equivalently sized wheels, lower seat height and pneumatic tires. See *id*. Because it was so much easier, and safer, to operate, the safety bicycle would become very popular in the U.S. and elsewhere, as is explained in the text.

45    Robert A. Smith, *A Social History of the Bicycle* (American Heritage Press, 1972), 25.

46    *Id*., 27.

47    *Id*., x.

48    For "defective implementation" as a legal and technical construct, see Chapter 3.

49    For the issue of preventing "harm," see Chapter 3. For the need for laws controlling the implementation of bicycle technology, see law intended to prevent the defective implementation of bicycle technology, see Smith, *A Social History of The Bicycle*, 183–203. For laws designed to control the defective implementation of bicycle technology, see *Taylor v. The Union Traction Company*, 20 Pa. C.C. 238, 6 Pa. D. 365, 1897 WL 3527 *3 (Pa.Com.Pl. 1897) ("The experience of almost everyone . . . emphasizes the importance of . . . reasonable regulations for the protection of the many thousands of people who use the modern vehicle known as the bicycle"). See also *State v. Bradford*, 78 Minn. 387, 388, 81 N.W. 202, 203 (Minn. 1899) (Section 1, c. 43, Laws 1899 made it a misdemeanor to obstruct "a bicycle path constructed exclusively for the use of bicyclists"); *State v. City of Millville*, 63 N.J.L. 123, 124–125, 43 A. 443, 444 (N.J. 1899) (Act of March 3, 1896 authorized cities to enact ordinances governing bicycles and mandated that they "require that all bicycles . . . when in use in the public highways . . . have a lamp, of such illuminating power as to

But because bicycle technology was pervasive *both* in its effects and in itself, these laws could not be context specific in the way such laws had been. Bicycle laws could not focus on a cadre of occupational specialists who engaged in activities segregated from everyday human experience because bicycle technology was "democratic," that is, could at least theoretically be used by anyone in the society.

To understand the approach lawmakers took to preventing the defective implementation, we first need to review the different strategies they employed. After we have done that, we will parse the approach that evolved from these strategies.

Legislators at first simply banned bicycles from major thoroughfares, including sidewalks.[50] These early enactments were at least ostensibly based on public

---

be plainly seen 100 yards ahead, attached thereto, and kept lighted, between one hour after sunset and one hour before sunrise"); *Doll v. Devery*, 27 Misc. 149, 57 N.Y.S. 767, 769–770 (N.Y. Sup. Ct. 1899) ("Laws 1893, c. 102, § 10, as amended by Laws 1894, c. 8" authorized the park department to exclude bicycles from the park speedway); *Toedtemeier v. Clackamas County*, 34 Or. 66, 68–69, 54 P. 954, 955 (Or. 1898) (Act of November 25, 1885 required anyone operating a bicycle on "the public highways or streets . . . to bring the said bicycle . . . to a stop when within one hundred yards of any person . . . going in the opposite direction with a team . . . and remain stationary until said team . . . shall have passed by"); *Rowland v. Wanamaker*, 20 Pa.C.C. 621, 7 Pa. D. 249, 1898 WL 3637 *1 (Pa.Com.Pl. 1898) (Act of April 23, 1889 declared that bicycles were "'entitled to the same rights and subject to the same restrictions in the use . . . as are prescribed by law in the case of persons using carriages drawn by horses'"); *State v. Yopp*, 97 N.C. 477, 2 S.E. 458, 459 (N.C. 1887) (1885 statute forbade using a bicycle on a private road "without the express permission of the superintendent of said road", the purpose being to prevent injury to those in "carriages and other ordinary vehicles drawn by horses"). For more on this, see, *e.g.*, Ross D. Petty, "The Impact of the Sport of Bicycle Riding on Safety Law," *American Business Law Journal 35* (1998): 185, 190–198.

As Robert Smith explains in his history of bicycle technology in the United States, local police sometimes used a minor level of criminal liability—mostly, fines—to enforce defective implementation laws like those noted above. See Smith, *A Social History of The Bicycle*, 183–203. Chapter 5 deals with a similar—though more exaggerated—use of criminal liability for a similar purpose, i.e., to control a certain category of defective implementation of automobile technology. In both instances, the rules are defective implementation rules, instead of "misuse" rules, because they target "harms" resulting from the inept or inadvertent implementation of the technology, rather than "harms" deliberately inflicted by implementing the technology. See Chapter 5. See also Chapter 3.

[50] See Petty, *The Impact of the Sport of Bicycle Riding*, 185, 196. In the early years of the bicycle craze, for example, Denver and Philadelphia banned bicycles from sidewalks, while Kentucky banned them "from most major roads," 192. Other states had similar prohibitions. See 192–193. As bicycle historian Robert Smith noted, these laws lead some police forces to institute "bicycle traps," precursors of the automotive "speed trap." See Smith, *A Social History of The Bicycle*, 188 (bicycle traps in Hackensack, New Jersey, and Long Island, New York). According to Smith, police in some cities were even accused of digging trenches and otherwise creating obstacles in the road to force bicyclists onto sidewalks, where they were cited for violating the antisidewalk riding prohibitions. See *id.*

safety considerations. As the North Carolina Supreme Court explained in 1887, regulations prohibiting the use of bicycles on public roads were a valid exercise of the police power of the state because the evidence before the court showed "that the use of the bicycle on the road materially interfered with the exercise of the rights and safety of others in the lawful use of their carriages and horses in passing over the road."[51] Many courts and legislators cited the concern about frightening horses as a justification for restricting, or outlawing, the use of bicycles in this early period.[52] The concern resulted in the adoption of measures requiring bicyclists either to avoid public roads or take certain precautions to avoid frightening horses when they encountered them.[53]

As bicycles became more ubiquitous, legislators could no longer ban them from roadways and other public areas. In 1888, the Rhode Island Supreme Court held that a bicycle was a "vehicle" subject to the same rules and entitled to the same rights as "any carriage or other vehicle."[54] Other state courts often cited this decision, which held that bicycles "had an equal right to use the road" and were not "a public nuisance."[55] In 1894, for example, the Minnesota Supreme Court explained that "a bicycle is a vehicle used now very extensively for convenience, recreation, pleasure, and business, and the riding of one upon the public highway in the ordinary manner as is now done is neither unlawful nor prohibited, and they cannot be banished because they were not . . . used in the Garden of Eden by Adam and Eve."[56]

As the nineteenth century waned, state legislators began to adopt similar views, and by the 1890s, many states had enacted laws that gave "bicyclists the same

---

[51]  *State v. Yopp*, 97 N.C. 477, 2 S.E. 458, 459 (N.C. 1887).

[52]  See Petty, *The Impact of the Sport of Bicycle Riding*, 185, 196; Smith, *A Social History of The Bicycle*, 183–187. "The first machine to panic horses, provoke pedestrians, and incur both urban and rural hatred was the relatively quiet and outwardly inoffensive bicycle," 183.

[53]  See *id.*, 183–185. The protective measures included requiring the cyclist to stop inquire whether a horse was likely to be frightened by a bicycle or to simply dismount and wheel the bicycle around the horse. For a summary of similar measures, see *supra* note xlix.

[54]  *State v. Collins*, 16 R.I. 371, 17 A. 131, 131 (R.I. 1888). The case involved a wagon driver who refused to drive to the right side of the road when approaching a bicyclist and thereby caused a collision. See Petty, *The Impact of the Sport of Bicycle Riding*, 185, 194. The Rhode Island Supreme Court held that the bicycle was a "vehicle" under a state statute that required those operating a carriage or other "vehicle" to move to the right to allow an approaching "vehicle" to pass. See *id.* See also *State v. Collins, supra.*

[55]  See Petty, *The Impact of the Sport of Bicycle Riding*, 185, 194–196. See also Local Government Act 1888, Ch. 41, s. 85(1) (Eng.) ("Bicycles . . . are hereby declared to be carriages within the meaning of the Highway Acts").

[56]  *Thompson v. Dodge*, 60 N.W. 545, 546 (Minn. 1894).

rights . . . as other roadway users."[57] Cities and towns soon followed suit by passing "ordinances governing the use of roads and sidewalks" by carriages and bicycles, ordinances that "paved the way for the elaborate codes controlling the use of automobiles" that would appear in the twentieth century.[58]

The acceptance of bicycling as a routine feature of daily life brought demands that bicyclists meet certain standards in the operation of their vehicles.[59] The goal was to control the defective implementation of this new, pervasive technology. The problem was that the need for such standards created a novel issue; context-specific laws were used to control specialists' implementation of nonpervasive technologies, but that approach would not work for bicycle technology.

Common law had evolved a few "rules of the road" for travel on horseback, in carriages, and on foot. As the Pennsylvania Supreme Court noted in 1868, "[b]y the law and custom of the land it is the duty of persons traveling in wagons or other vehicles meeting each other on a public road to pass on the right hand side of the road."[60] This and other, similar principles were codified in at least some states.[61] Bicycles, though, created issues that were not addressed by these statutes or the common law rules from which they derived.[62] As one author notes, the increased "traffic and speed" attributable to bicycles brought demands for new rules governing "road use behavior."[63]

The bicycle speeder—"the scorcher, who darted in and out through the traffic, head down, rump up in the air, and feet flashing in the pedal stirrups"—was a major concern to everyone, even other cyclists.[64] Cities responded by imposing

---

[57]  See Petty, *The Impact of the Sport of Bicycle Riding*, 185, 196.

[58]  Smith, *A Social History of The Bicycle*, 185.

[59]  See Petty, *The Impact of the Sport of Bicycle Riding* 185, 202–203.

[60]  *Waters v. Wing*, 59 Pa. 211, 1868 WL 7301 (Pa. 1868). See also *O'Maley v. Dorn*, 7 Wis. 236, 1859 WL 2775 (Wis. 1859).

[61]  See, *e.g.*, *Smith v. Dygert*, 12 Barb. 613 (N.Y. Sup. 1852) (New York statute required that when those traveling in carriages met "on any turnpike road or public highway . . . the persons so meeting shall . . . turn their carriages to the right of the center of the road, so as to permit such carriages to pass without interference"). See also *Hawkins v. Riley*, 17 B. Mon. 101, 1856 WL 4275 (Ky. App. 1856) (citing a Kentucky statute which provided that "when a fast vehicle overtakes one of slower movement, the latter shall leave to the right, so as to permit the other to pass on the left or near side").

[62]  See Petty, *The Impact of the Sport of Bicycle Riding* 185, 1203.

[63]  See *id.*

[64]  Smith, *A Social History of The Bicycle*, 192.

speed limits and other requirements on cyclists.[65] In 1897, for example, New York adopted a traffic code that established a speed limit of eight miles per hour and required cyclists to give pedestrians the right of way.[66] New York's new traffic code also forbade cyclists from coasting on city streets and required them to have "their feet on the pedals and both hands on the handlebars at all times."[67] A contemporaneous effort to require brakes on bicycles failed because of opposition from cyclists; they claimed that "if brakes were required, the bicyclist would . . . rely abjectly on the mechanism, never learning the "flying dismount" that the cyclemaniacs thought was necessary."[68] This particular debate ultimately became moot as improved technology resulted in the installation of brakes on all bicycles.[69]

Cities initially took the lead in adopting rules governing the implementation of bicycle technology, and state legislators eventually followed suit, adopting statutes that imposed speed limits and other obligations on bicycle riders.[70] Modern statutes regulate various aspects of cycling, such as limiting how many people can ride a bicycle at one time, specifying how bicycles are to be operated, and requiring helmets for operators and lamps for cycles being operated after dark.[71]

---

[65] See Petty, *The Impact of the Sport of Bicycle Riding*, 185, 204 (15 miles per hour in Washington, D.C., 10 miles per hour in Connecticut, and 8 miles per hour in New York).

[66] Smith, *A Social History of The Bicycle*, 202 The requirement that cyclists defer to pedestrians was actually quite important, as many pedestrians had been injured, and some killed, by careless cyclists. See *id.* at 194–196.

[67] *Id.*

[68] *Id.*, 203.

[69] *Id.*

[70] See, *e.g.*, *Hanscomb v. Goodale*, 81 N.H. 150, 124 A. 458 (N.H. 1923) (statute set bicycle speed limit of 10 miles per hour). Another approach state legislatures took was to adopt statutes delegating this authority to towns and cities. See, *e.g.*, *Simpson v. City of Whatcom*, 33 Wash. 392, 74 P. 577, 578 (Wash. 1903) ("the bicycle, with its capacity for extreme speed, its liability . . . to injure . . . as well as the riders themselves, is a particularly suggestive subject for public legislation; and the Legislature of this state, recognizing such necessity, passed a law . . . authorizing and empowering cities . . . to regulate and license by ordinance the riding of bicycles").

[71] See, *e.g.*, West's Florida Statutes Annotated § 316.2065:

    (1) Every person propelling a vehicle by human power has all of the rights and all of the duties applicable to the driver of any other vehicle. . . .

    (2) A person operating a bicycle may not ride other than upon or astride a permanent and regular seat attached thereto.

    (3) (a) A bicycle may not be used to carry more persons at one time than the number for which it is designed or equipped, except that an adult rider may carry a child securely attached to his . . . person in a backpack. . . .

As this review of bicycle law may demonstrate, legislatures, which had assumed primary responsibility for responding to the effects of new technologies, applied a variant of the logic they had used for prior technologies in their efforts to prevent the defective implementation of this different new technology. They retained the notion that laws addressing the consequences of technology should focus on a particular context but altered the context: Because the legislators could not target an occupational context (e.g., miners, railroad workers), they focused on the technology itself; bicycle technology became the context. The laws they adopted consequently focused on one's "use" of a bicycle; by riding a bicycle, I entered the context in which a set of bicycle-specific laws applied and, as a "user" of that technology, became subject to their requirements.[72]

Prior laws were also predicated on "using" certain technology, but the point of entry was different; under the tool technology and industrial technology laws, someone entered the context in which a set of technologically specific laws applied by mastering a specific occupational technology. Because access to these occupational specialties were limited in varying ways, these laws had, as we have seen, a far more limited applicability than the bicycle laws; the bicycle laws anticipated

---

(b) Except as provided in paragraph (a), a bicycle rider must carry any passenger who is a child under 4 years of age, or who weighs 40 pounds or less, in a . . . carrier that is designed to carry a child of that age or size and that secures . . . the child from the moving parts of the bicycle.

(c) A bicycle rider may not allow a passenger to remain in a . . . carrier on a bicycle when the rider is not in immediate control of the bicycle.

(d) A bicycle rider . . . who is under 16 years of age must wear a bicycle helmet that is properly fitted and is fastened securely upon the passenger's head by a strap. . . .

(6) Persons riding bicycles upon a roadway may not ride more than two abreast except on paths or parts of roadways set aside for the exclusive use of bicycles. . . .

(7) Any person operating a bicycle shall keep at least one hand upon the handlebars.

(8) Every bicycle in use between sunset and sunrise shall be equipped with a lamp on the front exhibiting a white light visible from a distance of at least 500 feet to the front and a lamp and reflector on the rear each exhibiting a red light visible from a distance of 600 feet to the rear. . . .

(9) No parent of any minor child . . . may authorize or knowingly permit any such minor . . . to violate any of the provisions of this section.

(10) A person propelling a vehicle by human power upon and along a sidewalk, or across a roadway upon and along a crosswalk, has all the rights and duties applicable to a pedestrian under the same circumstances.

(11) A person propelling a bicycle upon and along a sidewalk, or across a roadway upon and along a crosswalk, shall yield the right-of-way to any pedestrian.

(14) Every bicycle shall be equipped with a brake or brakes which will enable its rider to stop the bicycle within 25 feet from a speed of 10 miles per hour on dry, level, clean pavement.

[72] See *Twilley v. Perkins*, 77 Md. 252, 26 A. 286, 287 (Md. 1893) ("We do not suppose that it could be seriously disputed that it is competent to the legislature in the exercise of its . . . right to regulate the use of the highways of the state to restrict . . . the use of . . . bicycles . . . on the highways, if they . . . be dangerous to the general traveling public").

twentieth-century laws that would also apply to the civilian "users" of particular technologies, such as the automobile.[73]

The bicycle-technology-as-context strategy was an eminently reasonable way to address the consequences of implementing bicycle technology because it reflected the unique pervasiveness of that technology.[74] As I noted earlier, bicycle technology was unique at this point in being pervasive both in its effects and in itself; law's concern was still, as it had always been, with the implementation of a technology, not with its effects. That is, the focus was still on preventing defective implementation; the issue of improper implementation—misuse—had yet to arise. We will return to that issue in a moment.

First, though, we need to understand why law's sole concern to this point was with the implementation of a technology and to understand why that was true we need to consider how societies approach technology.[75] We are concerned only with societies that embrace technology because implementation issues do not arise in societies that reject technology.[76]

---

[73] See Petty, *The Impact of the Sport of Bicycle Riding*, 185, 196 ("towns passed ordinances governing the use of roads and sidewalks by both carriages and bicycles and so paved the way for the elaborate codes controlling the use of automobiles in the present century") (quoting Smith, *A Social History of The Bicycle*, 185.

[74] See *Thompson v. Dodge*, 58 Minn. 555, 557, 60 N.W. 545, 546 (Minn. 1894) ("A bicycle is a vehicle used now very extensively for convenience, recreation, pleasure, and business, and . . . they cannot be banished because they were not . . . used in the Garden of Eden").

[75] The notion of "technology" as a distinct phenomenon warranting the attentions of lawmakers was apparently not a common theme in U.S. law until the twentieth century. I ran a search of U.S. cases decided prior to 1870 and found only two that use the term to denote what *we* would consider technology. See *Funk v. Haldeman*, 53 Pa. 229 (Pa. 1866) ("technology of conveyancing"); *Upton v. Brazier*, 17 Iowa 153 (Iowa 1864) ("mining technology"). Nineteenth-century courts seemed more likely to couple the term "technology" with "law," as in "legal technology" or the "technology of law." See *Western Granite & Marble Co. v. Knickerbocker*, 103 Cal. 111 (Cal. 1894); *Weill v. Kenfield*, 54 Cal. 111 (Cal. 1880); *Hope v. Rusha*, 88 Pa. 127 (Pa. 1879); *The Raleigh*, 20 F. Cas. 195 (E.D. Va. 1876). The only pre-1860 case I find using the term "technology" uses it in referring to "legislative technology." See *In re McElroy*, 1843 WL 5177 (Pa. 1843).

[76] Historically, societies have not always been receptive to technology. See The Subcommittee on Technology, 39:

> It is clearly to man's advantage to be able to traverse distances with facility . . . yet. . . . [i]n the thirteenth century. . . . Philip the Fair ordered the wives of citizens of Paris not to ride in carriages . . . A law . . . sought to prevent the use of coaches in Hungary in 1593, and the Duke Julius of Brunswick in 1588 made riding in coaches . . . a felony, largely on the grounds that it would interfere with military preparedness, for men would lose their equestrian skill. Philip II, Duke of Pomerania-Stettin, also commanded his vassals in 1608 that they should use horses and not carriages. In England, coaches were not widely used until the time of Elizabeth, who rode only reluctantly in this effeminate conveyance which young men scorned. . . .

Societies that are receptive to technological innovation have historically tended to equate the introduction of new technologies with improvements in the quality of life, both individually and systemically.[77] They have consequently not concerned themselves with regulating the generalized *effects* of a technology; they have, instead, tended to assume its implementation will have generally beneficial effects.[78] This, after all, is why societies have been receptive to new technologies.

---

(notes omitted). For resistance to other technologies, see 40–59.

One reason there was little interest in technology among the Greeks and Romans was the wide availability of slaves: "When slaves are readily available, there are few incentives to invent and use labor-saving machinery." Rudi Volti, *Society and Technological Change*, 4th ed. (New York: Worth Publishers, 2001), 137–138.

As for tools, some are inanimate, others animate; . . . to the helmsman a steering oar is an inanimate tool, the lookout man an animate tool. . . . [A]n article of property is a tool . . . and the slave is an animate article of property. Every assistant is a . . . tool that takes the place of several tools. For if every tool were able to complete its own task when ordered . . . if shuttles could pass through the web by themselves . . . masters [would have] no need of slaves.'

John W. Humphrey, John P. Oleson, and Andrew N. Sherwood, *Greek and Roman Technology* (London: Routledge, 1998), 581 (quoting Aristotle, *Politics*, 1.2.4–5 [1253b–1254a]).

Issues involving the implementation of technology generally did not arise in societies that reject technology because those societies have historically been able to avoid technology. In ancient times, Greek and Roman societies avoided the need to deal with technology by ignoring it. In more recent times, societies have been able to close their borders to specific technologies—or to technology in general—and thereby avoid the need to deal with it. Modern technology can make it difficult to do this. Some technologically intolerant societies have responded to this circumstance in the only way possible, i.e., by adopting laws that prohibit their citizens' utilizing the technology. It is, for example, illegal to possess an unregistered modem in Myanmar. See U.S. Department of State, "Consular Information Sheet: Burma (Myanmar)" (March 15, 2006), http://travel.state.gov/travel/cis_pa_tw/cis/cis_1077.html.

[77] This is a modern attitude, one that tends to conflate the notions of "progress" and "technology." The tendency to associate technology with established itself in America in the nineteenth century:

While the agrarian philosophy of Jefferson and his supporters accepted the . . . balance . . . between . . . man and nature, the proponents of technological improvement . . . tended to think in terms of a man-made universe. . . . Technology . . . was becoming the norm, and the power of machinery was replacing . . . nature. . . . The old American faith in progress, based on the richness of the natural landscape plus the American political system, had to make room for the new belief that science and technology would be the chief foundation stones of future progress. . . .

Arthur A. Ekirch, Jr., *Man and Nature in America* (New York: Columbia University Press, 1963), 44–45. For more on the evolution of American receptivity to technological innovation, see Neil Longley York, *Mechanical Metamorphosis: Technological Change in Revolutionary America* (Westport, CT: Greenwood Press, 1985), 3–7, 213–223. See also Steven E. Goldberg and Charles R. Strain, *Technological Change and the Transformation of America* (Carbondale, IL: Southern Illinois University Press, 1987), 24–30.

[78] This has generally proven to be true (except, perhaps, for war technologies). See Volti, *Society and Technological Change*, 221–259 (war technology as "the dark side of technological progress").

Societies concentrate instead on controlling *how* a technology is implemented. They see this as the best way to limit the negative consequences of its implementation: The technology is presumptively beneficial, so it follows that any negative effects must be a product of defective (or improper) implementation.[79] Rules dealing with technology have consequently focused on those who "use" technology; since "users" are the ones who implement a technology, its implementation can be controlled by adopting rules that restrict access to a technology (limit "users," both quantitatively and qualitatively) and set standards for its implementation (structure their "use").[80]

Until the end of the nineteenth century, technologies were not pervasive in and of themselves; the implementation of these pervasive-only-in-their-effects technologies was assigned exclusively to occupational specialists. Because these specialists were the only "users" of a technology, it was possible to control the implementation of a technology by enacting rules that targeted its specialist-"users" and the occupational context in which they functioned. This is why context-specific rules were the exclusive method used to control technology for centuries, and it is why they still survive.

Bicycle technology was pervasive not only in its effects but as a technology, and so required a different approach. The notion that a technology was used in a specific societal context was gone; what remained was a purely egalitarian technology.[81] Because the bicycle was theoretically available to everyone, its "use" was purely haphazard, a matter of individual taste, aptitude, and finances. Its "users" were "civilians"—random, undifferentiated members of the general public—rather than specialists.

The *ad hoc* strategy law applied to deal with this democratization of "use" was to employ the same basic approach—rules directed at "users"—but focus these rules

---

79  For the distinction between "defective" and "improper" implementation, see Chapter 3. As explained later in this chapter, the potential negative consequences of implementing some technologies are so slight that societies may not find it necessary to institute rules designed to control defective or improper implementation

80  As Chapter 5 explains, the laws that were adopted to control access to automobiles and to set standards for their operation are a good example of this.

81  This, in fact, was touted as one of the advantages of this new technology. As an 1896 article explained: "[i]t is the great leveler, for not 'til all Americans got on bicycles was the great American principle of every man is just as good as any other man . . . fully realized. All are on equal terms." Smith, *A Social History of The Bicycle*, 112 (quoting *Scientific American*, June 27, 1896, p. 391).

on "using" bicycle technology as technology, not on participating in a specialized, context-specific endeavor based on a technology.[82] This strategy was practicable, and intuitively appealing, because the concern was still with preventing defective implementation.

The rules devised to control the implementation of bicycle technology, like those employed to control the implementation of prior, nonpervasive technologies, therefore focused on the "users"; unlike the rules employed to control prior technologies, however, the bicycle rules were generalized. They applied to anyone in the society if, and as long as, that person was "using" a bicycle; "using-bicycle-technology" became the empirical context in which these rules applied. That is significant because here there *is* still a context; though these rules *can* apply to everyone, they in fact do not and will not. Bicycle rules only apply when one enters the bicycle-as-technology context by "using" a bicycle; like their predecessors, they remain a specialized set of technology-specific rules.

As we saw above, these rules were concerned only with controlling the defective implementation of bicycle technology. The issue of improper implementation— "misuse"—did not arise because the technology did not lend itself to "misuse." More accurately, it did not lend itself to technologically specific "misuse:" Bicycles were stolen, were used to flee after committing robberies and other crimes, and, on at least a few occasions, were used to assault someone.[83] The theft of a bicycle in no way constituted the "misuse" of that technology; here, the bicycle plays a purely passive role, as an item analogous to any other item valuable enough to warrant stealing. Bicycle theft was merely a particular manifestation of the traditional crime of theft; a bicycle's status as "technology" was quite irrelevant to the "harm" being inflicted.

---

[82]  Law could not, for example, rely on guild rules to control access to and the use of this technology. See Chapter 3.

[83]  For bicycle assaults, see, *e.g.*, *Fishwick v. State*, 10 Ohio N.P. (N.S.) 110 (Ohio Com. Pl. 1910) ("One who rudely and in such a reckless manner as to show a disregard of consequences rides his bicycle against a person standing upon a town sidewalk is liable for an assault and battery"); *Mercer v. Corbin*, 117 Ind. 450, 20 N.E. 132 (Ind. 1889) (same).

It was far more common for bicycles to be stolen than for them to be employed in the commission of crimes. See Smith, *A Social History of The Bicycle*, 59. They were on occasion used in the commission of crimes such as bank robbery and burglary. See *id.* at 60–61. They could increase the speed with which certain types of criminals could act and facilitate their escape from the authorities. Robert Smith cited, for example, the "cycle burglar [who] was able to make five raids in one evening, an increase of about 50 per cent in efficiency," 60. He also mentions the bicycling bank robbers who successfully got away, and the one who did not because "he had a puncture" in one of his tires.

The same is true of bicycle assaults because here the bicycle's role is merely that of a weapon—an evolved blunt instrument. And, finally, though the bicycle's contribution to miscreants' fleeing the scene of a crime did implicate its technical functionality, its role here is analogous to that of, say, the horse; for millennia, criminals used horses to flee the scene of their depredations without law's even incorporating this circumstances into its criminal prohibitions. Every society in history has had theft laws, but none has ever seen the need to add a "theft by horseback" prohibition.[84] The reason is that criminal law's concern is with discouraging the infliction of certain "harms."[85] As I explain in the next chapter, criminal law consequently focuses its prohibitions on the "harm" being inflicted not on the collateral circumstances involved in the infliction of that "harm" in a particular instance.[86] Societies could therefore adequately address the "harms" inflicted upon or by bicycles by applying existing criminal prohibitions, such as those criminalizing theft, assault or, perhaps, even homicide.[87] As an early

---

[84]  As with bicycles, horses were stolen, which gave rise to prosecutions for theft. See, *e.g., Burger v. State,* 83 Ala. 36, 3 So. 319, 320 (Ala. 1887); *State v. Webb,* 2 N.C. 103, 1794 WL 98 (N.C. Super. L. & Eq. 1794). Providing a fleeing felon with a horse to use in his escape would make the person who produced the horse liable as an accessory after the fact to the crime the perpetrator had committed, but is simply holding the helpful individual liable for the "harm" she inflicted, i.e., helping a criminal flee justice. See, *e.g., People v. Dunn,* 53 Hun, 381, 6 N.Y.S. 805, 808 (N.Y. Sup. Ct. 1889).

[85]  See Brenner, Is There Such a Thing as Virtual Crime?, 1. http://www.boalt.org/CCLR/v4/v4brenner.htm.

[86]  See *id.*

[87]  For assault prosecutions involving bicycles, see, *e.g., Fishwick v. State,* 10 Ohio N.P. (N.S.) 110 (Ohio Com. Pl. 1910); *Mercer v. Corbin,* 117 Ind. 450, 20 N.E. 132 (Ind. 1889). For theft prosecutions involving bicycles, see, e.g., *State v. Nagel,* 136 Mo. 45, 37 S.W. 821, 822 (Mo. 1896); *People v. Wright,* 11 Utah. 41, 39 P. 477, 477 (Utah. Terr. 1895); Edmonds v. State, 42 Neb. 684, 60 N.W. 957, 957 (Neb. 1894). In *Johnson v. State,* 66 Ohio St. 59, 63 N.E. 607 (Ohio 1902), the defendant, Noah Johnson, was convicted of manslaughter on the following facts:

Noah Johnson, who is . . . about twenty-three years of age, and an expert bicycle rider, in the county of Scioto and state of Ohio, on the 25th day of May, 1901, as it was growing dusk in the evening, rode a bicycle, known as a "racing machine," noiselessly down the main street of a village containing about 1,200 inhabitants, and over one of its most prominent street crossings, at a speed of about twenty miles per hour. . . . [T]he evening was fair, and many people were walking up and down said street, and over its crossings. . . . [D]efendant was leaning forward, and over his bicycle, the handle bars being dropped, and was in the position commonly used in riding in bicycle races. There was no bell attached to his bicycle, no alarm was given by defendant, and he could have seen ahead of him. While riding over the aforesaid street crossing at said rate of speed, the defendant collided with Emory L. Barrows, who was at the time walking, at the usual and customary place, from one corner of said crossing over the street upon which said defendant was riding, to another corner, the force of which collision lifted said Emory L. Barrows from the ground, hurled him a distance of about fifteen feet through the air, and fractured and crushed his skull in several places, thereby causing his death.

66 Ohio St. at 60, 63 N.E. at 607.

twentieth-century Indiana court explained:

> If one should drive so rapidly . . . as to be unable to avoid running over any
> pedestrian who may happen to be in the middle of the road, it is that degree
> of negligence in the conduct of a horse and gig which amounts to an illegal
> act . . . and if death ensues from the injuries . . . the parties driving are guilty
> of manslaughter. . . .*Regina v. Longbottom*, 4 Cox, C. C. 449. . . . The general
> rule . . . is that the negligent performance of a duty . . . is . . . an unlawful
> act, which if it results in death is homicide . . . for which the perpetrator is
> criminally liable. . . . 4 Blackstone, *Com.* 191; 2 Bishop, *New Criminal Law*,
> 659; 1 Wharton, *Criminal Law* (9<sup>th</sup> ed.) 329, 336. . . . These rules apply with
> full force to homicides resulting from the negligent management of loco-
> motive engines, automobiles, bicycles, and other like dangerous agencies.
> The test of criminal liability lies in the negligent operation of the engine in
> view of all the conditions.[88]

## Communication Technologies

Communication technologies assumed an unheard-of importance during the
nineteenth century. A number of new technologies—such as telegraphy, typewriting and photography—were well-established by 1900; and printing, a centuries-
old technology, had vastly evolved in sophistication.[89] This section examines
the extent to which each of these four technologies was pervasive in the traditional sense (effects only) or in the newer sense (technology itself), and the efforts
societies made to control these technologies by adopting rules of the type discussed above.

We defer our examination of two ostensibly nineteenth-century technologies
until the next chapter. Although the telephone was invented in the nineteenth
century, and telephones were being "used" before 1900,[90] the telephone did not
become an influential technology until the twentieth century.[91] The same is true

---

[88]  *Pittsburgh, C., C. & St. L. Ry. Co. v. Ferrell*, 39 Ind.App. 515, 78 N.E. 988, 996–997 (Ind. App. 1906).

[89]  See Derry and Williams, *A Short History of Technology*, 235–242, 637–661.

[90]  See Oliver, *History of American Technology*, 435–439.

[91]  See The Subcommittee on Technology, 4:

> [T]here were not many telephones in use in 1900, around a million in number. Yet the telephone industry
> was destined to grow into the third largest public utility in the United States, with an investment of nearly
> $5,000,000,000 and giving employment to hundreds of thousands. Its influence has been far reaching.

of cinematography; while the technology used for "movies" existed by the end of the nineteenth century, "cinema as a major social force belonged to a later period than 1900."[92]

## Printing

Printing technology arrived in the West in the 1400s[93] and did not change in any noteworthy fashion until the early nineteenth century,[94] when the introduction of new type-setting machines dramatically accelerated the publishing process.[95] Printing had for centuries been used to publish books, newspapers, and other periodicals,[96] but the

> turn of the eighteenth to nineteenth centuries marks a decisive stage in the history of printing. It was not a break but rather a sudden leap forward. It affected the technique of printing, the methods of publication and distribution, and the habit of reading. Compositors and printers, publishers and booksellers, borrowers and buyers of books adopted, or were forced into, new ways of production and consumption. Technical progress, rationalized organization and compulsory education interacted one on another. New inventions lowered the cost of production; mass literacy created further demands, the national and international organization of the trade

---

It broke the isolation of the farms, increased the number of business transactions, and speeded the tempo of modern life. . . . It has tended to break down State lines, to eradicate regional differences, and to increase international contacts. It has been of aid in safety, in transportation, in fighting fires, and crime.

See also Trevor I. Williams, *A Short History of Twentieth-Century Technology* (New York: Clarendon Press, 1982), 301, "in 1900 . . . the telephone was beginning to be used . . . but it was yet to make a major social impact."

92  Derry and Williams, *A Short History of Technology*, 661.

93  See *id.*, 240, "In 1450 book-printing was still in its earliest infancy, but by 1500 there were nearly 40,000 recorded editions of books, and even though more than two-thirds of these came from the presses of Germany and Italy, there were twelve other European countries in which the art of printing was by this time established."

94  See *id.*, "no basic changes in the working of a printing-press between its first inception and the early nineteenth century."

95  See *id.*, 638–641, 643–648. See also S. H. Steinberg & John Trevitt, *Five Hundred Years of Printing* (London: British Library, 1996), 137–145.

96  See Derry and Williams, *A Short History of Technology*, 644. See also John W. Oliver, History of American Technology (Ronald Press, 1956), 58 (printing technology arrived in America with the colonists; the first newspaper appeared in 1636).

widened the channels and eased the flow of books from the publishers' stock departments to the retailers' shelves.[97]

The changes in printing technology had an immediate and profound influence in one particular area: By dramatically improving the speed and quality of publishing, the new technology changed "the function and position of the newspaper in American life."[98]

Until the nineteenth century, newspapers offered little in the way of "news." They were "small, blotchily printed . . . sheets, devoted to political polemics, with paddings from private correspondence and clippings from foreign papers brought by the mails."[99] The new printing technologies also improved content: "Greatly improved facilities for newsgathering were developed, and papers printed the news as soon as it happened."[100] Soon, a rivalry developed among newspapers.

> In their efforts to increase circulation, editors printed sensational news stories which were read by rich and poor alike. . . . Display heads were used, and illustrations were introduced. Newspapers and printers began to pride themselves on the speed with which they could serve the public. Improved transportation . . . stimulated this rivalry and demands for daily newspapers increased.[101]

---

[97] Steinberg and Trevitt, *Five Hundred Years of Printing*, 136.

[98] Oliver, *History of American Technology*, 206.

[99] *Id.*, 207. See also David A. Copeland, *Debating the Issues in Colonial Newspapers: Primary Documents on Events of the Period* (Wesport, CT: Greenwood Press, 2000), xii; Shing-ling Chien, Carl J. Couch, and David R. Maines, Information Technologies and Social Orders 138–140 (New York: Aldine de Gruyter, 1996); Steinberg and Trevitt, *Five Hundred Years of Printing*,120–125. Early newspapers also had a very limited circulation. See Clarence Brigham, *Journals and Journeymen* (Philadelphia, PA: University of Pennsylvania Press, 1950), 19–22; Jarvis Means Morse. Connecticut Newspapers in the Eighteenth Century (New Haven, CT: Yale University Press, 1935), 6–30.

[100] Oliver, *History of American Technology*, 212–213:

> [R]ivalry developed among . . . papers. . . . In their efforts to increase circulation, editors printed sensational news stories which were read by rich and poor alike. . . . Display heads were used, and illustrations were introduced. Newspapers and printers began to pride themselves on the speed with which they could serve the public. Improved transportation . . . stimulated this rivalry and demands for daily newspapers increased.

[101] *Id.*

But the greatest impetus for the growth of newspapers came from the "penny press":

> The *Sun* in 1833 started issuing a daily that sold for one cent, which meant that the newspaper was no longer confined to the seclusion of the bar room, the political salon, or the counting house. It . . . became the people's paper. *The Philadelphia Ledger* and the *Baltimore Sun* . . . followed . . . and within a few years the penny press was being read in several cities. By 1840 . . . the increase in newspaper circulation was estimated to be 187 per cent. [102]

By the mid-nineteenth century, "technological improvements had so facilitated printing that the press had become 'man's most trusted servant,' and the newspaper was hailed as `the poor man's college.'"[103] Related advancements improved the speed and quality of publishing for books and periodicals.[104] As one author noted, the

> Victorians virtually invented mass literature. High-speed presses, cheap wood-pulp paper, machines for typesetting, . . . railways to send printed material quickly all over the country, and the steadily growing number of people who were literate enough to read for pleasure encouraged the publication of newspapers, magazines, and novels at every price and for every taste.[105]

---

[102] *Id.,* 214–215. As one author explains, the term

penny paper is best taken as referring to papers made widely available to the public. This development did not take place overnight. It had been possible (but not easy) to buy single copies of newspapers before 1830, but this usually involved the reader going down to the printer's office and purchasing a copy (a few were usually kept on hand beyond those mailed to subscribers). Street sales were almost unknown. However, within a few years, street sales of newspapers would be commonplace in eastern cities. At first the price of single copies was seldom a penny—usually two or three cents was charged—and some of the older well-established papers charged five or six cents. But the phrase `penny paper' caught the public's fancy, and soon there would be papers that did indeed sell for only a penny.

George H. Douglas, *The Golden Age of the Newspaper* (Westport, CT: Greenwood Press, 1999), 3.

[103] Oliver, *History of American Technology,* 207.

[104] See Derry and Williams, *A Short History of Technology,* 640–648. See also Dean De La Motte and Jeannene M. Przyblyski, *Making the News: Modernity & the Mass Press in Nineteenth Century France* (Amherst, MA: University of Massachusetts Press, 1999), 160–181; Mitchell, *Daily Life in Victorian England,* 233–238.

[105] *Id.,* 233. For the historical evolution of periodicals, see, *e.g.,* Henry Mills Alden, *Magazine Writing and the New Literature* (New York: Harper, 1908), 4–9. For the history of magazines—the "multi-authored text"—see, *e.g.,* Margaret Beetham, *A Magazine of Her Own? Domesticity and Desire in the Woman's Magazine, 1800–1914* (New York: Routledge, 1996), 17–20.

The net effect of all this was to create a popular press, the precursor of modern media.

Printing technology, like all of the technologies we have examined so far, was pervasive in its effects; printing differed from the other technologies, however, in that its sole purpose was to generate these effects (and to do so in real-time). The tool and industrial technologies each had a primary, instrumental function—for example, transportation, building, mining—that sustained a society; these instrumental technologies supported a society's critical infrastructure by helping, directly or indirectly, to ensure its citizens were supplied with food, shelter, clothing, implements, and other items. The pervasive effects of these infrastructure technologies were intended, desired byproducts of the successful performance of a technology's primary function. Civilians "received" the effects of these technologies indirectly as their byproducts percolated throughout a society; the effects of these technologies were therefore more mediated than those of printing technology.

The same is at once true and not-true of the railroad and ship transportation technologies that are the closest analogues of tool and industrial technologies. It is true in that the rail and ship technologies both transported (a) materials to the specialists who operated the infrastructure technologies and (b) products generated by the infrastructure technologies to suppliers who distributed them to civilians.[106] Because neither technology interacted directly with civilians in fulfilling these quasi-infrastructure functions, the effects of this aspect of their respective roles were mediated.[107]

The increased sophistication print technology attained in the nineteenth century created something new: a technology the sole purpose of which was to interact directly with civilians and thereby generate effects that pervaded a society in real-time.[108] And its effects were little short of radical:

> [Creation] of the penny press . . . caused such fundamental changes in American newspapers that it can properly be termed revolutionary.

---

[106] See Robert P. Clark, *The Global Imperative: An Interpretative History of the Spread of Mankind* (Boulder, CO: Westview Press, 1997), 93–94 (railroad as supporting infrastructure).

[107] Both technologies had another function, as well: Railroads and ships transported civilians for recreational purposes that were irrelevant to maintaining a society's critical infrastructure. Their effects were, in this regard, direct, and represented a step toward the consumer technologies discussed in Chapter 5.

[108] See, *e.g.*, James L. Crouthamel, *Bennett's New York Herald and the Rise of the Popular Press* (Syracuse, NY: Syracuse University Press, 1989), 24.

The . . . phenomenal popularity of the *Sun* . . . and the *Herald* with their cash-and-carry sales policy created the independent newspaper, free of political and mercantile patronage and dependent only on its own wide audience. The wide circulation attracted advertisers and led to financial independence; the revenue . . . financed the technological improvements necessary to produce papers for a large readership. There were . . . two interacting parts to the newspaper revolution. One was a change in style and technique to appease the tastes of the readers. . . . The other was the improvement in technology and news-gathering, with an emphasis on news as a commodity.[109]

And one historian noted, these papers "packaged news as a product to appeal to a mass audience. . . . [T]hey changed the focus of news to report activities of ordinary people, wrote in an accessible style . . . and covered subjects that interested the masses rather than elites."[110]

The effects of print technology differed from the effects of prior technologies such as tool and industrial technologies: Print technology distributed information and, in so doing, had a subjective rather than an objective effect upon the members of a society. It kept them informed, amused, outraged, and educated.[111] The effects of print technology were therefore more ephemeral than those of tool and industrial technologies; because the effects of printing, particularly printing news, tended to be transitory, they required constant renewal.

Print technology was not an infrastructure technology; it did not perform a function essential for the survival of a society, at least not in the way tool and industrial technologies did. Societies and earlier social groupings had survived for millennia without a popular press (or a literate population).[112] Nineteenth-century print technology began the process of institutionalizing a practice that had always been endemic to social life but had remained informal and unstructured: sharing information within a society.[113] For most of human history, we did

---

[109]   *Id.*

[110]   William E. Huntzicker, William David Sloan, and James D. Startt, *The Popular Press, 1833–1865* (Westport, CT: Greenwood Press, 1999), 163.

[111]   See *id.*

[112]   See Alfred Burns, *The Power of the Written Word: The Role of Literacy in the History of Western Civilization* (New York: Peter Lang, 1989), 1–13.

[113]   See David Riesman, *The Oral and Written Traditions* in *Explorations in Communication: An Anthology,* ed. Edmund Carpenter & Marshall McLuhan (Boston: Beacon Press, 1960), 109–111.

this orally; we relied on conversations among members of a society or formal pronouncements—speeches—by those in authority to disseminate information about events and about each other.[114] Nineteenth-century print technology changed this by shifting our focus from individually based communication to technologically based communication, and began a process that is still evolving: the use of technology to disseminate information rapidly throughout a society.

This differs from the oral transmission of information in two ways: Although oral transmission can be quite accurate, it is a much slower process because it depends on interactions between individuals; one acquires information by interacting with another and passes it along to one or more others in one or more subsequent interactions. The pace at which information is disseminated is therefore a function of the pace at which particular individuals interact. Relying on individual interactions also affects what we will call information saturation, that is, the thoroughness with which information is disseminated throughout a society. Because information moves from acquaintance to acquaintance in this model, the level of information saturation is more or less haphazard; information is likely to spread thoroughly in some sectors of society and less thoroughly in others.[115] We will return to the interaction of technology and information dissemination in Chapters 5 and 6; now, we need to consider how law dealt with nineteenth century print technology.

---

[114] See, *e.g.*, Hanna M. Cotton, Fergus Millar, and Guy M. Rogers, *The Roman Republic and the Augustan Revolution* (Chapel Hill, NC: University of North Carolina Press, 2002), 123–124; Janet Watson, *Speaking Volumes: Orality and Literacy in the Greek and Roman World* (Boston: Brill Leiden, 2001). See also Riesman, *The Oral and Written Traditions*, 109, 111.

Writing was also used to disseminate information at some points in history. See "Acta Diurna," *Wikipedia*, http://en.wikipedia.org/wiki/Acta_Diurna (acta diurna "were daily Roman official notices. They were carved on stone or metal and presented in message boards in public places like the Forum of Rome"). See also "Acta," *The Columbia Encyclopedia*, 6th ed. (New York: Columbia University Press, 2004); William Stearns Davis, *A Day in Old Rome: A Picture of Roman Life* (Cheshire, CT: Biblio-Moser, 1961), 282.

Writing was of little importance in disseminating information until the nineteenth century because of limited access to printed sources and because literacy was so very limited in most societies. See R. A. Houston, *Literacy in Early Modern Europe: Culture and Education 1500–1800* (London: Longman, 1988), 177–200. See also Burns, *The Power of the Written Word*, 12 ("Printing . . . made universal literacy possible, at least theoretically, and almost a reality"); "Literacy history," *Wikipedia*, http://en.wikipedia.org/wiki/Literacy ("before the industrial revolution finally made cheap paper and cheap books available to all classes in industrialized countries, in the mid-nineteenth century, literacy existed only in a tiny minority of the world's different societies"). The acta diurna, for example, were available only to those in physical proximity to wherever the notices were posted.

[115] See Riesman, *The Oral and Written*, 109, 111.

Print technology's effectives were pervasive, but the technology was not. Like all of the technologies we have discussed, except for bicycle technology, print technology was the exclusive province of a cadre of specialists—printers, typesetters, reporters, editors, newsboys.[116]

The pervasiveness, immediacy and nature of its effects on civilians all made print technology a prime candidate for rules that would control its implementation. As Chapter 3 explained, societies adopt these rules in an effort to limit the negative consequences—the "harm"—that can result from implementing a new technology. Although the physical implementation of print technology, as such, was unlikely to pose any physical danger to a civilian populace, government officials feared that unrestrained publication threatened the stability of the social order and so instituted measures to control what was printed.[117]

> European authorities devoted immense amounts of time, energy, and personnel to attempting to control the press. . . . In Spain, at least fifteen major press laws were enacted between 1810 and 1853. A . . . Russian journalist complained that his newspaper had to hire a specialist to keep up with the over 13,000 bureaucratic circulars . . . authorities promulgated to provide the press with `guidance. . . . French censorship regulations were so complex that at least ten books were published between 1830 and 1880 to provide guidance to lawyers [and] journalists . . . who were trying to decipher them. In most nineteenth-century European countries, changes in censorship regulations accompanied almost every important change in regime, ruler, or domestic policy orientation.[118]

Because of the First Amendment, censorship laws, as such, were not enacted in the United States.[119] Like other countries, though, the United States used criminal

---

[116]  See Oliver, *History of American Technology*, 206–215.

[117]  See, *e.g.*, Robert Justin Goldstein, *The War for the Public Mind: Political Censorship in Nineteenth-Century Europe* (Westport, CT: Praeger, 2000), 127 ("shortly before the 1830 revolution Charles X's ministers declared . . . the press had been . . . 'an instrument of disorder and sedition' . . . that had prevented the establishment 'of a stable and regular regime of government'"). The officials who took this position presumably regarded unauthorized stories as an "improper" implementation of print technology. See *id.* at 127.

[118]  *Id.*, 13, 16 ("every major European country enforced prior press censorship during part of the nineteenth century"). As the nineteenth century progressed, some countries relaxed their censorship laws, no doubt because they had become accustomed to the notion of a popular press.

[119]  There was a notably unsuccessful effort to censor the publication of troop movements during the Civil War. See, *e.g.*, Robert S. Halper, *Lincoln and the Press* (New York: McGraw-Hill, 1951), 133.

law to discourage publication of certain types of "offensive" information: obscenity, blasphemy, seditious material, and libel directed at public officials.[120] This, however, was the extent of American efforts in this regard; though laws authorized the printing of public documents, none specifically sought to regulate the implementation of print technology.[121] There were, in other words, no analogues of the laws that set safety standards for railroads or controlled the implementation of industrial technologies.

Like the laws that controlled the implementation of the tool, industrial and mass transportation technologies, the laws that sought to control implementation of nineteenth-century print technology were context specific. They targeted the specialists responsible for implementing the technology.[122]

The laws were of two types: laws that forbade publishing unauthorized material; and laws that punished those who had published such material. The prior restraint laws were implemented by various means, including criminal liability;[123] they sought to prevent the publication of prohibited material. The laws that retroactively punished those who had published such material were criminal laws;[124] they were meant to discourage those who had published unauthorized material from further engaging in such activity and to deter others from following their example.[125] Other laws took a more indirect approach by requiring newspapers to post large security deposits or pay an onerous newspaper tax "to make it difficult for poor people . . . to buy newspapers."[126]

---

[120] See Susan W. Brenner, "Complicit Publication: When Should the Dissemination of Ideas and Data Be Criminalized?", *Albany Law Journal of Science & Technology* 13, (2003): 273, 287–321. See also Goldstein, *The War for the Public Mind*, 59 (Germany), 138 (France), 181 (Spain).

[121] See, *e.g.*, *Hicks v. King*, 21 Wash. 567, 569, 58 P. 1070, 1070 (Wash. 1899); *State v. Bartley*, 50 Neb. 874, 70 N.W. 367, 367–368 (Neb. 1897); *Carter v. State*, 8 S.D. 153, 65 N.W. 422, 422–423 (S.D. 1895).

[122] See, *e.g.*, *State v. Holedger*, 15 Wash. 443, 444, 46 P. 652, 652 (Wash. 1896) (defendant indicted for "publishing . . . obscene and indecent literature"); *Reyes v. State*, 34 Fla. 181, 182, 15 So. 875, 875 (Fla. 1894) (same); *Commonwealth v. Kneeland*, 37 Mass. 206, 206, 1838 WL 2655 *2 (Mass. 1838) (indictment charged that defendant "unlawfully and wickedly composed, printed and published in a newspaper . . . of which he was the editor and publisher, a . . . blasphemous and profane libel").

[123] See Goldstein, *The War for the Public Mind*, 138 (French law required the posting of a press security deposit but also authorized post-publication prosecution).

[124] For the distinction between civil and criminal laws, see Chapters 2 and 3.

[125] See Brenner, *Toward a Criminal Law for Cyberspace: Distributed Security*, 46–65. See also Goldstein, *The War for the Public Mind*, 54 (section of the Prussian Criminal Code "banning attacks on official institutions and measures, was stretched to cover almost any criticism; and some journalists spent as much time in prison . . . as at their desks").

[126] See *Id.*, 17, 148.

We need to decide how the nineteenth-century printing technology laws fit within the dichotomy outlined in Chapter 3. Chapter 3 explained that societies use laws to control the "harm" caused by the misimplementation of technologies. It also explained that misimplementation either of takes two forms: defective implementation or improper implementation. Laws directed at defective implementation seek to ensure technical precision in a technology's implementation; they are, as Chapter 3 explained, intended to prevent failures of "use." Improper implementation laws, on the other hand, target deliberately abusing a technology in order to cause "harm"; they are intended to prevent the misuse of technology.[127] Civil liability is used to enforce defective implementation laws, while criminal liability is used to enforce improper implementation laws.[128]

The nineteenth-century printing technology laws are somewhat ambiguous, insofar as the application of this dichotomy is concerned, because both civil and criminal liability were used in their enforcement. Even when civil liability was used, however, its purpose seems to have been punitive. Ultimately, the laws seem to have been improper implementation, or "misuse," laws. They did not target the physical implementation of printing technology qua technology; they were not concerned with physical "harms"—such as injured printers or readers poisoned by toxic inks—resulting from inept use of the technology.

Instead, they targeted a somewhat culturally sensitive conception of improper implementation, or misuse: As noted above, the United States, along with most other societies used criminal liability to inhibit the application of printing technology to disseminate material inflicting what are *generally* recognized as uniquely egregious "harms."[129] Other countries went further and used criminal liability (or civil liability or both) to inhibit the application of printing technology to disseminate what would be First-Amendment protected speech in the United States. Unconstrained by the First Amendment or similar guarantees, these countries were responding to what they perceived as the "misuse" of printing technology to inflict a compelling, distinct "harm:" what Metternich described "'the manifestation of ideas which disturb the peace of the state, its interest and its good order.'"[130]

---

[127]  See Chapter 3.
[128]  See Chapter 3.
[129]  See Brenner, "Complicit Publication," 273, 287–321.
[130]  Goldstein, *The War for the Public Mind*, 13.

We seem to have encountered our first improper implementation (or "misuse") laws. One could argue, though, that these nineteenth-century printing technology laws were not *really* "misuse" of technology laws—that they were, instead, an extrapolation of existing laws criminalizing "harmful" speech to encompass a particular "use" of printing technology. And it is true that the "harms" these laws targeted—obscenity, blasphemy, defaming public officials, and sedition—had long been criminalized, in varying degrees, in Europe, in the United States and elsewhere.[131] It is also true, though, that printing technology increased the scale on which the prohibited "harm" was inflicted; someone can, for example, disseminate seditious speech much more extensively if it is in a printed leaflet distributed by the thousands than if he/she relies on word of mouth.

The printing technology laws therefore raise issues we will grapple with later in this book: Should "misuse" laws *only* target the infliction of a technologically specific, unique type of "harm"? Or should they also target the "use" of a technology to inflict a level of conventional "harm" that would not be possible otherwise? The answers to these questions will depend upon how we conceptualize "misuse" and that is an issue the resolution of which we must defer until Chapter 7.

## Telegraphy

In 1844, Samuel Morse sent the first public telegram using technology he had developed in 1836.[132] Congress had passed legislation appropriating $30,000 to fund his demonstrating telegraphy.

> Lines were set up between Washington and Baltimore. . . . With Morse presiding at the key . . . the . . . first message . . . was sent . . . May 24, 1844.

> The fact that the Democratic Convention was meeting in Baltimore . . . had much to do with making the public aware of the new invention. . . . The proceedings were transmitted to . . . congressmen in Washington, and their messages wafted back. . . . *The New York Herald* declared, "It . . . is unquestionably the greatest invention of the age."[133]

---

[131]  See Brenner, "Complicit Publication," 273, 287–321.

[132]  See Oliver, *History of American Technology*, 216–219.

[133]  *Id.*, 218. See also Harold Evans with Gail Buckland and David Lefer, *They Made America: From the Steam Engine to the Search Engine* (New York: Back Bay Books, 2004), 74–80.

After Morse formed his telegraph company—Western Union—in 1845, the growth of "the telegraph network was . . . explosive."[134] As lines were strung around the world, telegraphy "revolutionized business practice, gave rise to new forms of crime, and inundated its users with information."[135]

Functionally, telegraph technology was the mirror image of print technology. Print technology was a one-to-many communication technology in which one source (newspaper, magazine, book) communicated with a wide, undifferentiated audience. Each member of that audience received identical, standard information delivered on the same schedule. Telegraphy was a one-to-one communication technology offering remote communication between individuals;[136] unlike print technology, the information it transmitted was idiosyncratic, unique to the parties to a particular communication.[137]

Like print technology, telegraphy was a technology that interfaced directly with civilians, albeit on a lesser scale. Telegraphy was analogous to postal mail in that it transmitted written messages. Unlike the post, however, it used wired (later wireless) technology instead of human beings to transmit messages; its messages consequently traveled much faster than those committed to the post. Telegraphy differed from the post in another important respect: To send a message, one wrote it out and gave it to a specialist, a telegrapher, who translated it into Morse Code and transmitted the contents to other telegraphers until the message reached its destination, was decoded and delivered to the intended recipient.[138]

---

134 Tom Standage, *The Victorian Internet* (New York: Walker & Company, 1998), 56–91.

135 *Id.*, vii. See also Oliver, *History of American Technology*, 219.; Mitchell, *Daily Life in Victorian England*, 81–82.

136 See Standage, *The Victorian Internet*, vii (telegraphy "allowed people to communicate almost instantly across great distances").

137 Telegraphy was an early form of mediated communication, i.e.,

> communication that takes place via and by virtue of some artificial medium . . .; it is to be distinguished from direct, or face-to-face, communication. Mediated communication can be specifically directed at one or more `known' parties, as in a telephone conversation, or it can be disseminated generally to an unidentified audience, as in radio or television broadcasts. Mediated communication can be interactive, such as a telephone conversation, or it can be the unilateral transmission of information, such as radio or television broadcasts.

> Susan W. Brenner, The Privacy Privilege: Law Enforcement, Technology and the Constitution, *Journal of Technology Law & Policy 7* (2002): 123, 125.

138 See Standage, *The Victorian Internet*, 63. See also Iwan Rhys Morus, "The Electric Ariel: Telegraphy and Commercial Culture in Early Victorian England," *Victorian Studies* 39 (1996): 339, 373. See, *e.g.*, *Koons v. Western Union Tel. Co.*, 102 Pa. 164, 1883 WL 14006 *2 (Pa. 1883) ("The well established rule is, that if a

Telegraph technology quickly became pervasive in its effects. Because it was much faster than the post, telegraphy was used by individuals, as well as by corporate and governmental entities.[139] But it was never as pervasive in its effects as print technology. One reason was cost: Printed materials were so inexpensive they were available to every segment of the population; while the cost of telegraphy was not exorbitant, it was sufficient to put telegrams beyond the resources of many people.[140]

Another reason telegraphy's effects were less pervasive lay in the differential modes of communication involved in the two technologies: Telegrams were private communication; the information they carried was conveyed, through intermediaries, from one individual to another. The systemic effects of telegraphic technology were therefore limited to its impact on *how* people communicated remotely; as people used telegrams instead of the post they became accustomed to technologically mediated personal communication and the advantages (speed, primarily) it offered. Printed materials were public communication; the content they delivered was shared, often simultaneously, with a wide audience. The systemic effects of print technology consequently encompassed both individual reliance on the technology for the delivery of information and the generalized dissemination of specific, often influential content throughout a society.

Unlike the telephone, which would eventually supersede telegraphy, telegraph technology was pervasive only in its effects, not in itself. Civilians could not use the technology themselves; they had to rely on the expertise of a series of

---

telegraph clerk cannot read a message, as written, he should not undertake to receive and transmit it; he should require it to be read by the sender, or, if necessary, re-written"). For a detailed explanation of the process involved in sending a telegram in nineteenth-century Britain, see 'How the Companies Worked,' Distant Writing, http://distantwriting.co.uk/howthecompaniesworked.aspx.

[139]  See Oliver, *History of American Technology*, 219; Mitchell, *Daily Life in Victorian England*, 81–82.

[140]  See Richard R. John, "The Politics of Innovation," *Daedalus 127* (1998): 187,

> In urging a government takeover of the industry, Wisconsin Congressman Cadwallader C. Washburn in 1869 posited that the cost of a telegram should be low enough that telegraphy, like letter writing, could be accessible to the poor. Why, he asked rhetorically, should it cost an immigrant servant girl in Illinois a week's hard labor to telegraph a ten-word greeting to her friends back in New York?

See also Standage, *The Victorian Internet*, 63, (because telegrams were expensive "only the rich could afford to use the network to send trivial messages; most people used the telegraph strictly to convey really urgent news"). See *generally* C. R. Perry, *The Victorian Post Office: The Growth of a Bureaucracy* (Woodbridge, England: Boydell Press, 1992), 122. Because the cost was based on the number of letters in a message, people devised a truncated system of communication for telegraph messages. See Morus, *The Electric Ariel*, 339, 372. For a detailed breakdown of telegram pricing in nineteenth-century Britain, see "What the Companies Charged," http://distantwriting.co.uk/whatthecompaniescharged.aspx.

specialists, beginning with the telegrapher to whom they gave their messages. Telegraphy was a context-specific technology, like most of the technologies we have examined; like those technologies, its implementation was the exclusive province of specialists. It followed that telegraphy, like most of those technologies, would become the subject of context-specific laws directed at these specialists.

The relatively circumscribed nature of telegraphy's effects meant it generated less concern about controlling possible negative effects resulting from its implementation than print technology. As a result, the laws societies directed at telegraphy conformed to the model they had used for most of the technologies we have discussed. The goal was to set standards that promoted the safe, effective implementation of this technology.[141] Telegraph laws consequently addressed matters such as ensuring that messages were delivered, that they were kept confidential, and that telegraphy equipment did not pose a safety hazard.[142] There were no telegraph "misuse" laws because telegraph technology really did not offer opportunities for "misuse."[143]

---

[141] These laws no doubt reflected the concerns of telegraphy's commercial customers. See John, "The Politics of Innovation," 187:

Western Union's critics generated little support among the merchants and manufacturers who were the principal users of the new technology. From their standpoint, speed and accuracy . . . were the overriding concerns. So long as Western Union transmitted time-sensitive commercial information quickly and accurately . . . its business customers had little cause for complaint.

[142] See Standage, *The Victorian Internet*, 121 (law made it "a crime to alter, delay, or disclose the contents of a telegram"). See also *Postal Telegraph-Cable Co. v. State*, 110 Md. 608, 73 A. 679 (Md. 1909) (company convicted of violating statute which required that "the time of filing the telegram at place of origin and the time received at . . . shall appear on each and every telegram'"); *Western Union Tel. Co. v. Todd*, 53 N.E. 194, 196 (Ind. App. 1899) (statute made telegraph company "liable for special damages occasioned by failure or negligence of their operators or servants in receiving, copying, transmitting or delivering of dispatches") (quoting Horner's Rev. St. 1897, § 4177; Burns' Rev. St. 1894, § 5513); *Western Union Tel. Co. v. Mellon*, 96 Tenn. 66, 33 S.W. 725, 726 (Tenn. 1896) (statute required that telegraph messages "be transmitted in the order of their delivery, correctly and without unreasonable delay and shall be kept strictly confidential") (quoting Mill. & V. Code, § 1542). See also *State v. East Jersey Telephone & Telegraph Co.*, 61 N.J.L. 136, 138–140, 38 A. 752, 753 (N.J. 1897) (statute required cities to give telegraph companies "a writing" designating the streets along which telegraph poles could be placed and the manner in which they would be placed "so as not to interfere with the safety . . . of any persons traveling along . . . such streets"); *City of Geneva v. Geneva Tel. Co.*, 30 Misc. 236, 62 N.Y.S. 172, 177 (N.Y. Sup. 1899) (legislature, "having control over telegraph . . . corporations . . ., may make such regulations to prevent the public evils and private injuries resulting from . . . their poles and wires as . . . are calculated to accomplish this end").

[143] Criminals did use telegraph technology in committing of fraud and other financial crimes. See Standage, *The Victorian Internet*, 105–109.

See also *Cordovano v. State*, 61 Ga.App. 590, 7 S.E.2d 45, 47 (Ga. 1940) (prosecution for the "telegram racket," a type of fraud scam); *People v. Carmen*, 9. N.E.2d 981, 986–987 (Ill. App. 1937) (fraud scam

## Typewriting

Prior to the development of the typewriter, one of the most common occupations in an office was that of "writer":

> These were clerks who wrote out documents in longhand. There were many attempts at inventing typewriters . . . but none . . . could overcome . . . the critical problems of document preparation: the difficulty of reading

---

involving falsified horse race results send by telegram). In the 1940s, West Virginia made it a crime to "operate a pool room," which was defined as "'any room where any pool ticket, chance . . . or certificate . . . purporting to entitle the holder . . . to money . . . contingent upon the result of any horse race, prize fight, game of chance, game of skill or science, or other sport or contest, the information of which result is obtained by telephone, telegraph, wireless telegraphy or radio, or other electrical device.'" *State v. McCoy*, 122 W. Va. 54, 7 S.E.2d 89, 89 (W. Va. 1940). Here, too, the telegraph and the other technologies play a very minor role in the commission of the offense. The traditional, generic "harm" being outlawed here is gambling; the use of the technologies is merely a circumstantial component of the infliction of that "harm." As such, neither the prosecution for this offense nor the prosecutions noted above would qualify as the "misuse" of telegraph technology. See Chapter 3.

The same is true for instances in which telegraphy was used to arrange other types of crime, such as robberies. See, *e.g.*, *State v. Chapman*, 6 Nev. 320, 1871 WL 3337 *5 (Nev. 1871):

> The evidence, if taken as true, proves the following state of facts, as to appellant: That in Sierra County, in California, on some day between the tenth and twenty-second days of October, 1870, he agreed with Jones, Davis and Cockerell . . . that on or about the fourth day of November . . . the express car of Wells, Fargo & Co. should be robbed of the treasure, . . . expected to be on it. That he would go to San Francisco, watch the office of Wells, Fargo & Co., and in an agreed cipher telegraph to Jones at Reno, in the State of Nevada, a point near where the robbery was to be attempted, when the large monthly shipment of coin for the use of the mines in Virginia City and vicinity should be made. That appellant sent the telegram which Jones received, and in connection with the other defendants, acted upon, and . . . on the morning of the fifth of November, 1870, robbed the express car of Wells, Fargo & Co., of forty thousand dollars.

See also *Yeager v. State*, 106 Tex. Crim. 462, 294 S.W. 200, 200–201 (Tex. Crim. App. 1927) (robbers used telegrams to arrange prerobbery meeting).

All of the cases I cite above are from the U.S. but Steven Roberts, an expert on the use of telegraphy in nineteenth-century Britain, speculates that similar malfeasance may have occurred there, as well:

> The obvious use of the telegraph in crime would seem to be the rigging of betting markets. The 1840s and 50's in London was an age of off-course horse race betting, with many betting shops being opened - according to one source, several hundred existed in one form or another before they were suppressed in 1854. These premises were targeted, much like gin-palaces, at the ignorant poor who were attracted by the high odds offered on major races. There were many instances of the shop-owners bolting before paying up. The telegraph would have assisted the swindlers in both providing information before the event and in informing of results before they were generally available.

> The other (slightly related) opportunity would have been in rigging the several stock and share markets that existed in mid-century Britain, where inside information or the perception of such easily motivates the immoral as much as the gullible to buy or sell. It was a period of share swindles; mostly, it must be said, of forgery, but market manipulation by speedily communicating information gained seems a good probability.

handwritten documents and the time it took a clerk to write them. In the nineteenth century . . . business documents were handwritten, and the . . . executive spent countless hours deciphering them. . . . [T]he major attraction of the typewriter was that typewritten documents could be read effortlessly at several times the speed of handwritten ones.[144]

By 1874, James Densmore had created a workable typewriter and persuaded the Remington firearms company to manufacture it.[145] Sales were slow at first because businesses "had not yet begun to use machines of any kind."[146] It took five years for Remington to sell a thousand machines, but by "1900 there were at least a dozen major manufacturers making 100,000 typewriters a year."[147]

The increasing popularity of typewriters created a need for trained "type-writers," or typists.[148] Schools opened to train students,[149] and by 1900, the census "recorded 112,000 typists and stenographers in the nation, of whom 86,000 were female."[150] The typewriter is credited with bringing women into the workforce for the first time.[151]

The nineteenth-century typewriter was pervasive in its effects, though much less so than print or telegraph technology. Along with helping to overcome biases

---

Email from Steven Roberts to Susan Brenner (May 26, 2007). See, *generally*, Distant Writing, http://distantwriting.co.uk/default.aspx. The telegraph, though, played such a minor part in the execution of these and other scams that its role cannot realistically be characterized as a "misuse" of the technology. See Chapter 3 (nature of "misuse"). As noted earlier, we will analyze the relationship between utilization of a technology and "misuse" in more detail in Chapter 7.

[144] William Aspray and Martin Campbell-Kelly, *Computer: A History of the Information Machine* (New York: Basic Books, 1996), 30. For early attempts to develop a viable typewriter, see, *e.g.*, Derry and Williams, *A Short History of Technology*, 642–643.

[145] See *id.*; Oliver, *History of American Technology*, 206–220, 440–442. After the Civil War, Remington branched out into manufacturing various items, including sewing machines and fire engines. See Aspray and Campbell-Kelly, *Computer*, 32.

[146] *Id.*, 31–32.

[147] *Id.*, 32–33. According to one source, "[b]usiness offices, correctly fearing the impression of impersonality, were slow to adopt the typewriter, but it came into use in big offices by 1880." Thomas C. Cochran, *200 Years of American Business* (New York: Basic Books, 1977), 79.

[148] Aspray and Campbell-Kelly, *Computer*, 33. ("Without training, a typewriter operator was not much more effective than an experienced writing clerk.")

[149] *Id.*

[150] *Id.*, 32–33.

[151] See *Id.* See also Oliver, *History of American Technology*, 442.

against employing women,[152] it fundamentally altered business practices by introducing the use of standardized text and acclimating businesses to using technology.[153] Its effects were, however, limited to the business sector;[154] unlike the print and telegraph technologies, typewriter technology was not used by "laymen" until well into the twentieth century for various reasons, one being that it was considered bad etiquette to use a machine for personal correspondence.[155]

During the nineteenth century, therefore, the typewriter was a context-specific technology. Like most of the technologies we have discussed, specialists operating in a discrete occupational context used it exclusively; because the occupational context was in part a product of self-imposed restrictions on access to the technology, it was less rigid than it had been for more dedicated technologies.

There do not seem to have been context-specific laws directed at the typewriter. The most likely reason[156] for this is that the potential negative consequences resulting from its implementation were negligible, at the most. The defective

---

[152]   See The Subcommittee on Technology, 49 ("The girl typist became a symbol of women's emancipation.")

[153]   See, *e.g.*, Courtney Robert Hall, *History of American Industrial Science* (New York: Library Publishers, 1954), 347. See also Roger Burlingame, *Engines of Democracy: Inventions and Society in Mature America* (New York: Charles Scribner's Sons, 1940), 137.

[154]   This included professionals of various types as well as commercial endeavors. See Aspray and Campbell-Kelly, *Computer*, 32 (users included "reporters, lawyers, editors, authors, and clergymen").

[155]   See The Subcommittee on Technology, 49.:

> As for etiquette, it was . . . considered bad taste to use the typewriter for personal letters. The machine was long looked upon as affectation . . . on the part of a layman. Some people looked upon the receipt of typed letters as an aspersion upon their literacy. All these factors tended to delay the wide utilization of the typewriter until recent years.

See also Burlingame, *Engines of Democracy*, 136 ("Many . . . were insulted by typewritten letters, some supposing the senders to believe that they could not read handwriting, others thinking that the letters must be some form of printed circular.")

Cost was another factor. See Oliver, *History of American Technology*, 441, public regarded the typewriter "as an interesting novelty, but few were willing to pay one hundred dollars for a typewriter when they could purchase a pen for a penny."

[156]   A related factor may have been that the generalized societal impact of the technology was slight; as noted above, its effects impacted on businesses but did not percolate down to the general public until well into the twentieth century.

implementation of typewriter technology would inflict no serious harm on civilians or on society;[157] and the rare instances in which it was misused could be addressed with existing laws, as with the misuse of bicycle technology.[158]

## Photography

Experiments with photography date back at least to the seventeenth century, but modern photography "begins with the work of the French physicist, Joseph Nicéphore Niepce, from which his partner, L. J. M. Daguerre, evolved the daguerreotype process in 1839."[159] Others modified their process in ways that improved the quality of photographs, made photography easier and opened it up to sophisticated amateurs.[160]

George Eastman made photography a popular pastime when he introduced the first hand-held camera—the "Kodak"—in 1888.[161] Advertised as a portable camera "for making instantaneous exposures," the Kodak used a roll of film that "was inserted at the factory. . . . When . . . the film was used, the camera was returned to the manufacturer to have the pictures developed and to be reloaded."[162] The phrase used to market the Kodak— " 'You press the button—we do the rest' "—became "a household slogan."[163]

> Eastman's invention changed photography. It was no longer the [exclusive] province of the professional and affluent amateur, but was practiced by thousands and thousands of people. . . . By 1889, the *New York Tribune*

---

[157] The consequences of a typist's ineptitude would redound to her detriment, and perhaps to the detriment of her employer. See *Mummenhoff v. Randall*, 19 Ind.App. 44, 49 N.E. 40, 40 (Ind. App. 1898). Unlike the defective implementation of, say, building or transportation technologies, defective typewriting posed little risk of harm to civilians or property.

[158] The deliberate misuse of typewriter technology to, say, write blackmail letters or forge documents could be folded into a prosecution for the underlying crime, e.g., blackmail or forgery. See Brenner, "Is There Such a Thing as Virtual Crime?", 1, http://boalt.org/CCLR/v4/v4brenner.htm. See also *Levy v. Rust*, 49 A. 1017, 1022–1027 (N.J. Ch. 1893) (court found typewritten documents were forgeries).

[159] Derry and Williams, *A Short History of Technology*, 651–652.

[160] See *id.*, 657–658.

[161] Oliver, *History of American Technology*, 444. Eastman called his camera "a Kodak because he liked the strength of the letter *K* and reckoned it was a word that would be pronounced the same in every language." Evans, *They Made America*, 313.

[162] Oliver, *History of American Technology*, 444.

[163] *Id.*

was able to report that "[a]mateur photography is rapidly approaching, if it has not already reached, the dignity of a craze."[164]

This had certain consequences for everyday life. The ease with which one could take surreptitious photographs, combined with advancements in printing technology, created a market for photographs "of prominent people at unguarded moments" and for "pictures of common, everyday members of the working class."[165] Professionals and amateurs alike took advantage of the opportunities this market offered;[166] the candid photographs they took were published in newspapers and magazines and sold in shops.[167]

By 1900, photography had become pervasive both in its effects and in itself. Both professionals and amateurs used cameras.[168] Photographs were a common feature in newspapers and magazines; and the availability of cheap, easily used cameras made photography an increasingly routine aspect of family and social life.[169] Its pervasiveness would become even more pronounced over the next century.

In terms of the analysis we are pursuing, photographic technology is at once like and unlike bicycle technology. Like bicycle technology, photography was pervasive in its effects and the technology itself was readily available to, and readily used by, civilians. Unlike bicycle technology, however, photography

---

[164] Benjamin E. Bratman, "Brandeis and Warren's 'The Right to Privacy and the Birth of the Right to Privacy,'" *Tennessee Law Review* 69 (2002): 623, 645 (quoting Robert E. Mensel, "'Kodakers Lying in Wait': Amateur Photography and the Right of Privacy in New York, 1885–1915," *American Quarterly* 43 (1991): 24, 28 [citing *New York Tribune*, September 5, 1889, at 6]). See also Evans, *They Made America*, 313–315.

A similar phenomenon occurred in other countries. See Mitchell, *Daily Life in Victorian England*, 232, "Cheap box cameras, introduced in 1888, were an instant sensation. They made photography possible for working people and even for children.". See also Trevor I. Williams, *A Short History of Twentieth-Century Technology* (New York: Clarendon Press, 1982), 324 ("By 1900 one person in ten in the USA and Britain owned a camera, though photography was less popular on the Continent").

[165] Bratman, *Brandeis and Warren's*, 623, 645–646.

[166] See, *e.g.*, Ken Gormley, "One Hundred Years of Privacy," *Wisconsin Law Review* (1992): 1335, 1352 ("stories of the press spying on President Grover Cleveland and his bride on their honeymoon were notorious.")

[167] See Bratman, *Brandeis and Warren's*, 623, 646.

[168] See M. Thomas Inge, *Handbook of American Popular Culture*, vol. 2 (Westport, CT: Greenwood Press, 1989), 887–893.

[169] See *Id.*

was also a matter for specialists; there was a division between hobby photographers and professional photographers.[170]

It is not surprising, then, that the only laws which were designed to control the defective implementation of this technology were directed at professionals.[171] In the nineteenth century, states required professional photographers to be licensed, and they held individuals criminally liable for "engaging in the practice of photography" without a license.[172] The statutes were apparently intended to protect (a) the general public from the chemicals professional photographers used and (b) customers from incompetent or dishonest professionals.[173] They were struck down in the twentieth century, as courts found they were an invalid exercise of the police power.[174]

---

[170]  There were professional bicyclists during the nineteenth century, but they were relatively few in number. See, *e.g.*, Robert Bedard, *"The History of the Bicycle* (1997), http://www.robert-bedard.com/bike/history/bikehist.html#note16 ("In 1895 there were over 600 professional bicycle racers in the United States.") And because professional bicyclists did not interact with the public, they posed little risk of injury to civilians.

[171]  See, *e.g.*, *State v. Schlier*, 50 Tenn. 281, 1871 WL 3596 *1 (Tenn. 1871) (Act of February 24th, 1870, c. 24, sec. 1 required "artists taking photographs" to "take out a license semi-annually, and pay a privilege tax therefore.")

[172]  *State v. Balance*, 229 N.C. 764, 766, 51 S.E.2d 731, 732 (N.C. 1949) ("Any person engaging in the practice of photography without being so licensed is guilty of a misdemeanor. . . . Any . . . person desiring to practice photography must undergo an examination by the Board [of Photographic Examiners] and qualify . . . 'as to competency, ability and integrity"). See also *State v. Cromwell*, 72 N.D. 565, 568, 9 N.W.2d 914, 915–916 (N.D. 1943) (defendant convicted of "attempting to practice photography without a license"); *State v. Manz*, 46 Tenn. 557, 1869 WL 2587 *2 (Tenn. 1869) (photographers guilty of a misdemeanor if they opened a gallery without paying required tax).

[173]  See *State v. Balance*, 229 N.C. at 771, 51 S.E.2d at 735–736:

> The arguments advanced to sustain the statute . . . as a valid exercise of the police power are without convincing force. . . . While there may be some fire risk incident to the practice of photography on account of combustible materials employed, such hazard is . . . no greater than that . . . from the things utilized daily in the home and in scores of other vocations. Any danger incidental to the practice of photography may threaten injury to the individual practitioner, but it does not imperil the public safety. . . .
>
> It is urged . . . that restricting the practice of photography to those whose competency and integrity is certified by a board of professional photographers will accomplish a public good because unskilled photographers may impose inferior pictures upon their customers, and dishonest photographers may practice fraud upon those who deal with them. . . . [T]his argument . . . runs counter to the economic philosophy . . . accepted in this country that ordinarily the public is best served by the free competition of free men in a free market. . . . [A] dishonest photographer may defraud those with whom he deals. So may a dishonest person in any other calling. . . .

See also *State v. Lawrence*, 213 N.C. 674, 197 S.E. 586, 587 (N.C. 1938).

[174]  See, *e.g.*, *State v. Balance*, 229 N.C. at 772, 51 S.E.2d at 735–736; *State v. Cromwell*, 72 N.D. 565, 581, 9 N.W.2d at 922. See also *Ralph v. City of Wenatchee*, 34 Wash.2d 638, 209 P.2d 270 (Wash. 1949).

There seemed no reason to adopt laws targeting amateur photography. While the defective implementation of bicycle technology could interfere with traffic on public roadways and cause accidents resulting in personal injury or property damage, the defective implementation of photographic technology by amateurs could not inflict any "systemic" injury. The most an incompetent amateur could accomplish would be to embarrass himself and/or those he photographed.[175]

The capacity for "misusing" photographic technology in the sense I articulated in Chapter 3 seems to have been, and to remain, essentially nonexistent. Like bicycles, camera equipment can be stolen, but this constitutes not a "misuse" of the technology but mere theft.[176] And as with most any implement, there was always

---

[175] By the end of the nineteenth century, some were calling for laws which would address negative consequences of photography that were more subtle and subjective than the physical hazards associated with other technologies. In 1890, Louis Brandeis and Samuel Warren argued for the recognition of a right to privacy that would protect civilians from what they saw as the improper implementation of photography. See Samuel Warren and Louis D. Brandeis, "The Right to Privacy," *Harvard Law Review 4* (1890): 193. Because Brandeis and Warren were primarily concerned about the use of an individual's image for commercial purposes, they lobbied for the creation of a civil cause of action that would let an aggrieved party seek damages or, in some instances, an injunction barring such use.

The Warren-Brandeis article is interesting insofar as it recognizes that technology can have hitherto unanticipated effects, but it is not relevant to this discussion for several reasons. The first and most significant is that the evil with which Brandeis and Warren were concerned did not involve a "misuse" of photographic technology.

Their complaint lay not with the technology, as such, or even with the way it was being implemented. Their complaint lay, instead, with the fact that the press published photographs, usually of "prominent" citizens:

> Instantaneous photographs and newspaper enterprise have invaded the sacred precincts of private and domestic life. . . . For years there has been a feeling that the law must afford some remedy for the unauthorized circulation of portraits of private persons. . . . The alleged facts of a somewhat notorious case brought before an inferior tribunal in New York a few months ago, directly involved the consideration of the right of circulating portraits; and the question whether our law will recognize and protect the right to privacy in this and in other respects must soon come before our courts for consideration.

This is not a "misuse" issue but an objection to a consequential effect of the "use" of photographic technology: the press' publishing what we would call candid photographs of people considered to be of interest to the general public. Essentially, Brandeis and Warren are anticipating complaints about the paparazzi.

Another reason the Warren-Brandeis analysis is not relevant to this discussion is that their proposal contemplated the use of civil liability, not the state's involvement in discouraging "misuse" of a technology; since the focus of this article is on using criminal law to control the negative consequences of technologies, purely civil remedies are inappropriate sources of analogy. And the final reason is that the Warren-Brandeis effort was ultimately unsuccessful See, *e.g.*, James Q. Whitman, "The Two Western Cultures of Privacy: Dignity Versus Liberty," *Yale Law Journal 113* (2004); 1151, 1204 ("after a century of legal history, it amounts to little in American practice today").

[176] See, *e.g.*, *Kelly v. State*, 31 Tex. Crim. 211, 214, 20 S.W. 365, 365 (Tex. Crim. App. 1892) (Kell "served a term in the penitentiary, for theft of photographic instruments).

the possibility that camera equipment could be used as a weapon,[177] but such a decided misapplication of photographic equipment could easily be addressed by using standard criminal law to charge the perpetrator with assault or homicide, depending on the outcome of the attack. As we saw earlier, this was true with bicycle technology.

## Electricity

Mankind had been observing static electricity since ancient times, and by the seventeenth century, scientists were attempting to fathom the nature of this mysterious phenomenon.[178] The first breakthrough came in 1831, when Michael Faraday created an electric motor and "pointed the way towards the conversion of mechanical into electrical power."[179] Devices for actually generating electricity had been developed by the 1860s, but it took time to perfect them; power-stations finally began to appear in the late 1870s and 1880s for the purpose of supplying illumination, which was initially assumed to be electricity's only use.[180] Its use for this purpose became much more common after Thomas Edison and Joseph Swan severally invented the "incandescent-filament lamp," or light bulb, in the 1880s.[181]

It is difficult for us to realize how extraordinary a phenomenon the incandescent lamp was. As one historian noted, in the 1880s electric light

> bordered on the supernatural . . . because it violated the natural order. . . .
> Light . . . had always implied consumption of oxygen, smoke, . . . heat, and

---

[177]  I am sure this has happened, but I cannot find a reported case or even a new story involving assault with a camera.

[178]  See Derry and Williams, *A Short History of Technology*, 607–609.

[179]  See *id.*, 610–611.

[180]  Derry and Williams, *A Short History of Technology*, 611–614:

> As early as 1875 a Gramme generator was installed . . . in Paris to supply power for arc-lamps. . . . Wanamaker's store in Philadelphia installed a generating plant in 1878 so that it could be illuminated with arc-lamps; in New York, Edison's Pearl Street generating station was in operation in 1882. . . . In 1883 a small powerstation . . . was built to light the Grosvenor Gallery, and surplus electricity was sold to local consumers. . . .

> *Id.* at 617. See also David E. Nye, *Electrifying America: Social Meanings of a New Technology* (Cambridge, MA: MIT Press, 1997), 29–37. Some were dubious about electricity's suitability for providing illumination, even after Edison's invention of the incandescent light. See, *e.g.*, The Subcommittee on Technology, 53.

[181]  See Derry and Williams, *A Short History of Technology*, 632–633.

danger of fire. . . . But inside the clear glass of an Edison lamp was a glowing orange filament, throwing off a light at once mild and intense, smokeless, fireless, steady, seemingly inexhaustible. The enclosed light bulb seemed an impossible paradox.[182]

Americans and Europeans rather quickly overcame their uncertainty about this new light source, and by

1900 the supremacy of incandescent lamps . . . was fully recognized: they were convenient, clean, safe, and reliable. Their adoption was, however, controlled by the rate of the development of public electric-supply services. Electric lighting was an accepted feature of urban life by 1900 . . . but its penetration into the countryside was necessarily slow.[183]

The federal government's efforts to promote rural electrification in the United States began in 1933 and continued, with some interruption, into the 1950s.[184] By 1949, "more than 78% of U.S. farms were receiving . . . electric power."[185] The figure rose to 90% a year later, and by the end of the 1950s, electrification in the United States was essentially complete.[186] It proceeded at a similar, though generally slower, pace in other parts of the world.[187]

Though a few electric appliances appeared prior to 1900,[188] the use of electricity for purposes other than illumination did not become common until well

---

[182]  Nye, *Electrifying America*, 2.

[183]  Derry and Williams, *A Short History of Technology*, 634.

[184]  See, *e.g.*, Bob Patton, "History of the Rural Electrification Industry," *Management* Quarterly 37 (1997): 7, 8.

[185]  See, *e.g.*, *id.*

[186]  See, *e.g.*, Gary A. Donaldson, *Abundance and Anxiety: America, 1945–1960* (Westport, CT: Praeger, 1997), 126–127.

[187]  See, *e.g.*, Joanna I. Lewis and Emily T. Yeh, "State Power and the Logic of Reform in China's Electricity Sector," *Pacific Affairs* 77 (2004), 437, 439; Navroz K. Dubash and James H. Williams, "Asian Electricity Reform in Historical Perspective," *Pacific Affairs* 77 (2004), 411, 413.

[188]  See Rick Szostak, *Technological Innovation and the Great Depression* (Boulder, CO: Westview Press, 1995), 189 (a number of electrical appliances appeared in the 1890s). See also Oliver, *History of American Technology*, 357–358. "Heating devices, such as hot plates, flat irons, and cooling devices like electric fans" were in urban homes by 1900.

into the twentieth century.[189] This was primarily due to the gradual pace of electrification and the cost of electricity, which began to decline in the 1920s.[190] There was also another, technical impediment to the broader use of electricity:

> While the advent of electric lighting had encouraged the development of a number of appliances in the 1890s, the dominance of lighting meant that these had generally to be plugged into light sockets . . . The cost and inconvenience of this was a major deterrent to appliance utilization. The modern two-prong plug and wall receptacle were creations of the early twentieth century; manufacturers only agreed to standardize these in 1917; the process of standardization was completed by the 1930s.[191]

As plug standardization progressed, so did appliance sales: Small appliances such as irons, toasters, percolators, and hotplates sold remarkably well in the 1920s, while vacuum cleaners, refrigerators, and washing machines were at least as popular in the 1930s.[192] Electricity was a driving factor in the "consumer durables revolution" of the 1920s, which "saw a startling diffusion of new products based on new technology."[193] We will return to the issue of consumer technology in Chapter 5, but for now our concern lies with electricity.

Electricity essentially changed everything.[194] As one author noted, it has been only a little more than a hundred years that we've harnessed this unique

---

[189] See *Id.* See also Evans, *They Made America*, 390–411. For a detailed treatment of electricity's proliferation throughout the United States and its effects on private and commercial life, see Nye, *Electrifying America*, 185–287.

[190] See Szostak, *Technological Innovation and the Great Depression*, 104.

> As utilities exploited the economies of scale and improved . . . efficiencies of newer power plants—along with higher-voltage transmission lines and improvements in other . . . equipment—the price of electricity declined. . . . [R]esidential customers in 1892 paid $4.52 (in 1996 dollars) for a kilowatt-hour of electricity, which explains why only the rich could afford the product. But in 1973, that same kilowatt-hour cost residential customers only about 8.4 cents.

> Richard F. Hirsch, "Revamping and Repowering," *Forum for Applied Research and Public Policy 15* (2000): 12. See also Nye, *Electrifying America*, 261. There was also a dramatic increase in output. See *The Subcommittee on Technology*, 50 (growth of electric power industry shown "by comparing the output of 92 billion kilowatt-hours in 1935 with 80 billion in 1927, 25.5 billion in 1917, 11.5 billion in 1912, 6 billion in 1907, and . . . 2.33 billion kilowatt-hours in 1902").

[191] Szostak, *Technological Innovation and the Great Depression*, 189.

[192] *Id.*, 191.

[193] *Id.*, 85. See also *id.* at 91.

[194] For a description of life in the pre-electrified world, see Robert Silverberg, *Light for the World: Edison and the Power Industry* (Princeton, NJ: Van Nostrand, 1967), 9–27.

form of energy. In that short period, electricity has changed our lives. Electric lights lengthened our days. Electric-power elevators and streetcars heightened and enlarged the cityscapes. Motors transformed industrial societies.[195]

As we sometimes appreciate, this elusive phenomenon has become essential to our lives. Without it, we could "no longer watch television, microwave dinners, obtain cash from ATM machines, pump water through sewage treatment plants, or check emails."[196]

I noted at the beginning of this chapter that electricity arguably should not be included in this section because though it is certainly a "technology," it is not a "machine." It is, as I also noted, a power source for machines and a product of machinery.[197] As to precisely *what* it is, for the average citizen, electricity is probably as inscrutable today as it was in the 1880s, when it "seemed to defy definition."[198] We, though, do not concern ourselves with defining what it is. Over the years, electricity became invisible, so we no longer even attempt to ascertain its nature.

Though it is not a machine, electricity became extremely important as a source of power we rely on for our machines. In the early twenty-first century, it is the life-blood of the devices that let us "stay connected," as well as of those that perform more mundane functions.[199] Chapter 5 examines consumer technologies, most of which use electrical power, and Chapter 6 explores developing "smart" technologies, which will also depend on electricity. Because electricity is the constant that

---

[195]  Richard Munson, "Electricity after Insull," *Management Quarterly 47* (2006): 6, 8.

[196]  *Id.*

[197]  The precise nature of electricity was a matter of some uncertainty when the technology was new. See Nye, *Electrifying America*, 138:

> The public encountered electrification in many guises. . . . Yet despite its ubiquity, electricity seemed to defy definition and remained a mystery to the citizenry who saw it every day in the street. As Charles W. Eliot wrote for inscription on the Union Depot in Washington, D.C., "Electricity: carrier of light and power, devourer of time and space; bearer of human speech over land and sea; greatest servant of man—yet itself unknown."

> Electricity was, as Nye (138) observes, "ubiquitous yet inscrutable." Over the years, electricity has become invisible to us, so we no longer speculate about its precise nature.

[198]  *Id.*

[199]  See Chapter 5.

makes these technologies possible, and because its use began in the nineteenth century, considering it at this point in our discussion seems appropriate.

In a sense, electricity is a metaphor for the consumer technologies we already employ and the "smart" technologies we will come to employ: Like those technologies, electricity connects us; we become accustomed to relying on an external source for support, amusement, and assistance.

We are "users" of electricity, but we do not "use" it in the same way specialists "use" most of the technologies discussed in this chapter. Most machine technologies are free-standing technologies; that is, each has a distinct, severable function and is implemented by a unique cadre of specialists. For modern, complex technologies, the specialists will be participants in a collaborative implementation process in which each plays a specific, segmented role.[200] The collaborative nature of the process does not alter the fact that the participating specialists "use" the technology; each manipulates an aspect of the technology in a way that gives her some control over its implementation.

For example, a telegrapher who "sends" a telegram does so in collaboration with (a) other telegraphers, (b) the telegraph clerk who took the message from the sender, and (c) the telegraph company employees who operate and maintain the equipment needed for the telegraph system to function. The same is true for transportation technologies: A railroad engineer operates a train engine as part of an occupational assemblage of specialists who ensure that the train is operational, is appropriately loaded, and that the other requisites of safe, effective transport are met.[201] As we saw earlier, each of the participants in such an assemblage is a specialist; each has knowledge and training that uniquely equips him or her to play an integral, essential role in the implementation of a particular technology. And

---

[200]  See *supra* note xx. For an example of this, see Chapter 2 (commercial air travel).

[201]  See, *e.g.*, "Conductor (transportation)," *Wikipedia*, http://en.wikipedia.org/wiki/Conductor_(transportation) (crew on board a railroad train includes engineer, conductor, brakeman, flagman, assistant conductor, onboard service personnel, fireman and pilot engineer). This list does not, of course, include those who are involved in the implementation of this technology but do so from a position external to the train itself. See, *e.g.*, "Centralized Traffic Control," *Wikipedia*, http://en.wikipedia.org/wiki/Centralized_Traffic_Control; "Employee Referral Program," Amtrak, http://amtrak.teamrewards.net/TR_PublicWeb/index.jsp.

though none of the discrete specialists participating in such an occupational assemblage controls the entire implementation process, each plays an active role in that process.

This means that a specialist's sole or collaborative "use" of a machine technology can give rise to negative consequences such as those noted earlier. To continue with the examples given above, a telegram "sent" by a telegrapher may never actually arrive because the specialist-employee responsible for maintaining the wires across which it would travel defaulted on his duty. The wire was down, so the telegram did not reach its intended recipient. Or the engineer operating a railroad engine tries to stop the train upon arrival at the station but cannot because the specialist whose job it is to maintain engine brakes was negligent, the result being that property is damaged and people are injured.

The structure and function of these complex occupational assemblages gave rise to the logic I outlined earlier: the premise that the best way to control the negative consequences resulting from the defective implementation of a technology is to adopt rules directed at the specialists who implement that technology. This logic applies to the specialists who implement the technology that produces electricity and laws have been enacted to control their defective implementation of that technology.[202] Here, though, we encounter a disconnect between implementation and "use." Implementation and "use" are synonymous for most of the technologies (e.g., transportation, industrial, communication) we have examined

---

[202] See, *e.g.*, 7 C.F.R. § 1724.50(a) (requiring that electrical systems, "including all electric distribution, transmission, and generating facilities" be "designed, constructed, operated, and maintained in accordance with . . . the most current . . . criteria of the National Electrical Safety Code (NESC) and all applicable and current electrical and safety requirements of any State or local governmental entity"). See also Cal. Pub. Util. Code §§ 362–363 (statutory provisions designed to ensure safety and reliability in the implementation of technology responsible for generating electricity); Neb. Rev. Stat. § 48–417 (safety regulations in electric power plants). The Federal Energy Regulatory Commission has been legislatively "directed to issue a final rule on new electricity reliability standards. . . . This rulemaking is . . . intended to establish a new electric reliability organization . . . that will enforce mandatory reliability standards" on electric power plants. Joseph P. Tomain, *Katrina's Energy Agenda*, Nat. Resources & Env't 20 (Spring, 2006): 43, 45. Safety regulations are particularly stringent for nuclear power plants. See, *e.g.*, Clinton J. Andrews, Regulating Regional Power Systems (Westport, CT: Quorum Books, 1995), 7, 305. For the staffing of electric power plants, see, *e.g.*, U.S. Department of Labor, "Power Plant Operators, Distributors, and Dispatchers," http://stats.bls.gov/oco/ocos227.htm; Commonwealth of Virginia – Department of Human Resource Management, "Utility Plant Operations #79710," http://www.dhrm.virginia.gov/compensation/careergroups/trades/UtilityPlantOper79170.htm.

in this chapter. They are not, however, synonymous for electricity; here, a cadre of specialists using appropriate technology implements electricity by creating it and delivering it to civilians, who are its ultimate "users."

The logic cited above does not apply to us—the civilian "users" of electricity. It cannot apply because our "use" of electricity is entirely passive: We cannot modify how much current—or what kind of current—goes into our appliances, nor can we alter how we access that current; we must accept what is distributed to us, rely on other power sources or do without.

The passivity of our "use" of electricity nullifies the applicability of the logic cited above. I exercise no control over the process that supplies me with electricity and very little over electricity once I receive it. Unless I do something drastic by, say, bombing a transformer, I cannot exert any control over the production—the actual implementation—of electricity.[203]

My ability to "misuse" electricity is also quite limited. There are "misuse" statutes that make it illegal to "tamper" with the availability of electricity, but they are not "misuse" statutes; these laws are concerned with what is generically known as the theft of services, that is, with arranging to get electricity without paying for it.[204] These theft laws have absolutely nothing to do with our actual "use"—or "misuse"—of electricity. It is, in fact, difficult to imagine how I could "misuse" electricity; I suppose if I were to use it to kill someone that could qualify as "misusing" electricity, but this literal kind of "misuse" can be discouraged without adopting specialized "misuse of electricity" laws. As with the "misuse" of bicycle technology, societies can quite adequately address the "harms" one could inflict here by applying existing "misuse" laws, such as those criminalizing homicide arson, assault, or whatever else seems appropriate.[205]

---

[203] See, e.g., CBU-94 "Blackout Bomb"– BLU-114/B "Soft-Bomb," Federation of American Scientists, http://www.fas.org/man/dod-101/sys/dumb/blu-114.htm. I have, in other words, little, if any, hope of introducing defects into the generation of electricity.

[204] See, e.g., Ark. Code § 5–36–104; Cal. Penal Code § 498; Conn. Gen. Stat. Ann. § 53a-127c(a); 11 Del. Code § 845; Hawaii Rev. Stat. Ann. § 708–839.5; Ky. Rev. Stat. Ann. § 514.060; Neb. Rev. Stat. § 28–515(1); Or. Rev. Stat. Ann. § 164.125; Utah Code Ann. § 76–6-409; Wy. Stat. Ann. § 6–3-408. See also Ala. Code § 13A-8-23 (tampering with availability of electricity); S.C. Code § 16–13–385 (tampering with electric meters).

[205] See, e.g., Templin v. State, 677 S.W.2d 541, (Tex. App. 1983) (defendant convicted of murder for "intentionally causing a 'live bare-wire electric cord'" to come into contact with his wife's body while she was bathing). See also Franks v. State, 1998 WL 760248 (Ark. 1998); People v. Murphy, 17 Bedell 595, 72 N.E. 1146, 1146 (N.Y. 1904). Existing criminal law can also be used to prosecute me if, say, I bomb a trans-

In a sense, electricity is "bridge" technology—an intermediate step between the "machine" technologies and the consumer technologies we will examine in Chapter 5. Like the "machine" technologies, a unique, sector-specific cadre of specialists implement—generate—it; like the consumer technologies, its ultimate "use" is in the hands of civilians, though the control they exert over that "use" is minimal.

former to shut down the power grid and interfere with the delivery of electricity to its ultimate "users." See, *e.g.*, 18 U.S. Code § 1030(a)(5)(B)(iv).

# CHAPTER 5

# Law and Consumer Technology

*. . . the transformation of American life into a fully engulfed technoculture . . .*
*is quickening.*[1]

For various reasons, the twentieth century saw the explosive development of thousands of preexisting and new technologies.[2] It also saw the emergence of a new variety of technology: consumer technology. The phrase denotes not a particular type of technology but a category that encompasses many different technologies, all of which civilians, not specialists, use.

Unlike early technologies, which were designed to promote our physical survival, consumer technologies are designed to make our experience of life easier and more enjoyable. They do this by automating essential but mundane tasks and by satisfying needs that had not crystallized a century ago, such as the "need" to

---

[1]   David Glen Mick and Susan Fournier, "Paradoxes of Technology: Consumer Cognizance, Emotions, and Coping Strategies," *Journal of Consumer Research 25* (September 1998): 123, 124, http://gates.comm. virginia.edu/dgm9t/Papers/Mick%20and%20Fournier%201998%20Paradoxes%20of%20Technology.pdf.

[2]   See Trevor I. Williams, *A Short History of Twentieth-Century Technology* (New York: Clarendon Press, 1982), 1–2:

   [T]echnology . . . was entering a new phase. Hitherto it had been based . . . on progress in mechanical engineering, but a new force was making itself felt[:]. . . . electricity. . . . [E]lectricity made little social impact until the 1880s, when the first public supply systems began to appear in the larger cities. From that time onward electricity became increasingly important. . . . [T]he allied science of electronics . . . was destined to bring about great changes before the middle of this century. The thermionic valve, of paramount importance in the early days of radio, paved the way to the transistor and the microprocessor, of profound significance in the development of computers and automatic control systems. . . .

   See also The Subcommittee on Technology to the National Resources Committee, *Technological Trends and National Policy* (U.S. Government Printing Office, 1937), 3–7.

listen to music while jogging, watch a movie at home, create a blog and share our thoughts with the world, or communicate on a whim with someone across town or half-way around the world.[3]

As these examples illustrate, choice is a defining characteristic of consumer technology; we tend to use a consumer technology because we choose to do so not because our individual or collective survival depends on it. Because they are meant to be used by civilians in the course of their everyday lives, consumer technologies are pervasive both in their effects and in themselves.[4] They are not intended to be, and are not, as pervasive as the technologies that will emerge in this century; as Chapter 6 explains, consumer technologies act as a conceptual "bridge" to the twenty-first century pervasive technologies.

The distinction between consumer and nonconsumer technologies is not always absolute; the notion of consumer technology has evolved gradually over roughly the last century and a half as the result of continuing advancements in technology. In the late nineteenth century, for example, gas lamps became available for use in

---

[3]    As many have noted, modern technology often

> creates needs rather than satisfying them. . . . There was no need . . . for the personal computer before it was invented (for who would have known to demand such a thing?) but once the computer took its place as a vital tool, it became necessary to own one . . . The same is true of nearly every other technological advancement in modern times: merely by coming into existence, they created a new need. . . .

"Why Study Equity?", The Center for the Study of Technology and Society, http://www.tecsoc.org/equity/whatsequity.htm. See also Yuval Levin, "Who Needs It?, Tech Central Station," http://www.consumersvoice.org/1051/techwrapper.jsp?PID=1051–250&CID=1051–091902A:

> *We are in great haste to construct a magnetic telegraph from Maine to Texas; but Maine and Texas, it may be, have nothing important to communicate.*

> So said Henry David Thoreau in *Walden* in 1854. . . . Thoreau. . . . saw no need for Maine and Texas to communicate. But as the march of modern technology has taught us, the ability to communicate would soon enough create the need. The idea that necessity is the mother of invention—that Maine and Texas would have to have something important to say to each other before someone would link them with a telegraph line—has not . . . been the governing logic of the modern age of invention.

> Modern technology creates needs at least as often as it serves them. . . . [T]hose . . . who happened to live before 1879 did not spend much time saying 'If only we had electric lighting.' But who among us now could live without it? No one could have imagined a real need for a radio or television before they were invented, but few of us could . . . give them up today. Maine would have serious trouble going on with life as normal if the information network that connects it to Texas was suddenly taken away. Invention is oftentimes the mother of necessity.

[4]    For the distinction between the two, see Chapter 2.

the home, where they provided a clean, easy to use light source.[5] Because gas lamps were used by civilians and were meant to make life easier and gave civilians a choice between lighting options, they qualify as a consumer technology. The same is true of other "domestic" technologies, such as central heating, hot water heaters, domestic refrigeration, vacuum cleaners, and laundry machines.[6]

As we saw in Chapter 4, this is also true of the bicycle and amateur photography. But though both were early versions of consumer technology, only amateur photography is truly analogous to modern consumer technologies. Unlike the gas lamp and the bicycle, both of which were technologically advanced ways of meeting basic needs (light and transport), photography met a new and nonessential need: the desire to capture images for sentiment, amusement, or self-fulfillment. As I noted above, modern technologies create needs as often as they satisfy them. Although many twentieth-century consumer technologies automated essential but mundane tasks, many others, including stereos, VCR's, DVD players, and iPods, satisfied needs that did not exist until the technology emerged to create, and then to fulfill, them.

It is neither possible nor necessary to review all of the consumer technologies that evolved after 1900 in this article. For the purposes of our analysis, the functional qualities each shares means that what is true of one consumer technology is also true of other consumer technologies. For this discussion, therefore, it is sufficient to review four influential consumer technologies: the automobile; the telephone; broadcast media; and computers.

## Automobile

> *The inventors of the automobile have had more influence than Caesar, Napoleon, and Ghengis Khan.*[7]

The automobile is a consumer technology as defined above: It was intended to improve the quality of our lives by automating personal transportation,[8] a task which it has accomplished. It was not the first automated transportation

---

[5]   See Sally Mitchell, Daily Life in Victorian England (Westport, CT: Greenwood Press, 1996), 81, 120–121.

[6]   See Williams, *A Short History of Twentieth-Century Technology*, 387–395.

[7]   The Subcommittee on Technology, 4.

[8]   *See, e.g.,* James J. Fink, America Adopts the Automobile, 1895–1910 11–55 (Cambridge, MA: MIT Press 1970).

technology; automated forms of transport had been available since at least the nineteenth century.[9] Rail and ship travel, however, were forms of mass transport, at least for all but the very rich. I could take a train, along with hundreds of other people, to one or more of the scheduled stops on its route,[10] but I could not customize the train's route to meet my own personal agenda.

The automobile introduced the concept of mechanized personal transport, that is, individualized control over automated transportation. Autonomy is an essential element of older modes of travel such as walking and animal transport, but it was absent from automated transportation until the appearance of the automobile. The bicycle was not automated; it relied on human motive power.[11] As we shall see, the automobile, like other consumer technologies, had a series of unintended effects, such as introducing the notions of driving for recreation and driving as a social activity.

Although experiments with motorized carriages date back to 1870, automobile manufacturing did not appear until "about the year 1890. By that time, Europeans and North Americans possessed the technology required to produce and successfully operate a mechanically powered road vehicle."[12] The popularity of bicycling created "a market for automobiles. Thousands of riders acquired a taste for speedy mechanical road transport, entirely under their own control."[13] French manufacturers dominated the world automobile market until 1908, when Henry Ford introduced the Model-T.[14] Ford's assembly-line production techniques and the Model-T's popularity quickly made the Ford Motor Company the dominant automobile manufacturer in the world.[15]

---

[9]   See Chapter 4.

[10]   See Chapter 4.

[11]   See Chapter 4.

[12]   Jean-Pierre Bardou, et al., *The Automobile Revolution: The Impact of an Industry* (Chapel Hill, NC: University of North Carolina Press, 1982), 3.

[13]   *Id.*, 6.

[14]   See *Id.*, 14–15, 54–55.

> Sturdy, simple in design, and easy to maintain, it had a wide appeal, especially to farmers who appreciated its high clearance, which made it easier to drive on unpaved rural roads. Its relatively high power-to-weight ratio gave it a long life, for most drivers could obtain all the performance they wanted without pushing the engine to its limit. Bardou, et al., *The Automobile Revolution* at 54.

In 1910, Ford slashed the price of the Model-T from $825 to $680, which made it even more accessible.

[15]   See *Id*. See also Harold Evans with Gail Buckland and David Lefer, *They Made America: From the Steam Engine to the Search Engine* (New York: Back Bay Books, 2004), 303–312.

Other American manufacturers emerged to compete with Ford, and by 1913, the United States was the world leader in automobile production.[16] In 1935, there was "one automobile to every five persons in the United States,"[17] and by 2000, more than eighty-two million U.S. households had at least one motor vehicle.[18] For over half a century, the automobile has been an unusually pervasive technology, far more so than its antecedent, the bicycle.[19]

The automobile's effects were equally pervasive. This excerpt gives a sense of the influence it had on U.S. society in the first part of the last century:

[A]utomobiles . . . . profoundly changed living styles. . . .

Physicians . . . made calls more quickly and visited more patients. . . . Automobiles allowed the replacement of the one-room schoolhouse by the large diversified school. . . . The post office . . . could offer rural free delivery, allowing farmers to receive mail every day. . . . Rural isolation ended, for easy travel now became available . . .

In . . . cities . . . the . . . car . . . became a family necessity. . . . It found a variety of uses: . . . as transportation to the job, but also to run errands, visit friends, and . . . schools, hospitals, and churches. Women began to drive . . . and the car became an aspect of their growing autonomy. Business began to adapt. . . . The first drive-in restaurants appeared. . . . On Sundays, owners took their cars . . . for pleasure drives. Gradually the weekend emerged as an institution. . . . When they began to receive vacations, city dwellers, as well as their rural cousins, traveled in their cars. Tourism . . . enjoyed an unprecedented popularity. . . .

Service stations, garages, restaurants, and hotels sprang up along the major routes. In addition to travel, cars encouraged the development of new residential suburbs . . . . People gave up apartment-house living for private dwellings, and before long would obtain household supplies from . . . shopping centers, situated away from the central business districts. . . .

---

16   See Bardou, et al., *The Automobile Revolution*, 74.

17   The Subcommittee on Technology, 4.

18   See U.S. Bureau of the Census: 2000 Census, Section 25 (Construction and Housing), Table 1220, http://www.census.gov/prod/2001pubs/statab/sec25.pdf (out of a total of 99,487,000).

19   See Chapter 4.

The car. . . . weakened parental authority. . . . Young drivers became much more mobile and found it easier to escape family control. Cars also reduced the supervision of the relations between the sexes [and] became a place for courtship.[20]

As the automobile pervaded society, it "quickly generated" opposition: "Some feared it as a danger to life and limb . . . because of careless driving or . . . the many accidents that occurred from horses panicking when confronted by these vehicles."[21] Here, once again, the implementation of a novel transportation technology gave rise to concerns about the danger of defective implementation by the "users"—the operators—of motor vehicles.[22]

Governments in the United States and in other countries sought to deal with the defective implementation issue by "registering cars and drivers" and "regulating driving, especially speed."[23] In the United States, motor vehicle owners opposed the imposition of special automobile speed limits, arguing that motor vehicles should be subject to the same rules as horse-drawn vehicles: that the only requirement on roads should be that the driver maintain a speech that was "'reasonable

---

[20] Bardou, et al., *The Automobile Revolution*, 114–116. See also James J. Fink, *America Adopts the Automobile,1895–1920* (Cambridge, MA: MIT Press, 1970), 100–112. The automobile brought other problems, as well. See Bardou, et al., *The Automobile Revolution* at 116 (increased noise, congestion and air pollution).

[21] *Id.*, at 22. Communities were also concerned about "the terrible dust and damage to . . . roads caused by fast-moving cars."

[22] See Chapter 4 for a discussion of similar concerns about bicycle technology. European countries also focused on defects in the manufacture of motor vehicles. Laws in Europe required government inspection of "'every type of automobile that is placed upon the market'" in order to ensure certain standards of quality in their construction. See Fink, *America Adopts the Automobile*, 115. Laws of this type did not appear in the United States for many decades. The only U.S. laws that sought to ensure some level of safety in automobile construction were city ordinances and some state laws mandating that automobiles be provided with certain equipment, such as horns and lamps. See *id.* These laws are discussed later in the text.

[23] Bardou, et al., *The Automobile Revolution*, at 23. Initially, U.S. states applied "the few laws regulating the ownership and use of horse-drawn vehicles" to motor vehicles, but by 1900 they had begun adopting "special motor vehicle legislation." Fink, *America Adopts the Automobile*, 166. In 1901, New York became the first state to require the registration of motor vehicles; other states quickly followed suit, so by 1915 every state had a motor vehicle registration law, at 166–169.

Violating the rules regulating speed and other aspects of motor vehicle operation was usually a crime, though generally a minor one. See *State v. Long*, 30 Del. 397, 108 A. 36, 38 (Del. Oyer Ter. 1919) (unlawful "to run an automobile upon any public street or highway . . . at a greater rate of speed than 25 miles an hour"). Governments paved roads to deal with the dust and damage problem. See Bardou, et al., *The Automobile Revolution* at 23.

and proper' with respect to road and traffic conditions."[24] This effort was successful until after the turn of the century, but the obvious disparities between the
speed of horse-drawn vehicles and automobiles, combined with the increased
overall potential of the latter to cause injury or damage, soon prompted states to
impose speed limits on the operation of motor vehicles.[25]

In the United States, states also adopted rules requiring owners of motor vehicles
to equip them with certain equipment and to take precautions when they encountered horses, pedestrians, or streetcars.[26] As one state court explained, these rules
were intended to protect the public from injury by

> placing certain . . . obligations upon the driver of these fast moving vehicles.
>
> That this statute was enacted for the benefit of the public is made manifest by
> all the provisions regulating the manner in which automobiles shall be used
> upon the public highway, such as having the same equipped with a bell or
> horn, or device for signaling; such provisions as require him, when approach-
> ing one riding or driving a horse, to stop when signaled to do so; the provision
> requiring him to stop when passing a street car which has stopped for the
> alighting of passengers; those requiring him to slow down and give timely sig-
> nals when approaching pedestrians . . . or when approaching the intersection
> of a highway, or a curve, or corner where the operator's view is obstructed.
>
> One of these duties . . . is that he display at least two lighted lamps on the
> front of his vehicle, which shall be visible at least 500 feet in the direction
> in which he is going. This is . . . for the purpose of protecting the public . . .
> in the nighttime.[27]

These automobile rules were analogues of the provisions we examined in
Chapter 4, the rules that were intended to address similar concerns resulting from

---

24  Fink, *America Adopts the Automobile*, 180. European countries were much more willing to adopt speed
and other restrictions than were Americans, at least initially. Perhaps the most extreme example of this is
England's "Locomotives on Highways Act," which was adopted in 1865 and not repealed until 1896. See
*id.* at 114. It set a speed limit of 2 miles per hour and 4 miles per hour on open roads for "self-propelled
road vehicles." See *id.*

25  See *Id.*, 182–186. By 1906 "most" of the states had adopted automobile speed limits, which ranged from
20 miles per hour (the most common) to as low as 8 or 9 miles per hour, 185.

26  See *State v. Read*, 162 Iowa 572, 144 N.W. 310, 312 (Iowa 1913).

27  *Id.*

the widespread use of bicycle technology. The automobile rules were in fact based on the bicycle statutes.[28]

Adopting rules prescribing equipment for automobiles and defining a few basic standards for their operation was not the extent of official efforts to protect citizens from the mass implementation of this new technology. In an initiative that went beyond what they had required of cyclists, governments adopted laws that were intended to ensure a measure of competence in the "use" of automobile technology:[29]

> Rhode Island passed the first driver's license law in 1908. . . . Driver's licenses were created for the purpose of protecting public safety by recognizing those individuals who met the necessary standards to receive state sanction to operate a motor vehicle. . . . [T]hose standards include age, knowledge of traffic laws, physical capability to drive, and . . . driving competence. . . . All states have required drivers to be licensed since 1954.[30]

As we saw in Chapter 4, requiring an operator's license went well beyond the measures states had adopted to control the implementation of bicycle technology.[31]

---

[28]  See, e.g., Robert A. Smith, *A Social History of The Bicycle* (New York: American Heritage Press, 1972), 203:

> [A]s the cycle began to disappear from downtown areas and no longer contributed so heavily to congestion, traffic and light ordinances were less frequently enforced. However, the course of the future had been laid out. When the automobile began to crowd streets, the ideas and concepts of the older cycle ordinances were applied to the new . . . situation.

[29]  See, e.g., Automobiles and Highway Traffic § 105, American Jurisprudence (2007) (noting that "the fundamental purpose" of driver's license laws "is to ensure a minimum of competence and skill on the part of drivers of motor vehicles . . . so as to protect third persons who might otherwise be injured or else have their property damaged by the negligent or reckless operation of vehicles on the public highways"). Government "certification of the competence of automobile operators was well established" in Europe by the turn of the twentieth century but was then unknown in the United States. Fink, *America Adopts the Automobile*, 174. Some cities, such as Chicago, began to adopt ordinances requiring automobile driver examinations and licenses around the turn of the twentieth century. See *id.* at 174–176.

[30]  "Driver's License Integrity," National Conference of State Legislatures, http://www.ncsl.org/statefed/DLRCSG.htm. For a history of state driver licensing rules, see, e.g., Fink, *America Adopts the Automobile*, 174–178. See also *Clesas v. Hurley Mach. Co.*, 52 R.I. 69, 157 A. 426, 427 (R.I. 1931) (noting that Rhode Island had required drivers' licenses since 1908).

[31]  At least some cities adopted ordinances requiring licenses to operate bicycles on city streets. See, e.g., *People v. Bruce*, 23 Wash. 777, 777, 63 P. 519, 520 (Wash. 1901):

> The town of Hoquiam . . . passed . . . an ordinance making it unlawful for any person to ride any bicycle, tricycle . . . or vehicle of like character within the corporate limits of the town . . . "until the owner thereof shall have paid unto the city of Hoquiam annually the sum of one dollar, and obtained a license therefor"; further making a violation of the ordinance a misdemeanor

The empirical rationale for the automobile operator's licensing laws lay in the increased dangers posed by motorized vehicles. Like the bicycle and like photography, nonspecialists—civilians—used the automobile. Like the bicycle, but unlike photography, the automobile was a technology the implementation of which created a potential for negative consequences; here, however, the potential for negative consequences was much greater than it had been for bicycle technology.[32]

> As cars increased in numbers and speed, accidents multiplied. Highway accident fatalities rose in the United States from 15,000 in 1922 to 32,000 in 1930, and in Great Britain from 4,886 in 1926 to 7,300 in 1934. Population experts stated that highway driving had become the principal cause of the currently rising rate of violent deaths.[33]

Aside from anything else, cars were faster, heavier, and harder to stop than bicycles; they were therefore far more likely to inflict serious damage on persons and/or property than were bicycles. This, legislatures decided, required more stringent measures than those used to control the defective implementation of bicycle technology.

As the Michigan Supreme Court noted in 1935, requiring someone "to secure an operator's license . . . before driving an automobile is a regulation for the protection of life and property, the wisdom of which can scarcely be questioned."[34] Doctrinally, these licensing laws were predicated on the "police power":

> The right of a citizen to travel upon the public highways is a common right, but the exercise of that right may be regulated . . . in the interest of public

---

punishable by fine. The respondents were charged . . . with having violated the ordinance, and upon a trial were convicted and fined.

See also *Anderson v. Sterrit*, 95 Kan. 483, 148 P. 635, 636 (Kan. 1915); *Simpson v. City of Whatcom*, 33 Wash. 392, 393, 74 P. 577, 577 (Wash. 1903). Other ordinances required licenses to operate bicycles on sidewalks. See, *e.g., Lee v. City of Port Huron*, 128 Mich. 533, 534, 87 N.W. 637, 637 (Mich. 1901); *Morrison v. City of Syracuse*, 53 A.D. 490, 65 N.Y.S. 939, 940 (N.Y.A.D. 1900).

As the passage quoted above demonstrates, however, these ordinances were not designed to ensure that bicyclists demonstrated a threshold level of competence in the operation of their machines. They were, instead, revenue-generating devices; one only needed to pay the requisite fee to obtain a license. See, *e.g., Densmore v. Erie City*, 20 Pa. C.C. 513, 1898 WL 3616 *3 (Pa. Com. Pl. 1898).

32   See Bardou, et al., *The Automobile Revolution*, at 114–116.

33   *Id.*, at 116.

34   *Zabonick v. Ralston*, 272 Mich. 247, 252, 261 N.W.2d 316, 318 (Mich. 1935). See also *supra* note 29.

safety under the police power of the State. The operation of a motor vehicle on such highways is not a natural right. It is a conditional privilege, which may be suspended or revoked under the police power.[35]

The police power is a fundamental constitutional principle that gives Congress and state legislatures the authority to adopt measures which are designed to promote "the general welfare" by ensuring public health or safety.[36] As a legal treatise explains, the "police power is exercised out of public necessity" and it gives a legislature the ability to "impose obligations and responsibilities otherwise nonexistent."[37]

To enforce the laws requiring a driver's license, states made it a crime—usually a minor crime—to operate a motor vehicle without a license.[38] They did the same with other rules designed to control the defective implementation of automobile technology, such as law setting speed limits for the operation of motor vehicles. These laws were rigorously enforced:

> In the last three months of 1906, the New York City police made 646 arrests for violations of laws and ordinances relating to motor vehicles. As early as 1905 in California, driving an unregistered vehicle was a misdemeanor. Soon afterward, driving without a license became another. In 1925, the minimum age for a driver's license was fixed at fourteen; and habitual

---

[35]  *Commonwealth v. Ellett*, 174 Va. 403, 414, 4 S.E.2d 762, 767 (Va. 1939). See also *Sullins v. Butler*, 11 Beeler 468, 135 S.W.2d 930, 932 (Tenn. 1940); *Meany v. Connor*, 7 Conn. Supp. 165, 1939 WL 906 *4 (Conn. Super. 1939). See *generally* Motor Vehicles § 25, Corpus Juris Secundum (2007).

[36]  See*, e.g.,* Constitutional Law § 616, Corpus Juris Secundum (2007) ("The police power is exercised out of public necessity, and the securing of the general welfare, comfort, and convenience of the people is the real object of the police power").

[37]  Constitutional Law § 616, Corpus Juris Secundum (2007).

[38]  See *State v. Denson*, 189 N.C. 173, 126 S.E. 517, 518–519 (N.C. 1925) (defendants convicted of operating a motor vehicle without a driver's license).

For some time, police were at a distinct disadvantage in enforcing traffic and other motor vehicle laws for two reasons: One is that automobile drivers did their best to avoid being apprehended and cited; they refused to stop when signaled to do so, fled the scene and even refused to show up in court when ordered to do so. See Fink, *America Adopts the Automobile*, 186–187. In the years before and shortly after the turn of the twentieth century, drivers seem to have regarded all this as something of a joke. See *id.*

The other reason police were at a disadvantage lay in their very limited access to this new technology. Officers "on foot, on horseback, or bicycles" could not possibly hope to apprehend a speeding motorist. See *id.*, 186–187. And even when police had automobiles, their vehicles were often not as sophisticated or as powerful as those of the scofflaws they sought to apprehend. See *id.* at 186–188.

---

drinkers, drug addicts, and the 'feeble-minded' were barred from licensure. In 1931, the minimum age was raised to sixteen. In New York in 1910, the law required all drivers to drive "in a careful and prudent manner and at a rate of speed so as not to endanger . . . property . . . or . . . life or limb'; any speed over thirty miles an hour. . . was 'presumptive evidence'" of careless, imprudent driving. . . .

By 1940, the. . . . volume of traffic offenses was astronomical. . . . At the beginning of the 1940s, 212 cities with a combined population of 45,420,696 reported more than 6,000,000 violations of traffic and motor vehicle laws.[39]

Although the use of criminal liability might make it appear that these laws were "misuse" rules,[40] they in fact were not. They were, as I noted earlier, intended to control the defective implementation of automobile technology by setting minimum standards of competence and by defining certain parameters for the operation of motor vehicles. The use of criminal liability here was a specific manifestation of a general phenomenon that emerged around the beginning of the last century.

At the beginning of the twentieth century, American legislators began using their police power to create a new kind of criminal liability: the "public welfare offense."[41] The creation of public welfare offenses resulted from a "shift in emphasis from the protection of individual interests which marked nineteenth century criminal administration to the protection of public and social interests."[42] While they impose criminal liability on those who failed to comport with legislatively mandated standards of conduct, public welfare offenses are really regulatory measures; they represent an "exercise of . . . the police power where the emphasis of the statute is . . . upon achievement of some social betterment rather than the

---

[39]  Lawrence M. Friedman, *Crime and Punishment in American History* (New York: Basic Books, 1993), 278. As Friedman notes, the numbers have only "continued to rise, as automobiles choke the roads and highways, and millions of people . . . use the automobile as their lifeline," 278.

 As I explained earlier, the only rules adopted to target negative consequences associated with the implementation of photographic technology were directed at professional photographers, not the civilian users of the technology.

[40]  See Chapter 3.

[41]  See Francis B. Sayre, Public Welfare Offenses, 33 Colum.L.Rev. 55, 67–68 (1933).

[42]  M. Diane Barber, Fair Warning: The Deterioration Of Scienter Under Environmental Criminal Statutes, 26 Loy. L.A. L. Rev. 105, 110 (1992).

punishment of the crimes as in cases of *mala in se*."[43] Traffic laws represent "a classic example of statutory public welfare offenses."[44]

The criminal liability legislatures impose in the exercise of their police power is actually an attenuated form of criminal liability. Public welfare offenses usually eliminate one or more of the elements that have traditionally been required for the imposition of criminal liability, such as *mens rea* and the actual infliction of a specified "harm."[45] They compensate for this by imposing only a minor level of criminal liability; public welfare offenses are usually at most misdemeanor offenses punishable by a small fine.[46] This has always been true of the laws adopted to regulate the operation of motor vehicles; even particularly egregious violations of these rules—such as operating a motor vehicle while intoxicated—only rise to the level of a felony if the offender has previously been convicted of similar violations.[47] All of this is consistent with the general use of the police power to adopt defective implementation rules.[48]

---

[43]  United *States v. Balint*, 258 U.S. 250, 252 (1922).

Criminal law has historically divided crimes into "crimes *mala in se* (wrong in themselves; inherently evil) and crimes *mala prohibita* (not inherently evil; wrong only because prohibited by legislation)." Wayne R. LaFave, Substantive Criminal Law § 1.6(b), 2d ed. (St. Paul: West, 2007). Traditional offenses involving the malicious infliction of "harm" upon person (homicide, rape, assault) or property (theft, burglary, arson) are *mala in se* offenses. Regulatory measures such as traffic laws and pure food and drug laws represent *malum prohibitum* offenses. See *id.*

[44]  Louis A. Ambrose and Darrell F. Cook, Criminal Law, 51 Md. L. Rev. 612, 617 (1992). See Francis B. Sayre, Public Welfare Offenses, 33 Colum.L.Rev. 55, 73 (1933). See, *e.g., United States v. Park*, 421 U.S. 658 (1975); *United States v. Dotterweich*, 320 U.S. 277 (1943). See also Catherine L. Carpenter, *On Statutory Rape, Strict Liability, and the Public Welfare Offense Model*, 53 Am. U. L. Rev. 313, 327 (2003) (public welfare offenses include "(1) illegal sales or transport of intoxicating liquor; (2) sales of impure or adulterated food; (3) sales of misbranded articles; (4) violations of anti-narcotics acts; (5) criminal nuisances; (6) violations of traffic regulations; (7) violations of motor-vehicle laws; and (8) violations of general police regulations passed for safety, health, or well being of the community").

Some courts have, for example, found that certain motor vehicle rules, such as those that penalize the operation of a vehicle while under the influence of an intoxicant, are, at most, quasi-criminal in nature because their primary purpose is controlling the defective implementation of automobile technology. See State v. Hanson, 543 N.W.2d 84 (Minn. 1996). See also Janis Mary Gomez, Comment, "The Potential Double Jeopardy Implications of Administrative License Revocation," *Emory Law Journal 46* (1997): 329.

[45]  See, *e.g., Staples v. United States*, 511 U.S. 600, 616–618 (1994).

[46]  See, *e.g., id.*, 617–618 (1994). See also *United States v. Ahmad*, 101 F.3d 386, 391 (5th Cir. 1996).

[47]  See, *e.g.,* Alaska Stat. § 28,35.030(n); Fla. Stat. Ann. § 316.193(3)(b); Va. Code Ann. § 18.2–270(C)(1).

[48]  Public welfare offenses, which originated in Britain, began as a reaction to the increased uses of technology associated with the Industrial Revolution. See, *e.g., United States v. Morissette*, 342 U.S. 246, 253–254 (1952) ("The industrial revolution multiplied the number of workmen exposed to injury from increasingly powerful and complex mechanisms, driven by freshly discovered sources of energy, requiring higher

There is a category of automobile rules that seems to represent "misuse," rather than defective implementation, rules: In the latter part of the twentieth century many states adopted statutes that made "vehicular homicide" a new, and distinct, offense.[49]

These statutes deviated from the approach taken by bicycle rules[50] and from the approach that had been followed for automobiles until then; for most of the last century, causing someone's death as the result of operating a motor vehicle recklessly or negligently was prosecuted as what it really was—manslaughter or negligent homicide.[51] The Model Penal Code, an influential set of model criminal laws drafted under the aegis of the American Law Institute, takes this approach.[52]

The "vehicular homicide" statutes that appeared in the last century all derived from the 1960s version of the Uniform Vehicle Code,[53] a set of model laws drafted by a nonprofit group dedicated to improving and standardizing state traffic laws.[54] The "vehicular homicide" statutes are ostensibly "misuse" laws because they impose criminal liability based on "harm" that results from one's implementation of a technology. As I explained in Chapter 3, we use civil liability to enforce the rules designed to control the defective implementation of technologies and reserve criminal liability for instances in which the "harm" resulting from the implementation of a technology is inflicted intentionally and is of a type specific to that technology.

---

precautions by employers"). They have since been adopted in many areas. One area in which they tend to directly impact on the implementation of particular technologies is that of environmental regulation. Many public welfare offenses target pollution resulting from the byproducts of technologies. See, e.g., Kepten D. Carmichael, *Strict Criminal Liability for Environmental Violations: A Need for Judicial Restraint*, 71 Ind. L.J. 729, 740 (1996) (Clean Water Act prohibits pollution resulting from chemical, biological or radiological waste). See also Peter J. Martinez, et al., "Environmental Crimes," *Am. Crim. L. Rev. 43* (2006), 381.

49   See *Commonwealth v. Heck*, 341 Pa.Super. 183, 491 A.2d 212, 216 (Pa. Super. 1985) ("numerous states" adopted vehicular homicide provisions).

50   See Chapter 4.

51   See Margaret A. Andruchek, Comment, "Homicide by Vehicle in Pennsylvania," *Dickinson Law Review* 90, 833, 837–838 (1986). See also *People v. Adams*, 289 Ill. 339, 124 N.E. 575 (Ill. 1919); *Bowen v. State*, 100 Ark. 232, 140 S.W. 28 (Ark. 1911); *State v. Campbell*, 82 Conn. 671, 74 A. 927 (Conn. 1910).

52   See American Law institute, Model Penal Code §§ 210.3 & 210.4. See also "About the American Law Institute," http://www.ali.org/ali/thisali.htm.

53   See *Commonwealth v. Heck*, 341 Pa.Super. 183, 491 A.2d 212, 216 (Pa. Super. 1985) (vehicular homicide statutes "derived from Section 11–903 of the Uniform Vehicle Code [1968 rev.]).

54   See "NCUTLO: Who We Are and What We Do," http://www.ncutlo.org/news.html.

"Vehicular homicide" statutes are not really "misuse" laws because they address what is actually the defective implementation of automobile technology. This is apparent from two aspects of these laws. First, and of less importance, is the fact that they do not target the intentional infliction of "harm"; instead, they impose criminal liability on those who are reckless or negligent in operating a motor vehicle and thereby cause the death of another human being.[55] This is a classic example of defective implementation rules; the goal here is not to deter contumacious, malicious conduct but, rather, to encourage competence in the operation of motor vehicles. The other reason why these laws are clearly defective implementation rather than "misuse" rules is that they do not target the infliction of a technologically specific "harm."[56] Instead, they address a generic "harm"—the death of a human being—that results from the defective implementation of a specific technology. I would argue that vehicular homicide laws are redundant and, therefore, unnecessary; it seems to me that prosecuting someone for manslaughter or negligent homicide should be at least as effective in discouraging the defective implementation of automobile technology as are prosecutions under these statutes. They presumably represent a symbolic effort to underscore the need to control the implementation of this now-mundane but still very dangerous technology.

Ironically, perhaps, American law continues to apply the approach it has used for the "misuse" of bicycle technology to the far more serious instances in which someone intentionally uses an automobile as a murder weapon. As I noted earlier, American law has not devised "misuse" rules for bicycle or other technologies (such as electricity) both (a) because of the relative unlikelihood that the technology *would* be "misused" and (b) because "misuse" can be addressed by applying existing law. In the rare instances in which "misuse" occurs, prosecutors charge one who intentionally "used" an automobile to kill another with murder,[57] that is, with intentionally causing the death of a human being.[58] As I have explained elsewhere, we do not have "method" crimes, that is, do not criminalize "homicide by poison," "homicide by strangulation," "homicide by gunshot," "homicide by

---

[55]   See Colo. Rev. Stat. § 18–3–106; Fla. Stat. Ann. § 782.071; Minn. Stat. Ann. § 609.21.

[56]   See Chapter 3.

[57]   See *Harris v. State*, 152 S.W.3d 786 (Tex. App. 2004); *Commonwealth v. Rosier*, 425 Mass. 807, 685 N.E.2d 739 (Mass. 1997).

[58]   See American Law institute, Model Penal Code § 210.1.

stabbing," and so forth.[59] The particular instrumentality one uses to take life is irrelevant to the offense itself, though it can play an aggravating role in sentencing an offender.[60]

(A motor vehicle is not a particularly good murder weapon: It is normally "used" outside—on a street or road or parking lot—which means the murderer either has to know the victim will be on a specific street or road or in a specific parking lot at a given time or has to arrange for the victim to be there. A murderer could "use" a motor vehicle to kill someone inside—in a garage, say—but this raises the same logistical issues: the murderer would have to know the victim would be in the garage at a particular time or would have to arrange for the victim to be there. And once the killer and her victim are in physical proximity to each other, the killer may have a limited opportunity to consummate the crime; the victim may be able to escape by running into a building and/or taking other evasive measures. Getting away with the crime is another problem; a motor vehicle is a very "public" way of committing homicide, which would presumably be a concern to any potential murderer wishing to avoid being caught. All in all, the automobile's capacity for "misuse" is very limited.[61])

I have focused this discussion exclusively on the use of automobile technology to commit homicide because this is really the only crime in which this technology can begin to play a significant substantive role. In criminal law, "substantive" refers to the elements that unite to create the definition of a particular

[59] See Susan W. Brenner, "Is There Such a Thing as Virtual Crime?", 1, http://www.boalt.org/CCLR/v4/v4brenner.htm.

[60] See *id.* As to treating the instrumentality used to commit homicide as an aggravating factor in sentencing, see N.C. Gen. Stat. Ann. § 15A-2000(e)(10).

[61] The text focuses on the "misuse" of automobile technology to commit murder because this is really the only crime in which this technology can even begin to play a significant substantive role. In criminal law, "substantive" refers to the elements that unite to create the definition of a particular crime, or offense. See *Black's Law Dictionary*, 8th ed., "Offense" (St. Paul, Minn.: Thomson/West, 2004). See also id., "substantive." As was noted in the text and in note 37 above, the instrumentality used to commit a particular crime is not an essential component of the "substance"—or legal definition—of that crime.

The discussion in the text above therefore focuses on the "misuse" of automobile technology to commit murder because this is the closest automobile technology comes or, rather, can be said to come—to playing a "substantive" role in the commission of an offense. As the text explains, it really does not play such a role—it is merely *a* method that can be employed to inflict the "harm" (death of a human being) encompassed by this particular offense. See note 37, above. The only role automobile technology plays in the commission of other crimes is as a means of fleeing from the scene and/or from apprehension for committing the crime.

crime or offense.[62] As I noted earlier, we generally do not have "method" crimes; we focus on the "harm" inflicted instead of on the methodology by which it was inflicted. The instrumentality someone used to commit a particular crime is therefore not an essential component of the "substance"—or legal definition—of that crime.

The reason this discussion focused on the "misuse" of automobile technology to commit murder is that this is the closest automobile technology comes—or can be said to come—to playing a "substantive" role in the commission of an offense. As I noted above, automobile technology really does not play such a role in homicide; it is merely one of many methods—some involving the use of technology, some not—that can be employed to inflict the "harm" (death of a human being) encompassed by this particular offense. The only role automobile technology can play in the commission of other crimes is as a means of fleeing the scene and/or apprehension for committing the crime.

The "vehicular homicide" defective-implementation-passing-as-"misuse" statutes are an example of a phenomenon we will analyze in Chapter 7: the tendency to adopt laws that conflate technology and "harm"-inducing behavior. Chapter 7 explains why this phenomenon has arisen and why it represents a fundamentally flawed approach to the "misuse" problem.

To recap, the laws societies adopted to deal with the civilian implementation of automobile technology applied the same approach they had used for bicycle technology. That is, like all of the rules we have so far considered, the rules devised to control the implementation of automobile technology focused on the "users" of that technology.[63] But unlike the rules that were adopted to control the implementation of "specialist" technologies, automobile rules were generalized. They applied to anyone in the society if, and as long as, that person operated a motor vehicle; using-automobile-technology was the empirical context in which these rules applied.[64] That is significant because it creates a clear line of demarcation; automobile rules *can* apply to everyone, but they in fact do not and will not. They apply only when someone enters the automobile-as-technology context

---

[62]  See *Black's Law Dictionary*, "offense" and "substantive."

[63]  See Chapters 3 and 4.

[64]  This, of course, was the same approach societies took to controlling the implementation of bicycle technology. See Chapter 4.

by operating a motor vehicle; like bicycle rules, automobile rules are a specialized set of technology-specific rules.[65]

## Telephone

*It is an interesting instrument . . . for professors of electricity and acoustics; but it can never be a practical necessity.*[66]

Alexander Graham Bell patented his telephone in 1876 and demonstrated it that same year at the Centennial Exhibition in Philadelphia.[67] Though people were fascinated by being able to speak with someone at a distance, the telephone's

> value as a communications device was . . . underrecognized due to its technical limitations. The very idea of talking at a piece of sheet iron was so . . . extraordinary that both ordinary people and scientists resisted it. In the beginning, the telephone was not as practical as it is today. Its usefulness was limited by the fact that people could only speak to those with whom they were directly connected and voice communications were limited to 20 miles between connected locations. Initially a person had to shout into the telephone in order to be heard. The telephone did not appear to be a threat to the dominance of Western Union.[68]

Over the next three decades, Bell and others developed a business model, improved the technology, and mastered long-distance communication.[69] By the end of the nineteenth century, telephones were competing successfully with telegraphy, a much slower means of communication.[70] "By the turn of the century, the telegraph had seen its heyday."[71]

---

[65]  See Chapter 4.

[66]  Herbert N. Casson, *The History of the Telephone* 42 (Chicago: A.C. McClurg, 1922), 42 (quoting critics of the telephone).

[67]  See Susan E. McMaster, *The Telecommunications Industry* (Westport, CT: Greenwood Press 2002), 6–7.

[68]  *Id.*, 7.

[69]  See *id.*, 7–32, 96–97.

[70]  See *id.*, 10, 18. Another factor in telephony's competitiveness was the declining cost of the service. See McMaster, at 60 (cost of service in the U.S. was "cut by at least half during the first two decades of the twentieth century").

[71]  Ronnie J. Phillips, "Digital Technology and Institutional Change from the Gilded Age to Modern Times: The Impact of the Telegraph and the Internet," *Journal of Economic Issues 34* (June, 2000): 267, 276–277, http://diglib.lib.utk.edu/utj/jei/34/jei-34-2-3.pdf.

As we know, the telephone did, in fact, become a "practical necessity." Writing in 1935, a government subcommittee noted the effects this technology had already had upon life in the United States:

> It broke the isolation of the farms, increased the number of business transactions, and speeded the tempo of modern life. Its importance to special industries, such as newspapers, has been of inestimable value. It has tended to break down State lines, to eradicate regional differences, and to increase international contacts. It has been of aid in safety, in transportation, in fighting fires, and crime.[72]

The telephone's ultimate pervasiveness as a technology is in large part attributable to Theodore Vail; in 1907, Vail became president of American Telephone and Telegraph [AT&T] a successor to the company Bell founded in 1885.[73] Vail was "convinced that, at some future time, AT&T would provide . . . telephone service to every household in the country'"[74] Under his direction, AT&T aggressively linked existing connections, added new ones, and expanded long-distance service.[75] By the 1970s, it had "successfully completed the movement toward universal service. In the 1980s, the percentage of U.S. households using AT&T service topped 90 percent."[76] By the end of the twentieth century, AT&T was gone, phone service was in the hands of many smaller companies,[77] and the Federal Communications Commission had assumed responsibility for ensuring universal telephone service, a task that had become much more complex with the development of mobile telephony and other technologies.[78]

---

[72] The Subcommittee on Technology, 4. For a review of the effects telephony had on U.S. business, see Alfred D. Chandler, Jr. and James W. Cortada, *A Nation Transformed by Information: How Information Has Shaped the United States from Colonial Times to the Present* (Oxford University Press, 2000), 100–102.

[73] See McMaster, *The Telecommunications Industry*, 89–90. Bell founded the American Bell Telephone Company in 1885. See McMaster at 87.

[74] *Id.*, 95–96. "This was . . . a highly unrealistic objective at a time when telephones could be found in fewer than 10 percent of American households," at 96.

[75] See *id*. The "theme was 'one system, one policy, universal service', which . . . expressed Vail's vision of an integrated telephone network under the supervision of AT&T," at 96.

[76] *Id.*, 116. By the 1980s, AT&T was "the largest corporation in the world," at 114.

[77] In 1984, AT&T underwent a massive restructuring pursuant to an agreement it reached with the U.S. Department of Justice. The agreement settled an antitrust case and divided AT&T into a series of smaller companies. See *id.*,121–133. The Telecommunications Act of 1996 removed barriers to local competition, which increased the number of companies providing phone service. See McMaster, *The Telecommunications Industry*, at 153–157.

[78] See *id.*, 121–133. The FCC had taken responsibility for this earlier, but the requirement was never codified. See McMaster, at 158. The Telecommunications Act of 1996 "codified the requirements for universal

By the end of the twentieth century, the telephone had become, if not *the* most pervasive technology of all time, certainly one of the most pervasive. Automobiles are a pervasive technology, but many who do not have a car have a telephone of some sort.[79] A 2007 CIA study reported, for example, that almost four billion telephones were in use around the world,[80] a number that will continue to rise for the foreseeable future.[81]

Notwithstanding its pervasiveness, telephone technology is not a technology that civilians implement exclusively. To understand why, a comparison between the telephone and the automobile is useful: Specialists usually manufacture, and maintain, automobiles but civilians operate them almost exclusively.[82] Specialists

---

service" and mandated that the FCC and state telecommunications commissions "ensure that affordable local service was available to everyone." McMaster, at 158.

[79] See Daniel Gross, "How Many Mobile Phones Does the World Need?", *Slate* (June 2, 2004), http://slate. msn.com/id/2101625/ (estimated "1.35 billion cell phones in use in the world today" with a projection of "2 billion wireless subscriber" by 2008). See also "Telephones – mobile cellular – density," Exxun.com, http://www.exxun.com/encm/wr_telephone_mob_densi_1.html (per capita density of mobile phones by country).

[80] See Central Intelligence Agency, "World" in *The World Factbook: 2007*, https://www.cia.gov/library/ publications/the-world-factbook/print/xx.html (2,168,433,600 mobile telephones and 1,263,367,600 main lines).

[81] See "Gartner Says Mobile Phone Sales Will Exceed One Billion in 2009," Gartner (2005), http://www. gartner.com/press_releases/asset_132473_11.html; "1.5 Billion Mobile Phone Users," MyMob (2004), http://www.mymob.com/mobile-news/mobile-phone-users.html.

[82] One could argue that professional motor vehicle racers are specialists in the use of automotive technology, but this really misses the point. Professional racers and the machines they operate are a behaviorally and technologically discrete category. Racing vehicles are the product of specialized, often advanced technology; automotive racers specialize in an activity that has little, if any, connection to the operation of a "civilian" motor vehicle.

One could also argue that law enforcement officers are specialists in the implementation of motor vehicles. Officers are specially trained in the operation of what are essentially civilian motor vehicles. See, *e.g.*, State of Minnesota - Department of Public Safety, "Law Enforcement In-Service Training in Emergency Vehicle Operation and Police Pursuits for Peace Officers and Part-Time Peace Officers" (August 26, 1999), http://www.dps.state.mn.us/Newpost/PDFs/In-Service%20Police%20Pursuit%20and%20EVO% 20Learning%20objectives.pdf. This argument fails, however, because law enforcement officers, like professional racers, are implementing what is actually a sub-category of the civilian technology. Professional motor vehicle racers implement their specialized technologies in a unique context, one that is quite separate from the context in which civilians utilize automotive technology. Law enforcement officers do operate their vehicles in the same physical context civilians occupy, but they do so for very limited, very specialized purposes. It would, therefore, be inaccurate to characterize either professional racers or law enforcement officers as specialists in the implementation of conventional automobile technology; they are specialists in the implementation of distinct but related technologies.

also manufacture and maintain (to the extent they are maintained) telephones,[83] and part of their implementation is in the hands of civilians. Telephones, though, are only a small part of telephone technology.[84]

Automobiles are free-standing technology, but a telephone is merely telephone technology's interface with an end-"user."[85] Civilian "users" share the implementation of telephone technology with specialists—telephone company employees who ensure the proper functioning of the networked technology that provides civilian telephone service.[86] This shared implementation creates two distinct categories of "users": One consists of civilian end-"users"; these civilian "users" implement the consumer version of telephone technology in the real, physical world and are in that sense analogous to "users" of tool and machine technologies. Using consumer equipment, they "use" the technology for its ultimate purpose: real-time communication between individuals.

Telephone company specialists are "users" at one remove; they do not, at least in their professional capacity, "use" the consumer version of telephone technology for its ultimate purpose.[87] They "use" the systems that underlie and animate the operation of the consumer version of telephone technology; in that sense, their role is analogous to that of the railroad employees who operate the transport system that moves people and goods or the employees of an electric company who generate power for civilian "use."

---

[83] See "Data Technical Support," Verizon Wireless, http://dts.vzw.com/index.html?m=LG. See also "Return Policy," Verizon Wireless http://www.verizonwireless.com/b2c/globalText?textName=RETURN_POLICY&jspName=footer/returnPolicy.jsp.

[84] See "Public Switched Telephone Network," *Wikipedia*, http://en.wikipedia.org/wiki/Public_Switched_Telephone_Network; "Integrated Services Digital Network," *Wikipedia*, http://en.wikipedia.org/wiki/Integrated_Services_Digital_Network.

[85] See "Telephone," *Wikipedia*, http://en.wikipedia.org/wiki/Telephone ("modern telephones operate as one part of a complex public switched telephone network of equipment which allows almost any phone user to speak to almost any other. . . . [W]ireless telephony transmits messages using radio").

[86] See "Investor Relations," SBC, http://www.sbc.com/gen/investor-relations?pid=5711 (telephone company serving thirteen states has 157,600 employees). See also "Ironton Telephone Company Employees," http://www.ironton.com/company/employees.html (directory of employees of small phone company).

[87] Telephone company specialists do "use" telephones for real-time communications as part of their professional endeavors. Civilian "use" of telephone technology is not limited to personal use; it encompasses professional and commercial use by any individual, including specialists employed by telephone companies. The reference in the text above is to specialized activity involved in orchestrating the delivery of telephone service, not to the "use" of a telephone for one-to-one communication.

It is impossible even to summarize the effects the telephone has had on society. As an author noted, it "passed from miraculous in the nineteenth century to mundane in the mid-twentieth century to mandatory by the end of the twentieth century."[88] Bell's invention changed how we do business, how we conduct our personal lives, how we learn, and how we keep safe. It is, as Chapter 6 explains, the foundation and the model for the pervasive technologies that will permeate our lives as this century progresses.

At a fundamental level, telephone technology changed how we communicate and how we think about communication.[89] Telegraphy was a slightly automated version of the postal service; it used technology to transmit messages, but users still had to rely on individual intermediaries to enter a message into the system, initiate its transmission, and retrieve and un-encode it once it had arrived. Telegraphy was faster than the post, but it was still cumbersome, expensive, and offered little in the way of privacy.[90]

Telephony offered something new and attractive: instantaneous, one-to-one remote communication. One-to-one communication is communication that takes place between two and only two individuals.[91] Face-to-face communication is the oldest and simplest form of one-to-one communication.[92] The development of writing created the possibility of mediated one-to-one communication, that is, one-to-one communication carried out by means other than face-to-face oral communication.[93] Later in this chapter and in Chapter 6 we will

---

[88]   Claude S. Fischer, *America Calling: A Social History of the Telephone to 1940* (Berkeley, CA: University of California Press, 1994), 191.

[89]   See Thomas A. Wikle, "Cellular Tower Proliferation in the United States," *The Geographical Review 92* (2002): 45, 46

> Until the . . . telegraph, long-distance communication required people to move messages physically from place to place, a time-consuming activity involving travel by horse, boat, stagecoach, or other vehicle. Because of the difficulty . . . messages were simple and utilitarian. The telegraph, and later the telephone, helped decrease the dependence of communication on transportation, making the space between people less important and their messages longer but often less consequential. . As a result of its privacy and convenience, the telephone revolutionized business and personal communication.

(citation omitted).

[90]   See *id*. See also Susan W. Brenner, "The Fourth Amendment in an Era of Ubiquitous Technology," *Miss. L.J. 74* (2005): 1 (lack of privacy).

[91]   See Susan W. Brenner, "The Privacy Privilege: Law Enforcement, Technology and the Constitution," *Journal of Technology Law & Policy 7* (2002); 123, 131–133.

[92]   See *id*.

[93]   See *id*.

examine other models, including one-to-many, many-to-many, and many-to-one communication.

(In its early years, the telephone was also used for one-to-many communication, that is, to broadcast news, lectures and even music.[94] The telephone could, therefore, have evolved into a medium that, like the Internet, offered both one-to-one and one-to-many communication. For various reasons, it did not.[95])

The post and telegraphy both offered remote communication, and the post offered one-to-one communication,[96] but neither could provide real-time communication. Along with the obvious advantage of speed, real-time communication offers something else: fluid, interactive communication.[97] Telegraphy and the post were based on written communication, which is necessarily static; I cannot revise what I wrote as it is being read or immediately supplement my thoughts in response to the reader's reaction.[98] I communicate but I do not converse. For better or worse, conversing is the essence of telephonic communication; in a mature telephone system, the parties to a call interact directly and for as long as they choose.

This is significant psychologically because it influences our relationship with the technology. Historically, the "users" of technology have manipulated a technology

---

[94] See Carolyn Marvin, *When Old Technologies Were New* (New York: Oxford University Press, 1988), 208–216.

[95] See *id.*

[96] The post offered one-to-one communication because of the privacy the mail offered after the adhesive envelope and the gummed stamp were introduced in the nineteenth century. Unlike letters sent with sealing wax, the sealed envelope offered a reliable guarantee that the contents of mail would not be revealed inadvertently to postal workers. See Robert Ellis Smith, Ben Franklin's Web Site: Privacy and Curiosity from Plymouth Rock to the Internet 23–26, 51–56 (*Privacy Journal*, 2000). And the postage stamp expedited the process by ensuring that, once in the system, mail would travel with all due expedition. See id., 23–26, 51–56.

Telegraphy offered a form of one-to-one communication: A telegram was, ultimately, a communication between Person A (sender) and Person B (recipient). However, unlike the post and, later, the telephone, telegraphy sent the contents of a communication via intermediaries, each of whom read the message and transmitted it along its path or decoded it and delivered it to the recipient. The participation of the intermediaries attenuated the one-to-one nature of the process, along with eroding privacy.

[97] By the early part of the twentieth century, telephonic communication, like the post but unlike telegraphy, was also offering privacy.

[98] More recent forms of written communication, such as online chatting, are less static, because one can respond essentially instantaneously to another's response. This is due to a difference in the transmission medium. For both telegraphy and the post, the written communication was drafted and given to personnel employed by a third-party entity, who would then transfer the written communication to its intended recipient; they then did the same with that person's response. It is the medium of transmission, rather than writing itself, which imports the static element into these forms of communication.

for a specific purpose; they "used" it to achieve a discrete, identifiable goal such as producing pottery or textiles, transporting people and goods over rail lines or simply riding a bicycle to work. The technology was an extension of human abilities and human effort; it let individuals accomplish essential tasks quickly and more effectively. Our relationship with these technologies was (and is) purely instrumental; we use them to accomplish our task and then set them aside.

Our relationship with telephone technology is more complex. When automated switching replaced human "operators" in the 1920s, we civilians assumed responsibility for placing our own calls.[99] Our relationship with telephone technology is in that regard analogous to our relationship with prior technologies; we approach telephone technology as an implement we use to accomplish a specific purpose— establishing real-time voice communication with someone. But there is also another dimension to our relationship with the telephone; unlike our relationship with the tool and machine technologies, our relationship with telephone technology is not purely instrumental. Once we establish communication with someone, the existence and operation of the technology recede into the background of our consciousness.[100] We focus on the real-time communicative experience, not the technology. This erodes the applicability of the principle that has historically structured our approach to controlling the implementation of technology: the assumption that technologies are utilized in a discrete empirical context. We will return to this issue in Chapter 6 and again in Chapter 7.

Because telephone technology is extraordinarily pervasive in its effects, societies find it prudent to ensure that the technology is implemented effectively, that is, is as free as possible from defective implementation. Although the defective implementation of telephone technology does not pose the direct physical hazards associated with, say, the defective implementation of rail or air travel, our dependence on the telephone as our means of communicating with the outside world brings its own hazards, including physical dangers. We rely on the telephone to notify the fire department if there is a fire at our home; we also "use" it to advise

---

[99]  See McMaster, *The Telecommunications Industry*, 58–59, 72–73. Automated switching lets callers dial their party directly, instead of going through an operator.

[100]  Innovations such as speakerphones, wireless landline phones, mobile phones, and Bluetooth headsets have made the technology even less obtrusive than it was, say, thirty years ago. We are no longer tied to a landline desk phone; we can talk while we walk the dog, while we shop at the grocery, while we wait in an airport, while we drive—essentially anywhere. The mobility we enjoy while using telephone technology means it is less and less a focused, singular, experience; instead, our use of telephony increasingly becomes an unremarked incident of our daily lives.

police of a crime that has been committed or is in progress. And for many, it is their exclusive means of contacting emergency personnel when they are in need of medical assistance. Aside from anything else, these and other negative consequences of the defective implementation of telephone technology justify rules that ensure systems are stable and as dependable as possible.

Societies therefore adopt rules designed to prevent defective implementation; because the systemic implementation of telephone technology is the exclusive responsibility of specialists, these rules target the specialists, not the civilian end-"users."[101] Civilians have no ability, absent extraordinary measures, to influence the implementation of the systemic aspects of telephone technology. They would have to, say, bomb a telephone switching station to affect the systemic aspects of this technology.[102] Civilians' status here is analogous to the position they occupy with regard to the generation of electrical power.[103]

Although civilians cannot orchestrate the defective implementation of systemic telephone technology, they can "misuse" the consumer aspect of the technology. When telephone technology is used to facilitate the commission of a criminal act, the conduct can be dealt with by applying existing criminal prohibitions, just as the intentional "use" of a motor vehicle to kill someone can be prosecuted as murder. If, for example, someone uses a telephone to transmit an extortion threat, the act of using the telephone can be folded into a prosecution for the underlying offense, that is, extortion.[104]

It rather quickly became apparent, though, that telephone technology could be "misused" in ways that were not within the compass of traditional criminal prohibitions. Making obscene or harassing telephone calls was not a crime when the last century began; there had never been a need for such prohibitions.[105] States

---

[101] See Ark. Code Ann. § 23-17-404 ("preservation and promotion of universal service"); Mich. Stat. Ann. § 237.011 (goals for telecommunication service).

[102] See Cisco Van Schaik, "Information Warfare in the 21st Century," South Africa Defence College (2002), http://www.mil.za/CSANDF/CJSupp/TrainingFormation/DefenceCollege/Researchpapers2000_02/vanschaik.htm.

[103] See Chapter 4.

[104] See Ala. Code 1975 § 13A-8-14 (extortion).

[105] Britain, for example, did not criminalize harassment until 1986, in a move that was controversial at the time. See Nathan Courtney, *British and United States Hate Speech Legislation: A Comparison,* 19 Brook. J. Int'l L. 727, 742 (1993) (citing Public Order Act, 1986, ch. 64, §§ 5-6 (Eng.)). Harassment seems to have begun to be criminalized in the United States in the 1960's. See, *e.g.,* People v. Nix, 131 Ill. App. 3d 973,

consequently began sporadically adopting new prohibitions that specifically targeted such activity; because it began to be perceived as an increasingly serious problem, the drive to adopt such laws accelerated around fifty years ago, and by 1968 "every American jurisdiction maintained a penal statute against obscene or harassing telephone calls."[106] These prohibitions have evolved as the technology has evolved and now encompass telephone stalking as well as the making of obscene or harassing calls.[107] Like the other implementation laws we have considered, these prohibitions are context specific, the context being the "use" of telephone technology. We will return to this issue in Chapter 7.

---

974, 476 N.E.2d 797, 798 (Ill. App. 1985); People v. Smolen, 69 Misc.2d 920, 922, 331 N.Y.S.2d 98, 100 (N.Y. City Crim. Ct. 1972). A New York court explained the rationale for the new offense: "This [harassment] statute was enacted in 1965 . . . to cover those wrongs and annoyances, which neither rise to the level of assault . . . nor are intended or calculated to produce public disorder so as to constitute disorderly conduct". People v. Smolen, 69 Misc.2d at 922, 331 N.Y.S.2d at 100.

The closest English common law came to criminalizing harassment was making it a misdemeanor to challenge "another to fight or attempting to provoke another to give such challenge." See American Law Institute, Model Penal Code § 250.4 commentary. The premise of this misdemeanor was later codified in English and American statutes that make it an offense to attempt to provoke a "breach of the peace." See American Law Institute, Model Penal Code § 250.4 commentary.

Another common law offense that captured conduct that was somewhat analogous to harassment was "watching and besetting." See *generally* Matthew Goode, *Stalking: Crime of the '90s?,* Australian Institute of Criminology—International Victimology, Selected Papers from the 8th International Symposium 193, 194 (Canberra, Australia: Australian Institute of Criminology, 1996), http://www.aic.gov.au/publications/proceedings/27/goode.pdf. Basically, "watching and besetting" outlawed picketing, at least certain types of picketing. See, *e.g., Mulholland v. Walters' Local Union No. 106,* 13 Ohio Dec. 342, 1902 WL 1025 *14 (Ohio Com. Pl. 1902). See also Rachel Vorspan, *The Political Power of Nuisance Law: Labor Picketing and the Courts in Modern England, 1871-Present,* 46 Buff. L. Rev. 593, (1998) (in nineteenth-century English law, unlawful picketing was known as "watching or besetting"). Some, at least, suggest that the "watching and besetting" offense helped influence the evolution of contemporary harassment and/or stalking laws. See Good, *Stalking: Crime of the '90s?, supra.*

Neither harassment nor the use of obscene language seem to have been criminalized prior to the implementation of telephone technology, presumably because such conduct could be dealt with under these statutes or, if actually produced a physical altercation, under assault statutes. See American Law Institute, Model Penal Code § 211.1 (assault).

[106] American Law Institute, Model Penal Code § 250.4 commentary. Section 250.4 criminalizes the use of the telephone to make such calls.

[107] See *Taylor v. State,* 76 Tex.Crim. 642, 643 177 S.W. 82, 83 (Tex. Crim. App. 1915) (1911 act made it a misdemeanor to use "vulgar, profane, obscene or indecent language over or through any telephone"). States subsequently outlawed using a telephone to make harassing calls and to stalk someone. See Jennifer L. Bradfield, Note, "Anti-Stalking Laws: Do They Adequately Protect Stalking Victims?," *Harvard Women's Law Journal 21* (1998): 229; Wayne F. Foster, *Validity, Construction, And Application Of State Criminal Statute Forbidding Use Of Telephone To Annoy Or Harass,* 95 A.L.R.3d 411. See also *supra* note cv.

Like the automobile, the telephone is a consumer technology. It was intended to improve the quality of our lives by improving personal and business communication, and it has done that. Like the automobile, it has also had unintended effects; perhaps the most important of these is that it led to the "invention" of cyberspace, an event that is examined in later in this chapter.

## Broadcast Media

*Few inventions have captured the imagination more than those ... associated with entertainment and information.*[108]

For our purposes, "broadcast media"[109] is an umbrella term encompassing three information/entertainment technologies that emerged in the twentieth century: radio, cinema, and television.[110] They are grouped together because each is a

---

[108] The Subcommittee on Technology, 29.

[109] "*Media* . . . is a contraction of the term *media of communication*, referring to those organized means of dissemination of fact, opinion, and entertainment such as newspapers, magazines, cinema films, radio [and] television." "Mass media," *Wikipedia*, http://en.wikipedia.org/wiki/Media.

[110] Radio technology originated in the nineteenth century, but commercial broadcasting did not begin until the 1920s. See Trevor I. Williams, A Short History of Twentieth-Century Technology 300–301 (New York: Clarendon Press, 1982); Oliver, *History of American Technology*, 540–542.

> By 1922, there were 600 commercial radio broadcasting stations and a million listeners in the United States of America alone. In 1924, an estimated twenty million Americans listened to the national election returns from more than 400 stations. . . . Between 1922 and 1932, the number of radio sets in America increased from less than 1 percent to 60 percent, and radio broadcasting was having a profound effect on American life and American business.

Maurice Estabrooks, *Electronic Technology, Corporate Strategy and World Transformation* (Westport, CT: Quorum Books, 1995), 30. See also Ray Barfield, *Listening to Radio, 1920-1950* (Westport, CT: Praeger, 1996), 3–32.

Radio continued to be very popular roughly until the 1950s, when television eclipsed its role as a home entertainment medium. The technology that would become television dates back to 1875, but the first remote broadcasts of visual signals did not come until the 1920s. See Oliver, *History of American Technology*, 543–545. A commercial version of television was introduced in the 1930s and revived after World War II. See Oliver, at 545–546. By "the late 1940's the public was clamoring for television sets" and by "the mid-1950's more than five hundred television stations were in operation, and an estimated twenty-seven million homes were equipped with television sets." Oliver, at 546. By 1955, "[h]alf of all U.S. households had TV sets", by the late 1980s "98% of all homes in the U.S. had at least one TV set", and ownership and viewing grew exponentially for the rest of the century. "Television in the United States," *Wikipedia*, http://en.wikipedia.org/wiki/Television_in_the_United_States; "Television," *Wikipedia*, http://en.wikipedia.org/wiki/Television.

The technology used in cinema can be traced back to the seventeenth century, but the origins of commercial cinema lie in the early twentieth century. See Oliver, History of American Technology at 504–508. In 1905, the Nickelodeon, the "'first all-moving picture theater,'" opened in Pittsburgh; for a nickel,

remote one-to-many communication technology. That is, each uses electronic technology to distribute "audio and[/or] video signals . . . to a number of recipients ('listeners' or 'viewers') that belong to a large group."[111] Unlike the telephone, these technologies are not interactive; the only choice the recipients have had, traditionally, is to receive the signals or decline to do so.[112] And as with print media, the content delivered to each recipient is identical.[113]

Radio, television, and cinema all began as electronic versions of older modes of communication. During the first decades of their respective existences, radio, and then television, provided their audiences with news and entertainment in the form of music, drama, and various types of comedic programming.[114] The notion of using an electronic medium to report news originated with radio and was later adopted by television.[115] It represented the extrapolation of an existing mode of communication—the newspaper—into an electronic environment.[116] The same is true for the other types of programming radio and then television offered, at least initially. Dramatic programming was derived from theater, comedic programming was based on vaudeville, and musical programming was derived, variously, from music halls, the symphony, and the opera.[117] As both media evolved, they

---

one could watch a 15–20 minute one-reel film. See Oliver, at 506–507. Within three years, there were 8,000 nickelodeons in the United States. See Oliver, at 507. Longer films featuring more complex stories began to appear, and by the 1920s an American film industry had been born. See Oliver, at 507–508. See also Douglas Gomery, "The Rise of Hollywood" (Geoffrey Nowell-Smith, ed.) in *The Oxford History of World Cinema* (Oxford: Oxford University Press, 1997), 43–53. Sound was introduced in the late 1920s and motion pictures became wildly popular, at least until the introduction of television in the 1950s. See Karel Dibberts, "The Introduction of Sound" in *The Oxford History of World Cinema*, 211–219; Michele Hilmes, "Television and the Film Industry" in *The Oxford History of World Cinema*, 466–475.

[111] "Broadcasting," *Wikipedia*, http://en.wikipedia.org/wiki/Broadcast_media.

[112] Technology has already begun to change this. See, *e.g.*, "Interactive Television," *Wikipedia*, http://en.wikipedia.org/wiki/Interactive_television.

[113] See Chapter 4.

[114] See Barfield, *Listening to Radio*, 107–184. See also Anthony R. Smith, *Television: An International History* (Oxford: Oxford University Press, 1995), 95–167.

[115] See *id.*, 95. ("From its very start . . . television used . . . existing forms—radio, film, music hall, theatre, literature—to create its own unique range of programme fare.")

[116] In the early years, radio news either came from newspapers or from newspaper wire services. See Gwenyth L. Jackaway, *Media at War: Radio's Challenge to the Newspapers, 1924–1939* (Westport, CT: Praeger, 1995), 14.

[117] See Barfield, Listening to Radio, 135. ("As vaudeville collapsed under the competition of Hollywood, its stage stars found their way to radio studios.") See also Christopher H. Sterling and John Michael Kitross, *Stay Tuned: A History of American Broadcasting* (Mahwah, NJ: Lawrence Erlbaum Associates, 2002), 80–88.

[V]audeville, both in its methods and ruling aesthetic, did not . . . perish, but rather resounded throughout the succeeding media of film, radio and television. Certainly, the screwball comedies of the 1930s . . .

developed their own, distinctive approaches to comedy, drama, and music and created new types of programming, such as audience participation programs, game shows, and "talk shows."[118]

Cinema was, and is, an electronic extrapolation of the theater, the opera, the music hall, and/or the vaudeville show.[119] Like radio and television, it takes the notion of a live performance by individuals and moves it into an electronic environment. But while radio and television broadcast live performances on various occasions, cinema is always "canned," that is, always offers prerecorded performances.[120] Cinema differs from radio and television in another notable respect: The one-to-many nature of radio and television communication derives from their practice of delivering identical content simultaneously to a large audience; a television show or a radio program scheduled for a particular time period is broadcast during that period and is not otherwise available, absent repetition or TiVo.[121] Motion pictures simultaneously deliver identical content discretely to a series of different audiences, each composed of a group of accidentally associated individuals. Some of the content delivery will be simultaneous across audiences, but this is generally inadvertent, a matter of theater scheduling; most of the specific deliveries of the content delivery will be at least slightly asynchronous, for the same reason.[122]

---

should be viewed as heirs of vaudeville's aesthetic. In form, the television variety show owed much to vaudeville. . . .

"Vaudeville," *Wikipedia*, http://en.wikipedia.org/wiki/Vaudeville.

[118] See Sterling and Kitross, *Stay Tuned*, 441; Anthony R. Smith, *Television: An International History* 111, 140–141 (Oxford University Press, 1995).

[119] See Geoffrey Nowell-Smith, *The Oxford History of World Cinema* (Oxford: Oxford University Press, 1997), 17–19 (noting how early motion pictures presented "a story as if it were being performed on a stage," instead of using a more complex narrative structure).

[120] See, e.g., "Film," *Wikipedia*, http://en.wikipedia.org/wiki/Film.

[121] By the end of the twentieth century, technological advances made it possible for members of the radio and television audience to record a program so it is available to those who were not present when it was originally broadcast. See "Videocassette recorder," *Wikipedia*, http://en.wikipedia.org/wiki/VCR; "Tape recorder," *Wikipedia*, http://en.wikipedia.org/wiki/Tape_recorder; "TiVo," *Wikipedia*, http://en.wikipedia.org/wiki/Tivo.

[122] The asynchronicity of the delivery of cinema content has been exacerbated by advances in home video technology (e.g., VCR's and DVD players) and by digital cable making movies available on demand. See "Videocassette recorder," *Wikipedia*, http://en.wikipedia.org/wiki/VCR; "DVD," *Wikipedia*, http://en.wikipedia.org/wiki/Dvd. See also "Movies on Demand Guide," Time Warner Cable, http://www.timewarnercable.com/CustomerService/OnDemand/Movies.ashx.

This difference in the timing of their respective content delivery does not alter the functional equivalence of the three media. In each, the audience is passive; its only role is to receive a stable, unalterable set of content.[123] The audience's role is analogous to that of the end-"users" of telephone technology in that both benefit from the efforts of a hierarchical cadre of specialists who implement a highly complex consumer technology; unlike the end-"users" of telephone technology, though, the only role audience members have is accepting the results of the specialists' efforts. They have no capacity to affect the implementation of these media technologies, absolutely no ability to initiate defective or improper implementation

It is that passivity which is most relevant to this discussion. Over many decades, we—as members of the audience—learned to rely on electronic sources for our news, entertainment, education and enlightenment. We became accustomed to "receiving" the content they provided, and so learned to take them for granted. In the respective early days of radio, television, and cinema, the content each media type delivered transfixed the audience; the novelty of the medium demanded the listener's full attention.[124] That is no longer true (except, perhaps, in movie theaters). We became so accustomed to media that it lost our attention and receded into the background; those of us who grew to adulthood in, say, the last thirty years are accustomed to having television, a movie, or music playing as our personal sound track in the background of our lives as we focus on other things.[125]

This is significant because it begins to erode the distinction between "using"-technology and not-"using"-technology that has been the empirical predicate of the approach we have taken to controlling the implementation of technology. The laws we have adopted to discourage the defective or improper implementation of technologies all assume that individuals consciously and deliberately "use" the

---

[123]  Conceptually, radio, television, and cinema are indistinguishable from the live performances and written media that were the only sources of entertainment until the twentieth century. This is because the technology available when these three types of media were developed could not sustain audience interactivity; as technology advances, these three media are likely to become more interactive and, perhaps, to morph into new and much less structured varieties of media.

[124]  See Barfield, *Listening to Radio*, 15–21; Smith, *Television*, 40–41.

[125]  See Ron Lembo, *Thinking Through Television* (Cambridge, England: Cambridge University Press, 2000), 4, 108, 131, 140–141; Jennings Bryant, *Television and the American Family* (Hillsdale, NJ: Lawrence Erlbaum Associates, 1990), 61. See also Matt Wells, "Children Who Can't Live without Constant TV," *The Guardian* (June 10, 2003), http://www.literacytrust.org.uk/Data base/TV.html#constant.

technology for a specific purpose.[126] "Use" is the point of demarcation for the applicability of the rules; they apply only as long as I "use" a technology.

If I have a television playing in the background as I shower and dress for work, am I "using" that technology? I am, of course, using it in a generic sense; I turned the television on and know, at some level, that it is "there" and that it is playing as I go about getting ready. I am not, however, "using" it in the way we "used" tool and machine technologies; it is part of my environment, not the focus of my efforts and intentions.

The discrepancy may seem insignificant and unimportant, especially because I have, as noted earlier, absolutely no ability to "misuse" any of the broadcast media. The passivity of our posture toward these technologies means we cannot manipulate them in socially unacceptable ways; I may attack my television, but I cannot use it to attack others. Societies have therefore never found it necessary to adopt rules designed to discourage audience "misuse" of the technologies that comprise broadcast media.[127]

Societies, particularly the United States, have criminalized the misappropriation of certain content disseminated via broadcast media.[128] These rules do not, however, criminalize the improper implementation of broadcast media technology; they are directed, instead, at the "misuse" of computer technology, which we will consider later in this chapter.

The import of the difference between how I "use" my television in the example given above and how an ancient textile worker "used" his loom lies not in the varying potential for defective implementation or "misuse" each scenario raises. It lies in what the example says about how our relationship with technology is evolving. We return to this issue in Chapters 6 and 7.

---

[126]  See Chapter 3.

[127]  They have, in varying degrees, adopted rules that are designed to control what might be characterized as the defective implementation of these three technologies. These rules, like the rules that attempted to control the implementation of printing technology, focus primarily on the content delivered by the broadcast media. See "EB–Broadcast Issues," Federal Communications Commission, http://www.fcc.gov/eb/broadcast/. As with print media, the First Amendment has been a limitation on the extent to which rules restrict the content these media disseminate in the United States. See Chapter 4.

[128]  See Ryan P. Wallace, Adam M. Lusthaus, and Jong Hwan (Justin) Kim, "Computer Crimes," *American Criminal Law Review 42* (2005): 223, 283–245.

# Computers

*How should we imagine a mechanical brain?*[129]

The modern origins of the computer date back to the early nineteenth century, when Charles Babbage invented the "difference engine."[130] Scientists continued their attempts to build a working computer, and in 1943, IBM constructed the first mainframe computer—the five-ton Harvard Mark I.[131] This initiated the era of the mainframe, which lasted until the early 1980s.[132]

The microprocessor, which would dramatically decrease the size and the cost of computers, was invented in 1971.[133] For various reasons, it was not until January 1975 that "the first microprocessor-based computer, the Altair 8800, was announced on the front cover of Popular Electronics."[134] The Altair 8800, which came in a kit and had to be assembled, was a very primitive device, but it generated interest in creating something new: "personal computers."[135] Hundreds of companies sprang up to customize the Altair or offer other alternatives.[136]

---

[129]  Edmund Callis Berkeley, *Giant Brains; Or, Machines that Think* (New York: Wiley, 1949), 6. See also Berkeley, at 5 ("a *mechanical brain* is a machine that handles information . . . and has a flexible control over . . . its operations").

[130]  See Aspray and Campbell-Kelly, *Computer*, 53. Babbage spent a decade, starting in the 1820s, working on the Difference Engine, but ultimately abandoned it for the Analytical Engine, which was to be capable of any mathematical computation. The idea . . . came to Babbage when he was considering how to eliminate human intervention in the Difference Engine by feeding back the results of a computation. . . . Babbage took this simple refinement . . . and from it evolved the design of the Analytical Engine, which embodies almost all the important functions of the modern digital computer. (53–54)

Versions of the computer date back to ancient times. See Chapter 3, antikythera machine.

[131]  See *id.*, 26–76.

[132]  See *id.*, 79–229. "Minicomputers" had appeared by 1970, but they cost around $20,000, which put them beyond the reach of most people, at 222, 237–238.

[133]  See *id.*, 229.("The allure of the microprocessor was that it would reduce the price of the central processor by vastly reducing the chip count in the . . . computer," 238).

[134]  *Id.*, 240.

[135]  See *id.*, 240–244.

A personal computer . . . is . . . a microcomputer . . . used by one person at a time . . . for general . . . tasks such as word processing . . . or game play. . . . Unlike minicomputers, a personal computer is often owned by the person using it, indicating a low cost of purchase and simplicity of operation. The user of a modern personal computer may have significant knowledge of the operating environment and application programs, but is not necessarily interested in programming nor even able to write programs for the computer. "Personal Computer," *Wikipedia*, http://en.wikipedia.org/wiki/Personal_computer.

[136]  See Aspray and Campbell-Kelly, Computer, 240–244.

Steve Jobs and Stephen Wozniak created their Apple II in 1976.[137] While Jobs and Wozniak's competitors concentrated on creating products for computer enthusiasts,[138] Jobs realized that a computer could be a consumer product

> if it were appropriately packaged. . . . [T]he microcomputer would have to be . . . a self-contained unit in a plastic case, able to be plugged into a stand-ard household outlet . . .; it would need a keyboard to enter data, a screen to view the results of a computation, and some form of . . . storage to hold data and programs. . . . [T]he machine would need software.[139]

Commodore Business Machines adopted a similar strategy, and if there was a "moment when the personal computer arrived in the public consciousness, then it was at the West Coast Computer Faire in April 1977, when the first two machines for the . . . consumer, the Apple II and the Commodore PET, were launched. Both . . . were instant hits."[140]

The expanded variety of software that was available by 1980 further increased interest in computers, as did the introduction of the IBM Personal Computer in 1981.[141] When Apple launched the Macintosh in 1984, its graphical user interface "made every other personal computer appear old-fashioned and lackluster",[142] and eventually led to Microsoft's developing its Windows software, which also provides a GUI interface.[143]

Computer hardware and software continued to evolve, and the popularization of the personal computer took a huge incremental step forward with the rise of the

---

[137] See *id.*, 244–246.

[138] See *id.*, 237–244. The computer enthusiast, or hobbyist, whom most of these companies targeted was "typically a young male technophile" with "some professional competence" in dealing with computers: "If not working with computers directly, they were often employed as technicians or engineers in the elec-tronics industry," at 237.

[139] *Id.*, 246.

[140] *Id.*, 247. Jobs marketed the Apple II as a "home/personal computer":

> The advertisement . . . produced to launch the Apple II showed a housewife doing kitchen chores, while in the background her husband sat at the kitchen table hunched over an Apple II . . . The copy read:
>
> > The home computer that's ready to work, play and grow with you. . . . You'll be able to organize, index and store data on household finances, income taxes, recipes, your biorhythms, balance your checking account, even control your home environment. (248)

[141] See *id.*, 248–257.

[142] *Id.*, 276.

[143] See *id.*, 276–282.

Internet in the 1990s.[144] ARPANET, precursor of the Internet, went online in 1969 but it "did not interact easily with other computer networks that did not share its own . . . protocol."[145] In 1983, the ARPANET's core networking protocol was changed to TCP/IP, which marked "the start of the Internet as we know it today."[146]

> In August 1991 Tim Berners-Lee publicized his new World Wide Web project, two years after he had begun creating HTML, HTTP and the first few web pages at CERN in Switzerland. A few academic and government institutions contributed pages but the public did not . . . see them yet. In 1993 the Mosaic web browser . . . was released, and by late 1994 there was growing public interest in the previously academic/technical internet. By 1996 the word `Internet' was common public currency.[147]

The popularity of the Internet, the personal computer and evolving variations on personal computer technology has increased exponentially in the last ten years. By 2006, there were at least billion personal computers in use around the world and, according to one estimate, just over a billion Internet users.[148]

If there had been no Internet, we would probably see personal computers as a glorified typewriter-calculator composite, a useful but unexciting way to process data, play games, and produce electronic versions of letters, reports, and term papers.[149] The transformative effects of the personal computer lie in its capacity to revolutionize how we communicate once it is linked to an interactive network.[150]

---

[144] "The Internet . . . is the publicly accessible worldwide system of interconnected computer networks that transmit data by packet switching using a standardized Internet Protocol (IP) and many other protocols. It is made up of thousands of smaller commercial, academic, domestic and government networks." Internet," *Wikipedia*, http://en.wikipedia.org/wiki/Internet.

[145] *Id.*

[146] *Id.*

[147] *Id.* See also Brian Winston, *Media Technology and Society: A History from the Telegraph to the Internet* (Routledge 1998), 321–336; Barry M. Leiner, et al., "A Brief History of the Internet," http://www.isoc.org/internet/history/brief.shtml.

[148] See "Twenty five Years of the IBM PC," *BBC News* (August 11, 2006), http://news.bbc.co.uk/2/hi/technology/4780963.stm; "Central Intelligence Agency," *The World Factbook, 2006*, https://www.cia.gov/cia/publications/factbook/geos/xx.html#Comm.

[149] This is, after all, what the pioneers in personal computing envisioned for their machines. And it is how the personal computer was perceived during the 1980s when it became popular both with consumers and business users. See "Personal Computer," *Wikipedia*, http://en.wikipedia.org/wiki/Personal_computer.

[150] See "Computer Networking," *Wikipedia*, http://en.wikipedia.org/wiki/Computer_networking.

Indeed, our desire to communicate is responsible for the Internet. As one source noted, the impetus for expanding the ARPANET lay not in "the economics of resource sharing, the ability to use remote computers, or even the pleasure of playing computer games."[151] Most ARPANET users never availed themselves of "any of these facilities. Instead it was the opportunity for communicating through electronic mail that attracted users."[152] This demand for e-mail drove the modification that let the ARPANET interact with other networks, which resulted in the proliferation of commercial, governmental and academic networks that combined to link thousands of computer users.[153]

> Taking just a few minutes to cross the continent, e-mail was much faster than the postal service. . . . Besides being cheaper than a long-distance phone call, e-mail eliminated the need for both parties . . . to synchronize their activities. . . . E-mail also eliminated . . . problems associated with . . . time zones. . . . [A] New Yorker arriving at . . . her office in the morning could e-mail a memo to a colleague in Los Angeles, . . . [and it] would be waiting in the recipient's electronic in-tray at the start of the business day.[154]

As the Internet evolved, communication moved beyond e-mail: People began exchanging "not just e-mail but whole documents. In effect a new electronic publishing medium had been created."[155] They could use hypertext and the World Wide Web to create websites, to post and exchange content and ideas.[156] There was no disconnect between consumers and publishers; consumers of content could also be publishers.[157] And the new medium was not only free, it was

---

[151] Aspray and Campbell-Kelly, *Computer*, 294.

[152] *Id.*

[153] See *id.*, 294–295.

[154] *Id.*, 295.

[155] *Id.*, 297.

[156] See *id.*, 297–298.

[157] See "World Wide Web," *Wikipedia*, http://en.wikipedia.org/wiki/World_wide_web ("The Web is available to individuals outside mass media. . . . [T]o 'publish' a web page, one does not have to go through a publisher or other media institution, and potential readers could be found in all corners of the globe"). See also Stephen Schwalger, "Electronic Publishing: Developments in and Orientation of the Industry," 2nd National Preservation Office Conference—Multimedia Preservation: Capturing the Rainbow (Brisbane, Australia, Nov. 28–30, 1995), http://www.nla.gov.au/niac/meetings/npo95ss.html:
> One of the key differences between the . . . Internet and other medias is . . . that there is not one small group in control . . . . [P]arallel development is being carried out by millions of users. . . . [T]he user is also able to be a contributor. Creators are also publishers and individuals are linked to millions of other individuals across the world at one time. . . .

borderless; people could communicate seamlessly with others around the world. It also transcended the strictures of one-to-one and one-to-many communication. As a librarian explained,

> using the Internet is . . . not merely one-to-one as in conversation, writing a letter or having a telephone conversation: it's not a predefined schedule of broadcast or publications—the from one-to-many model. . . . [I]t's a combination of one-to-one and one-to-many, many-to-one and many-to-many. In short, it's a new combination of possibilities.[158]

Cyberspace lets us communicate, in whatever combination, with those we know and with those we do not know. It lets us move beyond the passivity of the broadcast media to new, interactive modes of entertainment: We can create stories, videos, and music and share them with others; and we can interact with others in complex virtual worlds and online gaming.[159] We can shop, bank and conduct business online; we can also schedule travel, home repairs, personal grooming, and medical appointments.[160]

The Internet is a little over a decade old as this is written; our experience with cyberspace is still in its infancy and yet it has transformed many aspects of our lives.[161] The personal computer, our conduit to cyberspace, has been astonishingly pervasive in its effects and as a technology.[162] The influence of the personal computer and derivative technologies will accelerate as technology pervades more aspects of our lives;[163] we will return to this issue in the next chapter.

---

[158]   *Id.*

[159]   See J.D. Lasica, *Darknet: Hollywood's War against the Digital Generation* (New York: John Wiley & Sons, 2005), 11–12, 67–86 151–160, 243–255. See also "Second Life," http://secondlife.com; "Virtual World," *Wikipedia*, http://en.wikipedia.org/wiki/Virtual_world.

[160]   See Mary Madden, "America's Online Pursuits: The Changing Picture of Who's Online and What They Do," Pew Internet & American Life Project (December 22, 2003), i–vii, http://www.pewinternet.org/pdfs/PIP_Online_Pursuits_Final.PDF.

[161]   See *id.*:

Online activity has consistently grown. . . . Internet users discover more things to do online as they gain experience and as new applications become available. This momentum often fuels increasing reliance on the Internet in everyday life and higher expectations about the way the Internet can be used in matters both mundane and mighty.

[162]   See *id.* ("While there was once a time when the Internet was interesting because it was dazzling, it is now a normalized part of daily life for . . . the U.S. population.")

[163]   See "Trends 2005: Internet—The Mainstreaming of Online Life," 69, Pew Research Center (2005), http://pewresearch.org/trends/trends2005-internet.pdf (our relationship with the Internet "will only deepen over time as . . . communication technologies evolve. . . . [W]ireless connectivity will increase through . . . cell

Before we consider how our relationship with computer technology will evolve, we need to consider the efforts we have so far made to control the implementation of this technology. Like other consumer technologies, personal computer technology is a proletarian technology: It is designed for and "used" by civilians.

Until the personal computer was introduced, computer technology was the exclusive province of a cadre of specialists.[164] If personal computers had not been invented, computer technology would presumably have taken a course analogous to that of the machine technologies we examined in Chapter 3. It would have remained a specialized endeavor subject to specialized rules designed primarily to discourage defective implementation.

## Computers and "Misuse"

Personal computer technology is functionally analogous to telephone technology in that the civilian end-"users" of the technology are using what is, in effect, a service a cadre of specialists supply. For telephone technology the service is the capacity for telephonic communications; for personal computer "users" it is the operation of the networks that create and sustain cyberspace. Without these networks, a personal computer would be little more than a glorified typewriter-calculator-videogame console.

The specialists who are responsible for the networks that allow civilian "users" to access cyberspace are analogous to the specialists who are responsible for providing us with telephone service in that both implement a foundational, operational component of an interactive technology.[165] As with telephone technology, this operational component of personal computing can be implemented defectively. As with telephone technology, therefore, societies adopt rules that are designed to

---

phones and personal digital devices. . . . More things will become connected to the internet, from cars to home appliances to jewelry").

[164] See Aspray and Campbell-Kelly, *Computer*, 194–222. See also Scott McCartney, *Eniac: The Triumphs and Tragedies of the World's First Computer* (New York: Walker, 1999), 109–174.

[165] As long as dial-up (telephonic) access to the Internet is the norm, the two specialties collapse into one; the specialists charged with implementing telephone service also, by default, become responsible for implementing access to the Internet. The discussion above assumes that civilian "users" access cyberspace exclusively by means other than dial-up systems.

prevent defective implementation by the specialists who are responsible for these networks.[166]

Because civilians "use" personal computer technology independently, it—unlike most of the other consumer technologies we have examined—has a notable potential for improper implementation, or "misuse."[167] In this regard, personal computer technology is somewhat analogous to telephone technology.

As we saw earlier, telephone technology can be—and is—"misused" by civilian end-"users." As we also saw earlier, societies adopted telephone "misuse" laws— laws criminalizing obscene or harassing telephone calls—to control this capacity for "misuse." The laws were necessary because telephone "misuse" let one inflict "harm" in a way and of a type that had never before been possible. In crafting these "misuse" laws, societies applied the same approach they have historically utilized for controlling the defective implementation of technologies, that is, directing context-specific laws at the "users" of the technologies. Here, the context was the "use" of telephone technology.

As we will see in Chapter 7, the application of this approach to telephone—or other—"misuse" laws is based on a fallacious premise: that the laws are "about"

---

[166] See "The FCC's Proceeding Concerning High-Speed Internet Access Over Cable and Other Facilities, Federal Communications Commission," http://www.fcc.gov/mb/highspeedaccessnoi/. See also Final Rule: E911 Requirements for IP-Enabled Services, Federal Communications Commission, 70 FR 43323–01, 2005 WL 1749493 (F.R.) (July 27, 2005). As cyberspace evolves, societies may also find it necessary to adopt rules that are designed to ensure affordable, adequate access to the various civilian "user" constituencies. See Anne Broache, "Technologists Square Off on Net Neutrality," *CNET News* (July 17, 2006), http://news.com.com/Technologists+square+off+on+Net+neutrality/2100-1028_3-6094954.html?tag=nl.

[167] It is in this sense somewhat analogous to the automobile, which can at least arguably be "misused." The technologies differ, though, in the extent of their respective capacities for "misuse." Automobiles are a highly structured technology; they are "used" in specific ways, for specific purposes, and in specifically defined areas (streets, roads, parking lots, garages). Because the implementation of automobile technology takes place in a specific empirical context, its capacity for "misuse" is so limited that instances of "misuse" can, as we saw earlier, be addressed by applying existing criminal laws targeting the infliction of various types of "harm." There is consequently no need for specialized "automobile misuse" laws.

Many, many consumer technologies are not discussed in this chapter. Most have a very limited, if any, potential for improper use. It would, for example, be extraordinarily difficult to transform a vacuum cleaner, a dishwasher, an electric razor, or a coffee maker into a technologically specific instrument of crime. To the extent that such an item of technology is used as a mere implement to injure or kill another human being, this conduct can, as we saw earlier in this chapter, be prosecuted under existing laws governing assault or homicide.

the technology. Defective implementation laws *are* "about" particular technologies; they are technologically specific because their sole purpose is to regulate how a given technology is being implemented. "Misuse" laws are different; their fundamental concern is with controlling human behavior, not with controlling technology. Extrapolating the approach societies use for defective implementation to improper implementation (or "misuse") of technology misses the point and, as we shall see in Chapter 7, produces laws that may be antiquated and therefore inadequate when they are adopted; it can also result in the adoption of duplicative, overlapping and unnecessary "misuse" laws. In a moment, we will use personal computer technology to demonstrate how this happens. Before we do that, however, we need to note a conceptual issue that is to a great extent responsible for the flawed premise cited above.

The flawed premise is that improper implementation—or "misuse"—laws are, and should be, indistinguishable from "defective" implementation laws in that both are concerned with a socially undesirable "use" of a particular technology. Defective implementation laws are, essentially, concerned with the unintended inept "use" of a technology; improper implementation laws are concerned with the deliberate "misuse" of a technology to inflict "harm."[168] Defective and improper implementation can both result in the infliction of serious "harm"; the negligent operation or maintenance of a railroad or ship can result in a significant loss of life, for example. The critical differentiating factor is the *intent* to cause "harm."

Because defective implementation does not involve such intent, societies can control it by using civil, prescriptive laws[169] to structure—to regulate—how technologies are implemented. Societies use civil sanctions (e.g., civil fines, damages awarded to one "harmed" by an implementation default, loss of operating privileges) to enforce the laws. This system works, not perfectly, but adequately because defective implementation is the product of inadvertence not of malice. Civil damages and/or fines do a good enough job of controlling inadvertence to ensure that generalized, specialist technologies are implemented with an acceptable level of precision. (The effect of the proscriptive rules and concomitant sanctions is further enhanced by collateral factors, such as the desire to operate an effective and therefore profitable enterprise and to avoid negative publicity resulting from an implementation default.) The bottom line—the inevitable theme—in defective

---

[168]   See Chapter 3.
[169]   See Chapter 3.

implementation laws is therefore the technology. The technology—its nature, requirements, and limitations—is the exclusive focus of defective implementation laws because their goal is to ensure a level of quality in the implementation of a technology. This is why defective implementation laws target the "users" of a technology. Who else can control the implementation of the technology and prevent its inadvertently inflicting "harm"?

To understand why this focus on the "users" of a technology is not an effective way to address "misuse," we need to consider the implications consumer technologies have for "misuse." As we saw in Chapters 3 and 4, "misuse" is a relatively new phenomenon. It was not a significant issue as long as technology consisted only of tool and machine technologies because specialists who were unlikely (and/or unable) to employ a technology intentionally to inflict "harm" implemented these technologies.[170] Societies consequently did not need to devote much attention to controlling "misuse."

That changed with the appearance of consumer technologies, at least some of which can be "misused." Consumer technologies are implemented not by specialists, but by everyone, by anyone, which exponentially increases the likelihood that they *will* be "misused." Some of the consumer technologies that have appeared (so far, anyway) do not lend themselves to "misuse," but others do. Because "misuse" is still a relatively new phenomenon, and because it is still relatively rare (we are not, after all, "misusing" hair dryers, garage door openers, coffee makers, vacuum cleaners, and other routine technologies), societies have taken an *ad hoc* approach to dealing with "misuse" when it becomes problematic. They have—as we saw with telephone technology—extrapolated the conceptual approach they use for dealing with defective implementation to "misuse," adding criminal sanctions along the way.

---

[170] Specialists are generally unlikely to exploit a technology to inflict "harm" because of their training and professionalism. Their inability to exploit a technology for this purpose lies in the limitations of the technology itself (as we saw in Chapter 3, evolved tools do not lend themselves to the infliction of "harm" surpassing that possible by other, more mundane, methods) and in limitations that attend the implementation of more complex, machine technologies.

Commercial air travel is a good example of the latter issue: It is a complex machine technology and, as such, is implemented by a cadre of differentiated specialists, i.e., a cadre of individuals who have specialized expertise in various aspects of commercial air travel. Assume, hypothetically, that the pilot of a commercial airplane decides to crash the plane for some reason (to kill an enemy who is on the plane, say). Even if the pilot wants to do this, it would be very difficult for her to pull it off, given the mechanical complexity and redundant personnel involved in the implementation of this technology. We cannot, unfortunately, say that this scenario is impossible, only that the difficulty of its realization makes it unlikely.

Why is this unsatisfactory? It is unsatisfactory because the notion of "use" will become an increasingly unstable concept as technologies evolve in sophistication, in intelligence, and in how they are integrated into our lives. We address the evolution of technology in the next chapter. In the remainder of this chapter, we will examine how early twenty-first century technology is already eroding the traditional notion of "using" technology.

Consider two already-established consumer technologies: automobiles and personal computing. One could argue that "using" a personal computer is analogous to "using" an automobile in that the "use" of each technology occurs in a distinct empirical context. The "user" of the automobile implements the technology to travel from Point A to Point B; the empirical context of automobile implementation ("use") exists while the vehicle is being used for this purpose and ceases to exist when the trip is complete. As we saw earlier in this chapter, context-specific rules designed to control the defective implementation of automobile technology apply only as long as this context exists. As we saw earlier, the same is/would be true of context-specific rules designed to control the improper implementation ("misuse") of automobile technology.

The argument for applying the approach embodied in these rules to the personal computer posits that a functionally indistinguishable process occurs for computer "use." According to this view, the "user" enters the empirical context of personal computer implementation when she boots up the computer and goes online to surf the web, play a game, shop, or analyze her finances. A proponent of this argument would contend that context-specific rules designed to control the improper implementation ("misuse") of computer technology can be articulated and applied in the empirical context of personal computer implementation, just as rules of this type have been employed to control the implementation of other technologies.

The defect in this argument is that it ignores the already apparent difference between "using" computer technology and "using" older, less flexible technologies. In the example given above, the "user" of the personal computer is not "using" computing technology in the conscious, self-aware way the operator of an automobile "uses" motor vehicle technology. If the "user" of the vehicle were asked what he is doing, he would say he is driving ("using" a motor vehicle); if the "user" of the personal computer were asked the same question, she would not say she is "using" a personal computer. She would say she is surfing the web, playing a game, shopping, or balancing her budget; of the four, only surfing the web is a computer-specific endeavor. The other activities can be conducted with or without a computer; the person in our example "uses" a computer to conduct them because she has become accustomed to relying on it to do so.

Her doing so does not, however, mean that she perceives herself as having entered a unique empirical context: that of "personal computer user." The role the computer plays in this example—and in our lives—is increasingly analogous to my using a lamp to read in dim light. I am aware, at some level, that I am "using" the lamp (I probably had to turn it on), but if I were asked what I was doing I would say "I am reading," not "I am `using' a lamp" or "I am 'using' a lamp to read." Like the lamp, the personal computer is merging into our repertoire of mundane activities; operating an automobile is not merging into that repertoire—and will not—unless and until we turn the process over to automated systems.[171]

Those of us who routinely utilize computers are becoming increasingly oblivious to the fact that we are, indeed, "using" computer technology,[172] but the implications of this evolving phenomenon have yet to permeate the collective culture.[173] Societies have therefore not incorporated the difference between "using" computer technology and "using" antecedent technologies into their efforts to control the improper implementation ("misuse") of computer technology. Lawmakers in the United States and abroad have approached computer technology as if it were a context-specific technology, the "misuse" of which can be controlled by adopting context-specific rules.[174]

Beginning in the late 1970s, U.S. states adopted "computer crimes" laws that were intended to control the "misuse" of computer technology.[175] These laws

---

[171] We will return to this issue in Chapter 6.

[172] See William Shotts, Jr., Freedom, Rantings, http://linuxcommand.org/rantings.php ("Today, we take computers for granted"). See also Karnjana Karnjanatawe and Tony Waltham, "Digital Decade: Ten Critical Years," *Bangkok Post* (July 13, 2005), 2005 WLNR 10987891.

[173] See Jaan Valsiner, "Constructing the Personal Through the Cultural: Redundant Organization of Psychological Development" in *Change and Development: Issues of Theory, Method and Application*, ed. Eric Amsel and K. Ann Renninger (Mahah, NJ: Lawrence Erlbaum Associates, 1997), 27, 31 ("collective culture" encompasses "communally shared meanings, social norms, and everyday life practices").

[174] For a review of international cybercrime legislation, see Marc D. Goodman and Susan W. Brenner, "The Emerging Consensus on Criminal Conduct in Cyberspace," 2002 *UCLA J. L. & Tech.*: 3, 33–53.

[175] See Ryan P. Wallace, Adam M. Lusthaus, and Jong Hwan (Justin) Kim, "Computer Crimes," *Am. Crim. L. Rev. 42* (2005): 223, 268 ("In 1978 state legislatures began enacting computer crime statutes. . . Since then, every state has enacted some form of computer-specific legislation").

criminalize, among other things, "using" a computer to commit fraud;[176] "using" a computer to commit forgery;[177] "using" a computer to send harassing communications;[178] and "using" a computer to steal data, money, or services.[179] More recently, states have added "identity theft" statutes, which make it a crime to "use" a computer to obtain or utilize a means of identification belonging to another for the purposes of committing fraud.[180] A few states have also criminalized the "use" of a computer to send unsolicited bulk commercial email ("spam"),[181] and at least one has outlawed computer "phishing."[182] Every state outlaws hacking ("using" a computer to gain unauthorized access to a another computer) and cracking ("using" a computer to gain unauthorized access to a another computer to commit theft or other crimes).[183] States consistently make it a crime to "use" a computer to solicit a minor for sex[184] or to create, possess, or distribute child pornography.[185]

Federal computer crime legislation has similar prohibitions.[186] Section 1030 of title 18 of the U.S. Code is the general federal computer crime provision.[187]

---

[176]  See Ark. Code § 5-41-103; Haw. Rev. Stat. § 708-891W. Va. Code § 61-3C-4(a).

[177]  See Ga. Code § 16-9-93(d); Nev. Rev. Stat. § 205.481; Va. Code § 18.2-152.14; W. Va. Code § 61-3C-15.

[178]  See W. Va. Code § 61-3C-14a.

[179]  See Ca. Penal Code § 502(c)(2); Iowa Code § 714.1(8); N.J. Stat. § 2C:20-25(b); Va. Code § 18.2-152.6.

[180]  Ala. Code § 13A-8-192(a). See also Cal. Penal Code § 530.5; Conn. Gen. Stat. § 53a-129a; 11 Del. Code § 854; Ga. Code § 16-9-121; Iowa Code § 715A.8; Mass. Gen. Laws Ann. § 266 S 37E; Miss. Code Ann. § 97-45-19; Okla. Stat. Ann. § 1533.1; 18 Penn. Cons. Stat. Ann. § 4120.

[181]  See 11 Del. Code § 937; Ohio Rev. Code Ann. § 2913.421; Va. Code Ann. § 18.2-152.3.1(A).

[182]  See Virginia Code Annotated § 18.2-152.5:1. Phishing is

> attempting to fraudulently acquire sensitive information, such as passwords and credit card details, by masquerading as a trustworthy person or business with a real need for such information in a seemingly official electronic . . . message. . . . The term phishing comes from the fact that . . . scammers are using increasingly sophisticated lures as they `fish' for . . . financial information and password data.

"Phishing," *Wikipedia*, http://en.wikipedia.org/wiki/Phishing.

[183]  See Cal. Penal Code § 502(c). Conn. Gen. Stat. Ann. § 53a-251; Idaho Code § 18-2202; Kan. Stat. Ann. § 21-3755(b); Maryland Code – Criminal Law § 7-302(b); Mich. Comp. Laws Ann. § 752.794; N.H. Rev. Stat. Ann. § 638:17; South Carolina Code §§ 16-16-10(j) & 16-16-20 ;13 Vt. Stat. Ann. §§ 4102 & 4104; Wis. Stat. Ann. § 943.70.

[184]  See Ala. Code § 13A-6-110; 11 Del. Code Ann. § 1112A; Ga. Code Ann. § 16-12-100.2; 720 Ill. Comp. Stat. Ann. § 5/11-6; Ind. Code Ann. § 35-42-4-6; Iowa Code Ann. § 728.12; 17-A Me. Rev. Stat. Ann. § 259; Mich. Comp. Laws Ann. § 750.145a; Minn. Stat. Ann. § 609.352; N.H. Rev. Stat. Ann. § 649-B:4; N.C. Gen. Stat. Ann. § 14-202.3; 21 Okla. Stat. Ann. § 1040.13a; S.D. Codified Laws § 22-22-24.5; Texas Penal Code § 15.031; Utah Code Ann. § 76-4-401; W.Va. Code § 61-3C-14b.

[185]  See Alaska Stat. § 11.61.125; Ark. Code Ann. § 5-27-603; 11 Del. Code Ann. § 1109; Ind. Code Ann. § 35-42-4-4; R.I. General Laws Ann. § 11-9-1.3; Texas Penal Code § 43.26.

[186]  See Wallace et al., "Computer Crimes," *American Criminal Law Review 42* (2005): 223, 228–255.

[187]  See *Id.*, 223, 231–232.

Section 1030 makes it a federal crime (a) to "use" a computer to access classified government information, (b) to "use" a computer to hack a government or private computer and cause damage, (c) to "use" a computer to commit extortion, (d) to "use" a computer to commit fraud, and (e) to "use" a computer to transmit a computer virus, worm, or other code and intentionally damage a computer.[188] Other sections of title 18 outlaw "using" a computer (a) to possess, create, or distribute child pornography; (b) to transmit a threat in interstate commerce; (c) to send spam emails; (d) to commit identity theft; and (e) to commit any of a number of offenses against intellectual property.[189]

As this brief overview of computer crime provisions may illustrate, the "misuse" of computer technology has received a great deal of attention from legislators over the last two decades.[190] Much of this legislation has been reactive—a legislature's responding to an actual or perceived "new" threat (such as fraud or phishing). The newer legislation therefore tends both to be very specific in its prohibitions and to overlap with existing provisions.[191] In the federal system, for instance, we have (a) several statutes that make it a crime to commit fraud,[192] (b) a statute that makes it a crime to "use" a computer to commit fraud,[193] and (c) a statute that make it a crime to "use" another's identification to commit fraud.[194]

In an effort to take these prohibitions one step further, Senator Leahy proposed adding two more crimes to the federal criminal code: (a) creating a website that is to be used to "phish" (i.e., a site that would induce individuals "to divulge personal information" for the purposes of committing "a crime of fraud"); and (b) sending an email for the same purpose.[195] Because it is already a federal crime to use someone's personal identifying information to commit fraud (and also

---

[188]  See See *Id.*

[189]  See See *Id.*, 223, 237–255. See also 18 U.S. Code § 875.

[190]  See Wallace, *Computer Crimes,* 223, 267–270.

[191]  Some states, for example, have both "computer harassment" and "telephone harassment" statutes. See, *e.g.,* Ga. Code Ann. §§ 16-11-39.1 & 16-5-90; W. Va. Code §§ 61-3C-14A & 61-8-16. Like the federal statutes discussed later in the text, some states also have duplicative fraud provisions. See, *e.g.,* Ark. Code Ann. § 5-37-227 ("financial identity fraud") & § 5-41-103 ("computer fraud"). See also 11 Del. Code Ann. § 854 (identity theft) & § 2738 (computer fraud).

[192]  See, *e.g.,* 18 U.S. Code §§ 1341 & 1343.

[193]  See 18 U.S. Code § 1030(a).

[194]  See 18 U.S. Code § 1028(a).

[195]  "The Anti-Phishing Act Of 2005 Fact Sheet," Office of U.S. Senator Patrick Leahy, http://leahy.senate. gov/press/200503/030105.html.

already a crime to commit fraud, with or without a computer), it seems these proposed new crimes are meant to reach *attempts* to commit identity theft (or fraud or the "use" of a computer to commit fraud). (Modern criminal law outlaws attempts—crimes that have not been completed—so police can interrupt one who is preparing to commit a crime before he actually does so.)[196] If so, the new crimes still seem redundant because both § 1030—which makes it a federal crime to "use" a computer to commit fraud—and § 1028—which makes it a federal crime to commit identity theft—outlaw attempts.[197]

Senator Leahy's proposal—like other, similar proposals—is a product of the reaction noted earlier: a legislative response to a "misuse" of computer technology that has received a great deal of media attention. Such a response would be a reasonable strategy if we were dealing with a context-specific technology because context-specific technologies are stable; they are used in consistent ways in a specific, stable, empirical context.[198]

This is not the appropriate way to deal with the "misuse" of computer technology. Leaving aside the somewhat more esoteric issues of identity theft and phishing, why do we need a statute that makes it *another* crime to "use" a computer to

---

[196]   See Wayne R. LaFave, 2 Substantive Criminal Law § 11.2 (f) (2d ed. 2006).

[197]   See 18 U.S. Code §§ 1030(b) & 1028(f).

[198]   Drunk driving laws are a good example of context-specific laws addressing the "misuse" of a stable technology. These laws target those who operate a motor vehicle (stable technology) on the streets or roads of a jurisdiction while under the influence of drugs and/or alcohol ("misuse"). See Vernon's Ann. Missouri Stat. § 577.010. Because the technology is stable, it is reasonable to assume that this type of misuse will persist (as it has); and since operating a motor vehicle while intoxicated poses hazards that did not arise with the drunken operation of a bicycle or a horse, it was reasonable to adopt laws targeting this type of misuse.

Given the analysis of "vehicular homicide" laws presented earlier, one could argue that drunk driving laws are defective implementation laws, not "misuse" (or improper implementation) laws because drunk drivers usually do not become intoxicated and then drive with the specific intention of causing "harm" to persons or property. The "harm" results because their impaired condition results in their operating the motor vehicle in a defective manner.

We are, though, assuming drunk driving laws are "misuse" laws for this reason: "Vehicular homicide" statutes are defective implementation laws because they target the reckless or negligent (inadvertent, defective) implementation of an automobile. Drunk driving laws are "misuse" laws because they target intentional conduct—the act of consuming intoxicants (drugs and/or alcohol) and then operating a motor vehicle. While the person who consumes intoxicants usually acts recklessly or negligently at the time he actually *causes* "harm," he intentionally got himself into an impaired state in which it was foreseeable that he would do so. The "misuse" here, then, is prefatory—it occurs before the person gets behind the wheel of the motor vehicle.

commit fraud when it is already a crime to commit fraud? Historically, we have directed prohibitions at the undesirable result (homicide), not at the method "used" to achieve this result (homicide-by-poison, homicide-by-knifing, and so on).[199] And some of the rules we have adopted to control the "misuse" of technology comport with this principle; that is, they target not the method used to achieve a result, but the result: "harm" resulting from the "misuse" of a technology.

Drunk driving laws, for example, target a result: operating a motor vehicle under the influence of alcohol. We will assume, for the purposes of this analysis, that drunk driving laws *are* "misuse" rules.[200] A "motor vehicle" is an essential element of this law in the same way "human being" is an essential element of a homicide law; each element is intrinsically bound up with the "harm" the law seeks prevent.[201] Drunk driving laws are intended to prevent the "harm" to persons and/or property that can result from one's operating a motor vehicle in an impaired condition; they consequently do not proscribe "operating" a horse while intoxicated.[202]

The federal provision that makes it a crime to "use" a computer to commit fraud is not a rule that targets a context-specific activity. Statutes that criminalize the "misuse" of a telephone to make obscene or harassing phone calls *are* rules that target a context-specific activity; these laws have no meaning outside the unique technological context they address. One can make a phone call without its being obscene, but one cannot make an obscene phone call without using a telephone.

The federal provision that makes it a crime to "use" a computer to commit fraud is a "method" rule, instead of a rule targeting a context-specific activity. It outlaws the "use" of a particular methodology to commit fraud.[203] Legislatures have targeted the "use" of certain methodologies—notably firearms—in the commission

---

[199] See, *e.g.*, Brenner, "Is There Such a Thing as Virtual Crime?" For crimes such as homicide or theft, the proscribed result is a change in some empirical condition; homicide results in the death of a once-living human being, and theft results in Person A's losing her property to Person B. The factual landscape has altered materially, and detrimentally, in both instances. Other criminal prohibitions target conduct as the proscribed result.

[200] See supra note cxcviii.

[201] See American Law Institute, Model Penal Code § 1.13(9)(ii).

[202] See *State v. Blowers*, 717 P.2d 1321, 1323 (Utah 1986); *State v. Williams*, 449 So.2d 744, 748 (La. App. 1984).

[203] See Brenner, "Is There Such a Thing as Virtual Crime?"

of generic offenses, such as theft. These provisions, however, are concerned not with the method employed in the commission of the crime, as such, but with the heightened risk of "harm" the use of firearms poses.[204] They are therefore best understood as sentence enhancers.[205] This was clearly not Congress' goal in criminalizing the "use" of a computer to commit fraud; the provision was adopted as part of an effort to target "a new type of criminal—one who uses computers . . . to defraud . . . others."[206] This offense, like the proposed phishing offenses, consequently represents an effort to employ context-specific laws to control the "misuse" of a particular technology, computer technology in this instance.

We will return to this issue in Chapter 7. Chapter 6 adds an essential empirical layer to the analysis we have begun in this discussion; it describes how our "use" of computer technology will change over the next decade or four (or five). At this point in our history it is still possible—inadvisable, but still possible—to construe our relationship with computer technology as one of "use"—"use" denoting the conscious, instrumental utilization of a technology for the achievement of particular ends. This is still possible, notwithstanding the ever-increasing sophistication of computer technology because computers are still in a "box"—still a detached, free-standing technological artifact. As Chapter 6 explains, this will change in the near future (is changing, in fact); computers will migrate out of the "box" and into the fabric of our lives. This, as Chapter 7 explains, will make it impossible to continue to construe our relationship with this technology as one of "use." We will, as that chapter also explains, have to reinterpret our relationship with computer technology and rethink how we should go about controlling the "misuse" of evolved, twenty-first-century computer technology.

Before we go to the next chapter, though, I need to note yet another reason why context-specific laws are not an appropriate way to deal with the "misuse" of computer technology.

---

[204]  See Ga. Code Ann. § 16-8-41.

[205]  See Wayne R. LaFave, 2 Substantive Criminal Law § 20.3(f) (2d ed. 2006).

One could argue that since the use of computers in the commission of crimes increases the level of "harm" a perpetrator can inflict, it is reasonable to define computer method offenses as a sentencing enhancement device analogous to armed robbery laws. See Brenner, "Is There Such a Thing as Virtual Crime?." The better view, however, is that the aggravated harm made possible by computer technology can be adequately addressed either (a) by charging an offender with multiple offenses, each representing the infliction of a discrete harm, (b) by factoring the level of harm into our sentencing standards or (c) by making the use of a computer an aggravating factor in sentencing. See ¶¶ 122–123.

[206]  S. Rep. No. 432, 99th Cong., 2d Sess. 1986, 1986 U.S.C.C.A.N. 2479, 2480, 1986 WL 31918.

The discussion, above, of drunk driving laws explained that context-specific laws are an appropriate way to deal with the "misuse" of stable technologies, such as automobile technology. As Chapter 6 demonstrates, computer technology is not a stable technology; it is evolving constantly and rapidly. As computer technology evolves, its capacity for "misuse" also evolves-—taking new and different forms. Senator Leahy's proposal to criminalize phishing came at a time when the Anti-Phishing Working Group—a law enforcement-industry group that tracks fraud and phishing [207]—reported that phishing is on its way out, that it is being replaced by newer, more sophisticated techniques.[208] If, therefore, Senator Leahy's proposed legislation were adopted, it would be an instance of "too much, too late." The legislation would criminalize a type of "misuse" that is already on the wane and might have disappeared by the time it was outlawed. As this possibility illustrates, the evanescence of computer "misuse" is another reason why we should not rely on traditional, context-specific laws to deal with this phenomenon.

---

[207]  See Anti-Phishing Working Group, http://www.antiphishing.org/.

[208]  See "Phishing Activity Trends Report," Anti-Phishing Working Group (June, 2005), http://antiphishing.org/APWG_Phishing_Activity_Report_Jun_05.pdf ("phishers will . . . adopt more automated attack systems based on technical subterfuge to supplement social engineering schemes—or replace them."

# CHAPTER 6

# "Smart" Technology

*[C]omputers disappear and the world becomes our interface.*[1]

As I explained in Chapter 1, this book analyzes the evolving intersection of law and a new kind of technology: "smart," ambient technology. The last three chapters surveyed our history with older, "dumb" technologies. This chapter provides an overview of what "smart," ambient technology is and how it differs from the technologies we have dealt with to this point in our history.

"Smart" technology is an extrapolation of computer technology, the evolution of which we reviewed in Chapter 6. Mark Weiser, formerly Chief Technologist at Xerox PARC,[2] is considered the "father" of "smart," ambient technology.[3] Weiser said "smart" technology is the

> third wave in computing, just now beginning. First were mainframes, each shared by lots of people. Now we are in the personal computing era, person and machine staring uneasily at each other across the desktop. Next comes . . . the age of calm technology, when technology recedes into the background of our lives.[4]

Technology's receding into the background of our lives has several purposes and several dimensions. We start with the latter.

---

1    Neil Gershenfeld, *When Things Start to Think* (New York: Henry Holt, 1999), xi.
2    Mark Weiser, http://www.ubiq.com/weiser/. Xerox PARC is the Xerox Corporation's Palo Alto Research Center, its "renowned high-technology incubator." Xerox Press Release (August 14, 1996), http://www.ubiq.com/weiser/weiserannc.htm. See PARC. http://www.parc.xerox.com/. Weiser, unfortunately, died in 1999. See "In Memoriam: Mark Weiser," *Usenix News* (1999), http://www.usenix.org/publications/login/1999–8/weiser.html.
3    See Ubiquitous Computing, PARC, http://sandbox.xerox.com/ubicomp/.
4    *Id.*

## Dimensions

For one thing, it means computer technology will move "out of the box"[5] and into the recesses of our environment.[6] Adam Greenfield, who refers to this phenomenon as "everyware," says computer technology would not only be

> "in every place" but also "in every thing." Ordinary objects, from coffee cups to raincoats to the paint on the walls, would be . . . sites for the sensing and processing of information. . . . [P]eople would interact with these systems fluently and naturally, barely noticing the . . . informatics they were engaging.[7]

As Greenfield notes, this will involve extending "information-sensing, -processing and -networking capabilities to . . . things we've never thought of as 'technology' "— things like "clothing, furniture, walls and doorways."[8]

The reason for moving technology "out of the box" and into our environment is to improve its overall functioning. The premise is that the limitations—and attendant "user" frustrations—associated with personal computing technology are attributable to the fact that it attempts to be everything to everyone. Don Norman argues that these limitations (and frustrations) are "artifacts" of the "general-purpose nature" of "dumb," "boxed" computer technology.[9]

---

[5]  See Chapter 5.

[6]  See Adam Greenfield, *Everyware: The Dawning Age of Ubiquitous Computing* (New York: New Riders, 2006), xi (computing that "'does not live on a personal device of any sort, but is in the woodwork everywhere'"). Embedded technology will be in public environments, as well as in private spaces:

> Not only would rooms . . . have . . . embedded intelligence . . . but . . . streets, malls, and towns. . . . Writing . . . is . . . embedded into our environment. Writing is everywhere, . . . passively waiting to be read. Now imagine . . . computation . . . embedded . . . to the same degree. Street signs would communicate to car navigation systems or a map in your hands. . . . Point to a billboard . . . and it would send you more information on its advertised product. . . .

> Kevin Kelly, *Out of Control: The New Biology of Machines, Social Systems and the Economic World* (Cambridge, MA: Perseus Books, 1995), 172.

> A European Union-sponsored project known as Ambient Agoras is working on the implementation of this concept. See Ambient Agoras, http://www.ambient-agoras.org/ ("Dynamic Information Clouds in a Hybrid World"). According to the project's goal statement, Ambient Agoras "integrates information into the architectural environment by means of smart artefacts. The computer as a device disappears, but the functionality is available in a ubiquitous and invisible fashion." Ambient Agoras, *supra*.

[7]  Greenfield, *Everyware*, 11.

[8]  *Id.*, 38.

[9]  *Id.*, 22. See Don Norman, *The Invisible Computer* (Cambridge, MA: MIT Press, 1999), viii. See also Gershenfeld, *When Things Start to Think*, 7. ("the limitation is the box," not the technology).

He maintains that computing technology should be "quiet, invisible, and unobtrusive," and should disappear "behind the scenes into task-specific devices."[10] This is precisely the approach that is being, and will be, taken—exploding "the computer's many functions into [an] . . . array of networked objects scattered throughout" our homes, our offices, our vehicles, and our public spaces.[11] Embedded ambient technology will also become personal; projects are focusing on developing wearable wireless devices that will allow us consciously, or unconsciously, to interact with embedded environmental technology.[12]

As Weiser explained, the goal is to make computer technology "so fitting, so natural, that we use it without even thinking about it."[13] He analogized ambient computer technology to writing and electricity, technologies that have "become so commonplace, so unremarkable, that we forget their huge impact on everyday life."[14] "Smart," ambient technology will be functionally invisible.

It will also be intelligent. In *When Things Start to Think*, Neil Gershenfeld explains why it will be useful for these technologies to be "smart" as well as environmentally pervasive:

> A VCR insistently flashing 12:00 is annoying, but . . . it doesn't know that it is a VCR, that the job of a VCR is to tell the time rather than ask it, that there are atomic clocks available on the Internet that can give it the exact time, or even that you might have left the room and have no interest in what it thinks the time is. . . . [We will] be frustrated by our creations if they lack the rudimentary abilities we take for granted—having an identity, knowing something about our environment, and being able to communicate.[15]

---

10  Norman, The Invisible Computer, viii.

11  Greenfield, *Everyware*, 22 . Workspace is a European Union-funded project the goals of which are to do this in the office and in other workplaces. See "Workspace," http://www.daimi.au.dk/workspace/index.htm. See also "Objectives, Workspace," http://www.daimi.au.dk/workspace/site/navigation/index_01.htm.

12  See, e.g., 2WEAR, http://2wear.ics.forth.gr/ (European Union-funded project researching wearable computing devices).

13  "Ubiquitous Computing," PARC, http://sandbox.xerox.com/ubicomp/.

14  Mark Weiser and John Seely Brown, "The Coming Age of Calm Technology," Xerox PARC (October 5, 1996), http://www.ubiq.com/hypertext/weiser/acmfuture2endnote.htm.

15  Gershenfeld, *When Things Start to Think*, 8. For an example of what one might expect from a rather basic example of "smart," ambient technology, see id., 201 ("A coffeemaker that has access to my bed, and my calendar, and my coffee cup, and my last few years of coffee consumption, can do a pretty good job of recognizing when I'm likely to come downstairs looking for a cup of coffee").

The embedded computer technologies will use artificial intelligence; indeed, they are often referred to as "ambient intelligence."[16] One company that is in working to develop ambient intelligence technologies describes the result as "people living easily in digital environments in which the electronics are sensitive to people's needs, personalized to their requirements, anticipatory of their behavior and responsive to their presence."[17] Another research project describes its goal as developing "extrovert gadgets"—"objects with communicative abilities" that are "enhanced by intelligence."[18]

Weiser's view of "calm technology" receding into our environment also means that the various components of this technology will not only be "smart," they will also be able to communicate with us and with each other.[19] One paper, for example, describes how offices encompassing interlinked "smart" devices will be able to

> learn their occupants' patterns of behavior. . . . [C]ameras . . . track how a
> subject uses the space. Once the system understands how people's locations

---

[16]  See, *e.g.*, "What Is Ambient Intelligence?", Phillips Research, http://www.research.philips.com/technologies/syst_softw/ami/index.html:

> We believe that current inventions . . . will make electronics "smart." Technological breakthroughs will also allow us to integrate 'smart electronics' into more friendly environments.
>
> This is our vision of "Ambient Intelligence": people living easily in digital environments in which the electronics are sensitive to people's needs, personalized to their requirements, anticipatory of their behavior and responsive to their presence.

> IBM calls this phenomenon "autonomic computing," on the premise that it will use "computer systems that regulate themselves much in the same way our autonomic nervous system regulates . . . our bodies." "IBM's Perspective on the State of Information Technology," IBM, http://www.research.ibm.com/autonomic/overview/.

[17]  "What Is Ambient Intelligence?", Royal Philips Electronics of the Netherlands, http://www.research.philips.com/technologies/syst_softw/ami/index.html.

[18]  e-Gadgets, http://www.extrovert-gadgets.net/public/about.asp. These researchers also define "e-gadgets" (or "extrovert gadgets") as "everyday objects, augmented with a digital self." "Survival Guide," http://www.extrovert-gadgets.net/public/about.asp#.

[19]  See Greenfield, *Everyware*, 23 ("things are endowed with the ability to sense their environment, store metada reflecting their own . . . location, status, and use history, and share that information with other such objects"). See also 37 ("by entering a room, you trigger a cascade of responses on the part of embedded systems around you. Systems in the flooring register your presence, your needs are inferred . . . and conditions in the room altered accordingly").

> Smart-Its, a European Union-funded research project, is working on developing "smart" artifacts that can be utilized for this purpose. See "The Smart-Its Vision," http://www.smart-its.org/vision/vision.html (goal is to develop small, "smart" devices that can be attached to "mundane everyday artifacts to augment these with a 'digital self,' " i.e., to enable them to perceive their environment and communicate with other artifacts, "such as scattered personal belongings, toys in the playroom, and objects in collaborative interactive experiences").

correspond to their needs, computers, lights, and even radios can react to their movements. . . . [A] vision-enabled room could direct a . . . call to voice mail if it recognized that the recipient was sitting at a table with three other people and . . . likely having a meeting.[20]

Another source explains that in a "smart" office the telephone "rings slightly louder if the stereo is on; the stereo lowers itself when you answer the phone. Your office voice mail unit knows your car is not in the parking lot so it tells the caller you haven't arrived."[21] An incremental aspect of incorporating embedded "smart" technology into our offices is that the spatial context in which we do our work evolves from the "literal/-concrete space" that is currently our only option to "metaphorical/abstract spaces".[22]

The other context that is often used to illustrate how "smart," ambient technology will affect our daily lives is the "aware" (or "smart") home. A *Wall Street Journal* reporter offered this description of life in such a home:

At 6:45 a.m., the house turns up the heat . . . because it has learned . . . it needs 15 minutes to warm up before your alarm goes off. At 7 a.m., when your alarm sounds, it signals the bedroom light and kitchen coffee maker to turn on. When you step into the bathroom, the morning news pops up on a video screen, and the shower turns on automatically. While you shave, the house senses (through the floor) that you are two pounds over

---

20  Lisa Scanlon, "Rethinking the Computer," *Technology Review* (July/August 2004), http://www. technologyreview.com/articles/04/07/scanlon0704.3.asp.

21  Kevin Kelly, *Out of Control: The New Biology of Machines, Social Systems and the Economic World* (Cambridge, MA: Perseus Books, 1995), 171.

22  See "Design Principles," Workspace, http://www.daimi.au.dk/workspace/site/navigation/index_02.htm:

Currently, embodied aspects of the social and spatial organisation of work are restricted . . . to the physical environment. We take a multi-layered approach to support the embodied social and spatial organisation of work across the digital and physical environment, utilising collaborative virtual environments, computational augmentation, hypermedial relationships, connectivity between devices, sensors, actuators, projection and display technologies, new interaction devices and metaphors.

These researchers define "metaphorical spatiality" as moving activity into "abstract spaces with no direct correspondence to real world space." *Id.* They cite spatial hypermedia systems and Collaborative Virtual Environments as examples of current technology that are capable of providing metaphorical spatial support. See *id.*

your ideal weight; it adjusts your suggested menu and displays it in the kitchen.

When you leave home . . . the house locks itself. Later that morning, it notes that the refrigerator is low on milk and cheese, and it places a grocery order to be delivered just before you get home. When you arrive, the food is there—and the house has cranked up the hot tub for you.[23]

Various initiatives are underway to develop "aware" homes,[24] and "smart" offices will not be far behind.[25]

A South Korean initiative is even more ambitious. As I write this in the summer of 2006, KT, South Korea's "dominant" telecommunications company, is building five "U-cities"—digital municipalities where computer technology will be embedded in every part of the environment and "lifeless objects . . . will have intelligence".[26] The "U" in U-cities is an abbreviated reference to "ubiquitous" and denotes the extent to which intelligent technology will permeate these towns.[27]

---

[23] Kelly Greene, "Take A Glimpse Inside the Home of the Future," *Real Estate Journal* (May 24, 2004), http://www.realestatejournal.com/housegarden/indoorliving/20040524-greene.html.

[24] See, *e.g.*, "Gator Tech Smart House," University of Florida, http://www.icta.ufl.edu/gt.htm; HomeLab, Phillips Research, http://www.research.philips.com/technologies/misc/homelab/index.html; "The Aware Home," Georgia Institute of Technology, http://www.awarehome.gatech.edu/.

[25] See Jan Petzold, et al., *Next Location Prediction Within A Smart Office Building*, 3rd International Conference on Pervasive Computing (Munich, 2005), http://webspace.ulbsibiu.ro/lucian.vintan/html/Citare_Teo_2005.pdf.

[26] Kim Tae-gyu, "KT Plans to Build 60 Ubiquitous Cities by 2015," *Asia Media* (July 28, 2006), http://www.asiamedia.ucla.edu/article.asp?parentid=49984.

[27] See *id.*:

"[M]any lifeless objects in U-Cities will have intelligence with incorporated chips or sensors. Plus, data provided by them will travel and be shared through lightning-fast networks.

Residents, who some call Digital Homo Sapiens, will be able to enjoy access to the high-speed networks that carry all the information from people or objects at any time and at any place.

See also Pamela Licallzi O'Connell, "Korea's High-Tech Utopia, Where Everything Is Observed," *New York Times* (October 5, 2005), http://www.nytimes.com/2005/10/05/technology/techspecial/05oconnell.html?ei=5088&en=4a368c49e8f30bd2&ex=1286164800&adxnnl=1&adxnnlx=1156360124-WKhrcx2+eQzlJ4DCmTMCIA ("A ubiquitous city is where all major information systems (residential, medical, business, governmental and the like share data, and computers are built into the houses, streets and office buildings").

KT plans to have twelve U-cities built by 2010 and "more than 60" in place by 2015.[28]

As these examples may illustrate, the purpose of all this is to enhance computer technology's ability to serve us (an issue we will return to in the next section). Adam Greenfield describes this process as "information processing dissolving in behavior" and gives several examples of how unobtrusive technology will become:

> You close the door to your office because you want privacy, and your phone and IM channel are automatically set to "unavailable." You point to an unfamiliar word in a text, and a definition appears. You sit down to lunch with three friends, and the restaurant plays only music that you've all rated highly.[29]

Computer technology—in its myriad evolved, complex forms—becomes as invisible to us as the electricity I "use" in writing this sentence.[30]

And that will have profound consequences for our relationship with these "smart," ambient technologies. As we saw in earlier chapters, our "use" of prior technologies has been one of focused, transient intention; we consciously "use" a particular technology—an automobile or a camera—for a specific purpose and for a specific period of time. And this is still, to some extent, at least, true of contemporary personal computing: As Adam Greenfield notes, a personal computer "user" chooses "the time, manner, and duration of her involvement with her machine. . . . [T]he interaction [falls] into a call-and-response rhythm: user actions followed by system events."[31]

This dynamic disappears when we come to rely on environmental changes. In a world of "smart," ambient technologies, the "system precedes the user. You walk

---

[28]  See Tae-gyu, *KT Plans to Build 60 Ubiquitous Cities.*

[29]  Greenfield, *Everyware*, 26–27.

[30]  As one source notes, there are two ways in which computing technology can disappear into our environments: "via the "physical disappearance" by becoming very small due to miniaturization; via the "mental disappearance" of devices by becoming "invisible" because they are integrated/embedded in the physical environment (e.g., walls, doors, tables) around us." Approach, Ambient Agoras, http://www.ambient-agoras.org/.

[31]  Greenfield, *Everyware*, 38.

into a room, and something happens in response: The lights come on, your e-mails are routed to a local wall screen, a menu of options . . . appears on the display sewn into your left sleeve."[32] We do not "use" these technologies in the conventional, historical sense. As Adam Greenfield explains in *Everyware*, the concept of "use"

> stumbles and fails in the context of everyware. As a description of someone encountering ubiquitous systems, it's simply not accurate.
>
> . . . [O]ne no more "uses" everyware than one would . . . the floor to stand on. . . . [T]he whole point of . . . ubiquitous systems was that they would be ambient, peripheral and *not* focally attended to in the way that something actively "used" must be.
>
> Perhaps more importantly, "user" also fails to reflect the sharply reduced volitionality that is . . . bound up with such encounters. We've . . . seen that everyware . . . may be engaged by the act of stepping into a room, so the word carries along with it the implication of an agency that simply may not exist.[33]

We will return to the future of "use" in Chapter 7. Before we analyze how the relationship between law and "smart" technology should adapt to the decline of "use," we need to briefly consider the reasons for moving to "smart," ambient technologies.

## Purposes

While you may find the notion of "smart," ambient technologies intriguing, you are probably wondering "Why? Why would we want to do this?"

As the discussion in the previous section may indicate, the primary reason for moving to "smart" technology is to make our lives easier. As Neil Gershenfeld noted, the "real promise" of these technologies is "to free people, by embedding the means to solve problems in the things around us."[34] Instead of our having to

---

32   *Id.*

33   *Id.*, 70.

34   Gershenfeld, *When Things Start to Think*, 7.

program a device—like the VCR Gershenfeld mentioned or a TiVo or the climate control system in our homes—that will be taken care of for us by systems that anticipate our needs and desires.[35]

These "smart" systems will redefine the "division of labor between people" and technology.[36] Our lives will become easier—and, one hopes, more productive and more rewarding—because we will be freed from dealing with many (most?) of the mundane tasks that currently occupy our time.[37] This is why ambient technology is sometimes referred to as "calm" technology: "As technology becomes more imbedded and invisible, it calms our lives by removing annoyances while keeping us connected with what is truly important."[38]

This general desire to make all of our lives easier and more rewarding is the global driver for the development and incorporation of "smart," embedded technologies into our environment. A more specific, more immediate catalyst for the development of "smart homes" comes from the overall aging of our populations.[39]

---

35   See Ed Zander, "The Invisible Internet," Tomorrow's Professor Listserv, http://sll.stanford.edu/projects/tomprof/newtomprof/postings/311.html:

> [D]evices [will] communicate with each other. Your sprinkler system will modify its settings based on weather . . . data, your dishwasher will search for times when electricity is cheapest before washing a load, and your house will help your hotel room preset the temperature, music settings and TV channels. And you'll never even think about it. . . .

See also Jack Cox, "Futurists Foresee Flying Cars and Packed Preschools," *Seattle Post-Intelligencer*, 2004 WLNR 3183606 (January 4, 2005). For the statute of current climate control systems, see "Message from the President," National Building Museum, http://www.nbm.org/blueprints/95s/summer99/contents/contents.htm (air conditioning as a "ubiquitous yet invisible technology").

36   See Gershenfeld, *When Things Start to Think*, 8.

37   This process will to a great extent undo the effects of twentieth century personal computing. As the architects of Project Oxygen, a Massachusetts Institute of Technology initiative, explained:

> computation has centered about machines, not people. We have catered to . . . computers. . . . Purporting to serve us, they have actually forced us to serve them. They have been difficult to use. . . .
>
> In the future, computation will be human-centered. It will be freely available everywhere, like . . . oxygen in the air. . . . [D]evices . . . will bring computation to us, whenever we . . . might be. [W]e'll communicate naturally, using speech and gestures . . . ( "send this to Hari"or "print that picture . . . "), and leave it to the computer to carry out our will.

"Vision," Project Oxygen – Massachusetts Institute of Technology, http://oxygen.lcs.mit.edu/Overview.html.

38   Alexandru Tugui, "Calm Technologies in a Multimedia World," *Ubiquity* (March 23, 2004): 5, http://www.acm.org/ubiquity/views/v5i4_tugui.html (quoting Mark Weiser).

39   See "Digital Home Technologies for Aging in Place," Intel Corporation, http://www.intel.com/research/exploratory/digital_home.htm.

---

"Smart homes" are seen as a way to let the elderly, and infirm, live in their own "home" instead of having to go into a nursing home or other care facility.[40]

## Cyborg

So far, we have been talking about "smart" technology that is embedded in our physical environment. And this will probably be the first type of embedded technology we will encounter, at least on a large scale.

Twenty-first century "smart" technology will, though, almost certainly encompass another approach, as well: one we will call the "cyborg alternative," because it involves embedding computer technology not in our environments but in ourselves. "Cyborg" is the term "used to designate an organism which adds to or enhances its abilities by using technology."[41]

Cyborgs used to exist only in speculative fiction, but cyborgs—at least in a sense—already live among us.[42] Technology can already give people artificial limbs, artificial hearts, and cochlear implants to improve their hearing.[43] A clinical trial is exploring the possibility of using "neuromotor prostheses" to "replace or restore lost motor function in paralysed humans,"[44] and efforts are well under way to use retinal implants or implanted electronic devices to let blind people see.[45]

"Personal" embedded technology will not, however, only be used to make up for missing limbs, defective hearts and problems with sight, hearing or motor function. It will become far more important as a way to enhance our natural human abilities.

Experiments to that effect have been underway for some time. In 1998, Kevin Warwick, a Professor of Cybernetics at the University of Reading in England,

---

[40] See Dave Gussow, "Home, Smart Home," *St. Petersburg Times* (September 12, 2005), http://www.sptimes.com/2005/09/12/Technology/Home__smart_home.shtml.

[41] "Cyborg," *Wikipedia*, http://en.wikipedia.org/wiki/Cyborg.

[42] See "Cyborg," *Future Wiki*, http://future.wikia.com/wiki/Cyborg.

[43] See *id*.

[44] "Cyberkinetics Neurotechnology Systems, Inc.," http://www.cyberkineticsinc.com/ (quoting "Editor's Summary," *Nature* [July 13, 2006]: 305–308, story about Matt Nagle, first person to participate in the BrainGate pilot clinical trial).

[45] See "Cyborg," *Future Wiki*, http://future.wikia.com/wiki/Cyborg. For more on these and similar efforts, see Ray Kurzweil, *The Singularity is Near* (New York: Viking, 2005), 305–308.

had an RFID chip implanted under his skin and used it to "control doors, lights, heaters, and other computer-controlled devices based on his proximity. The main purpose of this experiment was to test the limits of what the body would accept, and how easy it would be to receive a meaningful signal from the chip."[46] In 2002, Warwick had a more complex chip implanted that "interfaced directly with . . . [his] nervous system."[47] It was used to have an external robot arm mimic the movements of Professor Warwick's own arm and in other experiments.[48]

In a related, albeit somewhat different, vein, University of Toronto Engineering Professor Steve Mann spends hours every day viewing the world through a "wearable computer" that gives him a 360 degree visual perspective and can alter how he sees colors, among other things.[49] Although he is sometimes described as a cyborg, Mann does not fit within the usual conception of the term, both because it assumes the surgical implantation of technology and because it contemplates technology that enhances one's senses and other abilities.[50] As noted above, Mann's computer equipment is something he wears, not something he has had implanted; and he apparently believes wearable computer technology should be used to mediate, but not enhance, our perceptions and abilities.[51]

In a similar vein, the Victoria and Albert Museum hosted a 2005 exhibition of "hearwear:" hearing devices for the nonhearing impaired.[52] Some of the devices muted "annoying sounds," others improved communication and one, a "pair of glasses with a tiny speaker at the end of each arm" gives the wearer "surround sound on demand—an ability that, until now, was unique to animals like the coyote."[53]

---

[46]  "Kevin Warwick," *Wikipedia*, http://en.wikipedia.org/wiki/Kevin_Warwick. See also Professor Kevin Warwick, http://www.kevinwarwick.com/.

[47]  *Id.*

[48]  *Id.*

[49]  See "Why Life As a Cyborg Is Better," *CNN News* (January 14, 2004), http://edition.cnn.com/2004/TECH/internet/01/14/internet.cyborb.ap/.

[50]  See Kurzweil, The Singularity is Near, 305–308.

[51]  See "Why Life As A Cyborg Is Better." See also Steve Mann, "Hyper-Textual Ontology" (August 10, 2004), http://wearcam.org/tv04/hyper-textual_ontology.htm.

[52]  See Martina Smit, "Hear's to the New Fashion," *This Is Local London* (August 4, 2005), http://www.thisislocallondon.co.uk/news/topstories/display.var.619371.0.hears_to_the_new_fashion.php.

[53]  See *id.*

Many very credible people believe that, instead of wearing this type of enhancing technology, we will be implanting it within the next decade or two. Ray Kurzweil, a noted futurist, calls this the "human body version 2.0 scenario," that is, a future in which we use implanted computer and related technologies to vastly enhance our physical and mental capabilities.[54] And in August of 2005, the BT Group issued a detailed future timeline that says "sensory augmentation implants" and surgical implants which give us direct access to cyberspace will be possible, and perhaps routine, between 2013 and 2017.[55] Another way we can achieve this is via nanotechnology; we could inject or implant nanobots that would then give us direct access to cyberspace and to intelligent systems in our external environment.[56]

Another, more radical cyborg scenario is "uploading": decanting our brains into "a computer or other substrate" that gives us "more speed, processing power, memory, longevity, and room to grow than the original biological equipment."[57] It would also let us avoid "tedious journeys" by transmitting our consciousness into a suitable "substrate" in an alternate geographical location.[58] And we could make "backup copies" of ourselves to preserve our existence in case something drastic happened to the original, decanted version.[59]

Whenever it happens (and modern technology usually evolves much faster than is anticipated), it is very likely we will embed technology in ourselves, as well as in our environments. And our move toward becoming cyborgs will raise many difficult issues, including legal issues.

We will not, however, incorporate the "cyborg scenario" into our analysis of how the relationship between law and technology should evolve to accommodate the rise and proliferation of "smart," ambient technologies. We will not include it for two reasons: One is that "smart" environmental technologies are a near-future phenomenon and, as such, are of more pressing concern. The other reason

---

54  See Kurzweil, *The Singularity is Near*. See also Rodney Brooks, "Toward a Brain-Internet Link," *NewsFactor* (December 10, 2003), http://www.newsfactor.com/perl/story/22841.html.

55  See "2005 BT Technology Timeline" (August, 2005), http://www.btplc.com/Innovation/News/timeline/TechnologyTimeline.pdf.

56  See, *e.g.,* "Brain Chips," Soft Machines (March 1, 2007), http://www.softmachines.org/wordpress/?p=283; J. Storrs Hall, Nanofuture (Amherst, NY: Prometheus Books, 2005), 258–259.

57  *Id.,* 283.

58  *Id.*

59  *Id.*

is that the approach outlined in Chapter 7 can accommodate both the near-future embedded environmental technologies and the further-future embedded personal technologies. If, as I argue in Chapter 7, we shift the focus of our "misuse" laws from technology to behavior, then those laws should be able to accommodate cyborg "misuse" as well as unenhanced human "misuse."[60]

---

[60]  This should still be true even if, as some speculate, our use of cyber- and nano-technologies to enhance our bodies and our minds results in our becoming something an early twenty-first century individual might well not recognize as a "human." See, e.g., Id., 266–268. If we indeed surpass or even discard the biological selves that currently define our identities and capacities, we will still need rules to channel our behaviors into acceptable modes . . . unless and until we completely abandon collective association.

As long as we congregate in structured social groupings, we will need rules—laws—that define what is, and is not, acceptable behavior. As I noted earlier, the need for such rules derives from our capacity for intelligent, independent action; with volition comes the possibility for transgression, in varying degrees The contours of the rules we implement if and when we become transhuman will no doubt differ from those we have traditionally enforced, but their function will almost certainly remain the same.

CHAPTER 7

# Law and "Smart" Technologies

*. . . technology dissolves into behavior . . .* [1]

As we track the evolution of our relationship with technology toward the "smart," ambient technologies that will come to dominate in the twenty-first century, we find there are two very different ways in which we unenhanced humans[2] relate to technology. The first two sections below review both. They analyze how our relationship with technology changes as we move from "use" to "interaction," a shift driven by the development of ever-more sophisticated "civilian" technologies. ("Civilian" technologies are, as we saw earlier, implemented by "civilians," instead of by a cadre of specialists.)[3]

The remainder of this chapter analyzes how we can best go about developing rules—criminal laws—that effectively and efficiently address the problem of "misuse."[4] As we saw in Chapter 6, the concept of "misusing" a technology becomes meaningless when our relationship with technology shifts from "use" to "interaction." These sections argue that, in dealing with what has been treated as the "misuse" of *a* technology, our focus should be on the underlying behavior, not on the technology.

## "Use"

For pre-twentieth-century technologies, "using" technology was a conscious, intentional process of manipulating the artifacts or techniques of a given technology.[5]

---

[1]   This phrase is adapted from a phrase attributed to Naoto Fukasawa: "design dissolves in behavior." See "Design Dissolving in Behavior," *ICC Online* (2001), http://www.ntticc.or.jp/Archive/2001/NewSchool/design.html.

[2]   See Chapter 6. Ultimately, the relationship cyborgs have with "their" technology may be something other than "interaction" (or "use"). Analyzing that relationship, however, will have to wait until we have more data—until we have cyborgs of a sophistication far surpassing what we have seen so far. See Chapter 6.

[3]   See Chapters 3 and 6.

[4]   See Chapters 2 and 3.

[5]   See Chapter 3.

An ancient artisan consciously used the specialized tools and techniques he needed to create pottery, weave textiles, or refine metals. The tool and, later, machine technologies were fundamentally passive instrumentalities, an extension of deliberate human effort that was directed toward accomplishing a particular task, such as operating a railroad engine.[6] This is also true of most consumer technologies; when we operate a motor vehicle or play a DVD, for example, we consciously "use" that technology for specific purposes.[7]

This conception of "use" underlies the strategy societies devised to control the negative consequences of various technologies. It produced the context-specific rules we examined in Chapters 3—6. Implicit in this conception is the notion that our posture toward technology consists of two and only two states: "use" and not-"use." We are either "using" a technology or we are not; if we are not-"using" a technology, it is a nullity for all practical purposes. This defined break between "use" and not-"use" made context-specific laws practicable; it was reasonable to hold individuals to certain performance standards once they consciously embarked on the process of "using" a technology. As was explained earlier, their "use" of the technology marked their entry into the empirical context in which these laws applied (a context that became increasingly fluid as early ambient, or consumer, technologies began to appear).[8] And they in effect assumed the risk of abiding by those standards by embarking on the process of "using" a technology.

This conception of "use" as a conscious process will not apply to twenty-first century "smart," ambient technologies. As we saw in Chapter 6, one of the underlying premises of these technologies is that they are invisible; we become so accustomed to their presence and operation that we do not consciously "use" them. Indeed, we will not "use" them at all in the traditional sense; that is, we will not consciously manipulate the artifacts and techniques of "smart," ambient technology to achieve a particular purpose, in a manner analogous to fashioning a piece of pottery. As Adam Greenfield notes, the intelligent, invisible technologies that will become routine in this century can be "engaged inadvertently, unknowingly, or even unwillingly."[9]

---

6    See Chapters 3 and 4.
7    See Chapter 6.
8    See Chapter 3. See also Chapters 4–6.
9    Adam Greenfield, *Everyware: The Dawning Age of Ubiquitous Computing* (New York: New Riders, 2006), 66. Greenfield offers scenarios illustrating inadvertent, unknowing, and unwilling implementation of everyware, 66–67. And he notes "[h]ow different this is from . . . the . . . systems we're accustomed to,

Instead of "using" this technology, we will "interact" with it. "Interaction" differs from "use" in that one is reciprocal and the other is not.[10] When a carpenter cuts timber with a saw or John mows his lawn, each is "using" a technology; each is manipulating a more or less complex but passive device to accomplish a task. The relationship between the "user" and the technology is one sided; the device plays its role in accomplishing the task only as long as, and to the extent that, the "user" intentionally implements it for its intended purpose. And most "user" technologies have only one intended purpose; we cannot, for example, "use" a camera to record sound or "use" a lawnmower to sweep the floors.

"Interacting" with technology is a very different process because it involves at least some level of reciprocity between technology and us. The "interactive" conception of our relationship with technology differs from the traditional conception of "use" in two essential ways: One is that we do not make a conscious decision to utilize technology; technology is part of our environment, and we "interact" with it just as we "interact" with our environment.

Assume, for example, that it is 2015 and I live in an "aware home."[11] As I enter my driveway the home opens the garage door so I can park my car; after I am safely inside, it closes and locks the garage door and opens the entry door to the kitchen. As I enter the kitchen, appropriate lighting goes on, the room temperature is suitably adjusted and the home waits for my next move. If I head for the stairs, the home provides appropriate lighting and, perhaps, ensures there is plenty of hot water in case I want a shower. (It may actually anticipate my heading for the shower, based on my past pattern of behavior upon returning home at a particular time.) If I remain in the kitchen, the home may offer to play back important messages that came in while I was gone (it would presumably have screened out voice or text spam, again because it knows my preferences) or raise "housekeeping" issues with me. If it is clear that I am in for the evening, the home will arm the alarm system and take other security measures.

---

which . . . require conscious action even if we are to betray ourselves," 67. For more on this evolving relationship with technology, see Chapter 6.

10    *Compare* "interact," *Concise Oxford English Dictionary*, rev. 10th ed. (New York: Oxford University Press, 2002), 736, defining "interact" as "to act in such a way as to have an effect on another" and defining "interaction" as "reciprocal action or influence" *with* "use," 1579, defining "use" as to "take, hold, or deploy as a means of accomplishing . . . something."

11    See Chapter 6.

The home's respective action or inaction in this scenario is not the result of my intentionally manipulating the artifactual components that combine to constitute my "aware home." The home's "conduct" is, instead, the result of its responding to me, of its having observed my behavior over whatever period of time we have been "together" and having evolved specific reactions it deems appropriate based on what it has observed of my behavior and on its programming. (Its programming is relevant insofar as it shapes the level of intelligence and other capacities the home has to act autonomously, not because it has been "programmed" to conduct itself in a rigid, predetermined fashion.)

I am the catalyst for the home's "behavior"; I will probably be at least vaguely aware of that when I first move into an "aware home," but as I live there, it will all recede into the background. I will come to assume the home will take care of various matters without my having to consciously intervene or verbalize my desires. And many of the matters the home deals with will always be quite outside my consciousness; the home may, for example, call a service and arrange to have the driveway shoveled early in the morning after a heavy snowfall so it will be clear for me when I am ready to leave for work.[12]

The "aware home" scenario will represent one of the most "personal" modes of interacting with pervasive technology, but we will interact with technology in a similar fashion at our places of employment, in shops and stores, and in restaurants and public places. Something similar will occur as automobiles become increasingly automated; instead of consciously manipulating my Honda CRV to get to my law school, I will climb into an automated version, tell it where I want to go (or assume it knows, based on my past pattern of behavior), and leave the process of getting me there to the vehicle, as I daydream, read, listen to music, or watch the onboard video feed.[13] The car will decide the best route to take and will adapt to road conditions to minimize the possibility of accidents or other hazards; it will maintain an appropriate interior climate for me and let me know when I have arrived at my destination.[14] (If this sounds farfetched, keep in mind that as

---

[12] See Julie Clothier, "Smart" Homes Not Far Away," *CNN* (May 31, 2005), http://www.cnn.com/2005/TECH/05/27/vision.home/index.html; "when the washing machine leaks", the aware home "will automatically turn off the water at the mains, and alert you that a plumber may need calling."

[13] See Bruce McCall, "Will We Still Drive Our Cars, or Will Our Cars Drive Us?", *Time - Visions of the 21st Century*, http://www.time.com/time/reports/v21/tech/mag_cars.html.

[14] See "The Future Is in the Past," *Express–Berkeley, 2005 WLNR 10110310* (May), 235, 2005; Dick Pelletier, "Cars Drive Themselves; Trains Go 4,000 mph in Future," Better Humans (June 15, 2005),

this is written in the summer of 2007, Volkswagen has a prototype vehicle that can "drive itself at speeds up to 150 mph, several vehicles already on the market can park themselves and GM has announced it will market a semiautonomous vehicle with the 2008 model of the Opel Vectra.)[15]

This brings us to the second, related way in which the interactive conception of "using" technology differs from the traditional, instrumental conception of "use": Unlike prior technologies, the new "smart," ambient technologies are not passive. Whether standing alone or incorporated into a system, the components of twenty-first-century ambient technologies will incorporate artificial intelligence.[16] Artificial intelligence gives them the "ability" to (a) act with a degree of autonomy and (b) interact with humans.[17] Unlike tool or machine technologies, they are not

---

http://www.betterhumans.com/Members/futuretalk/BlogPost/777/Default.aspx; Alexandra Kahn, "MIT Group Presents Research on City Car of the Future," Massachusetts Institute of Technology—New Office (September 1, 2004), http://web.mit.edu/newsoffice/2004/smartcars.html.

[15] See Ray Massey, "The Self-Driving Golf That Would Give Herbie A Run For Its Money," *Daily Mail* (July 4, 2006), http://www.dailymail.co.uk/pages/live/articles/news/news.html?in_article_id=393401&in_page_id=1770; "2007 Lexus LS460—Tech Highlight," *Car and Driver* (October, 2006), http://www.carand-driver.com/roadtests/11601/2007-lexus-ls460-tech-highlight-page3.html; "Volvo Cars Self-Parking System," Automotoportal (2007), http://www.automotoportal.com/article/Volvo_Cars_self-parking_system. The 2008 Opel Vectra actually seems to be designed to help with the driving of a vehicle rather than to take over this function entirely. See, *e.g.*, "New Vectra Makes Its Approach," Carsales.com (May, 2007), http://editorial.carsales.com.au/car-review/2648106.aspx; new Vectra will come with the Traffic Assist system, which uses "video and laser functions to monitor the environment around the car for warning signs, lane markings and other vehicles" and "will apply brakes to avoid collisions." See also "Opel Vectra," *Auto Express* (May 22, 2007), http://www.autoexpress.co.uk/news/spyshots/208774/opel_vectra.html; "A Car That (Really) Drives Itself: The 2008 Open Vectra," Edmunds—*Inside Line* (August 25, 2005), http://www.edmunds.com/insideline/do/News/articleId=107011.

In 2005, an autonomous Volkswagen Touareg developed by the Stanford Racing team won the DARPA Grand Challenge by being the first to complete a 132-mile race; four other autonomous vehicles also completed the race. See "DARPA Grant Challenge," *Wikipedia*, http://en.wikipedia.org/wiki/DARPA_Grand_Challenge. The 2007 DARPA Urban Challenge is designed for vehicles that move a step closer to the kind of urban autonomous vehicle I hypothesize in the text. It will involve a race through a 60-mile urban course with the robotically operated vehicles being required to observe all traffic laws "while nego-tiating with other traffic and obstacles and merging into traffic." See *id.* See also "Urban Challenge," DARPA, http://www.darpa.mil/grandchallenge/index.asp.

[16] See Chapter 6.

[17] See European Commission IST Advisory Group, "Scenarios for Ambient Intelligence in 2010" (2001), 8; http://www.research.philips.com/technologies/misc/homelab/downloads/eur19763en.pdf:

The emphasis . . . is on . . . user-empowerment, and support for human interactions. In all four scenarios people are surrounded by intelligent intuitive interfaces that are embedded in all kinds of objects. The Ambient Intelligence environment is capable of recognising and responding to the presence of different individuals. And, most important, Ambient Intelligence works in a seamless, unobtrusive and often invisible way.

a passive extension of conscious human effort; they are, in effect, partners with whom I collaborate in achieving certain ends.

We return to this interactive conception of "use" in § III, where we consider its implications for how we can employ legal rules to prevent the misuse of sophisticated emerging technologies. Before we do that, however, we need to describe what the peculiarly pervasive technologies of the twenty-first century will be like.

## "Interacting"

Although it seems reasonably certain, absent some extraordinary turn of events, that we are on the fast track to an environment populated by pervasive technology, we are not there yet. Microsoft may have an "aware home,"[18] but most of us live in regular houses; "smart offices" are in development, but most of us still have regular offices; and even as the technology exists that would let our vehicles do the driving for us, we have not quite taken that next step (though it seems we are about to do so).[19]

The last observation encapsulates our current relationship with technology: We think of ourselves as "users" of technology because we really have no experience with the semi-autonomous, interactive technologies described above. And because we think of ourselves as "users," we are loath to surrender control to an automated vehicle. We *want* to be "in charge" of the vehicle; we think we are *supposed* to be "in charge" of the vehicle, even though it is clear that driving would be much easier and much safer if it were in the virtual "hands" of an automated system.[20] (Whatever problems they may have, automated vehicles will not cut each other off, will not drive while intoxicated, and are exceedingly unlikely to suffer from road rage.)

---

For the scenarios, see *id.*, at 4–8. "Like "ambient technology," ambient intelligence refers to environments in which "humans are surrounded by computing and networking technology unobtrusively embedded in their surroundings." See Chapter 6. See also "Ambient Intelligence," *Wikipedia*, http://en.wikipedia.org/wiki/Ambient_intelligence.

[18] See "The Microsoft Home: The Ultimate "Smart" Home—With Personality," MSN.com, http://houseandhome.msn.com/Improve/MicrosoftHome0.aspx.

[19] See note 15. See also Alan Boyle, "Pentagon Unveils Urban Robo-Race," MSNBC (May 1, 2006), http://www.msnbc.msn.com/id/12583619/.

[20] See *id.*, "autonomously driven passenger vehicles could revolutionize transportation" by, among other things, "drastically reduc[ing] the average annual traffic death toll of 42,000 Americans."

We are on the threshold of a fundamental transformation in our relationship with technology.[21] Most of the technologies we encounter (automobiles, televisions, vacuum cleaners, cameras, coffee-makers, elevators) are still "user" technologies; implementing any of them requires us to consciously manipulate the artifacts and techniques of a particular technology. There are, though, a few technologies with which we have a more ambiguous relationship. We will call them "transitional technologies" because while we are not completely oblivious to the functioning of these technologies, our "use" of them tends to recede into the background of our consciousness.[22]

Transitional technologies may be precursors of "smart," ambient technologies. As the previous section explained, we "interact" with "smart," ambient technologies, instead of "using" them. As it also explained, "interacting" differs from "using" in two respects: One is that our "use" of a technology is unconscious, rather than intentional. The other is that the technology plays an active, rather than a passive, role in the process.

Telephones, personal computers, and climate control systems are examples of transitional technologies;[23] we tend to take each of them for granted and so are only residually aware that we are "using" a technology when we rely on them. Our "use" of transitional technology therefore satisfies the first requirement for "interacting" with technology; we implement a transitional technology carelessly, not deliberately. The second requirement is more problematic; because these technologies are not designed to be truly intelligent, they have—at most—a very limited capacity for playing an active role in the utilization process.[24] We therefore do not—indeed cannot—"interact" with transitional technologies because they are all "dumb," passive technologies; we "use" them, but with increasing inattention.

Our inability to "interact" with transitional technologies does not mean they are not precursors of "interactive" technologies. There are two reasons why

---

[21]   See Raymond Kurzweil, *The Age of Intelligent Machines* (Cambridge, MA: MIT Press, 1990), 9, "The revolution manifest in the age of intelligent machines is in its earliest stages. The impact of this new age will be greater than the . . . technological and social changes that have come before it." For an assessment of where we are and where we are about to go, see Donald Norman, "Cautious Cars, Cranky Kitchens, Demanding Devices," Lecture–UC Berkeley School of Information (March 1, 2006), http://www.sims. berkeley.edu/about/events/dls03012006 (audio file of lecture).

[22]   See Chapters 5 and 6.

[23]   See Chapters 5 and 6.

[24]   See Chapters 5 and 6.

transitional technologies probably *are* precursors of the "smart," ambient technologies we reviewed in Chapter 6. One is that they no doubt provided the empirical basis for conceptualizing truly ambient technologies; the "invisibility" computer scientists and others seek for "smart," ambient technologies seems to be an extrapolation of our existing relationship with transitional technologies. The other reason is that our evolving experience with transitional technologies will probably help socialize us so we will eventually be ready to embrace "smart," ambient technologies.

Transitional technologies can also help us decide how to modify the strategy we have so far used to control the "misuse" of technology so that it can accommodate the new "smart," ambient technologies. Chapter 5 explained why the traditional strategy is increasingly inappropriate for one transitional technology—personal computers. And the previous section explained that adopting context-specific "misuse" rules directed at the "users" of a technology succeeds only when those "users" consciously implement that technology in a discrete empirical context.[25]

These "misuse" rules are designed to control my behavior as a deliberate "user" of technology; they assume the intentionality of my conduct.[26] If I am oblivious to the fact that I am "using" a technology, the rules fail. They fail because they are predicated on the derivative assumption that my act of deliberately utilizing a technology produces both (a) the realization that I am now subject to certain standards governing the "use" of that technology and (b) a decision to abide by those standards in order to avoid the consequences that are attendant on not doing so.[27] Absent deliberate use, there can be no realization and no decision.

Context-specific rules work quite well in, say, discouraging drunk driving.[28] We may tend to take automobiles for granted, but we are still aware that when we drive (a) we are operating a motor vehicle, (b) by doing so we enter an empirical context in which specific set of rules apply, and (c) our failure to abide by those rules can cause us to suffer certain consequences, for example, fines, loss of our driving privileges, even jail in more extreme instances.[29] These rules do not, of

---

[25]  See Chapters 3 and 5.

[26]  See "Intentionality," *Wikipedia*, http://en.wikipedia.org/wiki/Intentionality; a behavior is intentional when "it . . . is based on reasons . . . and performed with skill and awareness."

[27]  See Chapter 3.

[28]  See Chapter 5 (drunk driving laws as "misuse" rules).

[29]  See *id.*

course, work perfectly; people do drive while intoxicated. But the rules are effective enough; they ensure that most people follow the standards set out for operating a motor vehicle and, in so doing, minimize the "misuse" of this technology.

Imagine, on the other hand, that we adopt context-specific rules to control the "misuse" of electric light. Like all "misuse" rules, they prohibit utilizing the technology in various ways, each of which involves the infliction of prohibited "harm." One enters the context in which the rules apply by "using" electric light, and violates the rules by "using" electric light improperly. One very dark December night, John Doe consciously "uses" streetlights to follow and then rob Susan Smith. When we say Doe "consciously" "used" this technology, we do not mean that it was his *goal* to "use" electric light for a specific, prohibited purpose. We mean only that he acted with a base level of awareness, that is, Doe knew the illumination coming from the streetlights made it possible for him to follow Smith and rob her.[30]

Since Doe "used" the technology to inflict a prohibited "harm,"[31] he would be liable for violating the "misuse of electric light" rules. This no doubt seems an absurd example, but that is precisely the point: Its absurdity derives from the fact that electricity is a consummately "invisible" ambient technology. We are so accustomed to electric light, it so blends into the background of our lives, that it seems ridiculous to think Doe "misuses" electric light when he exploits it to rob Susan Smith. And yet, in this example Doe did consciously "use" electric light technology for a prohibited purpose, that is, to rob Smith.

Consider a less-absurd but still analogous real-world example. A variation of the Doe scenario may explain why online file-sharing persists even though it is blatantly illegal.[32] As most of us know, millions of people around the world violate copyright laws by downloading music from the Internet.[33] Most of them would

---

30  See American Law Institute, Model Penal Code § 2.02.

31  We are assuming, in this truly far-fetched hypothetical, that "using" electric light to commit robbery is a "harm" within the postulated "misuse" rules.

32  See, *e.g.,* "Recording Industry Starts Legal Actions against Illegal File-sharing Internationally," *IFPI* (March 30, 2004), http://www.ifpi.org/site-content/press/20040330.html.

33  See Marc Perlman, "Why File-Sharing Doesn't Feel Like Stealing," Brown UniversityOp-Ed, http://www.brown.edu/Administration/News_Bureau/2003-04/03-008.html; "File-sharing involves an estimated 57 million people . . . the largest group ever assembled for . . . law-breaking."

never steal a CD from a real-world store because they would see this as "theft."[34] How, then, can we explain their actions online?

This may be an instance in which context-specific "misuse" rules (copyright laws) designed to control conduct in the real world are coming into conflict with the effects of a transitional technology—personal computing. Copyright law originally applied only to written works but was expanded to encompass sound recordings in 1909; music piracy did not, however, become a real issue until the 1960s because copying vinyl recordings was expensive and difficult.[35] And although the process became much easier with the "introduction of the compact cassette in the 1960s," one still had to deliberately copy a physical item, a copyrighted record or tape.[36]

Online file-sharing has moved far beyond that.[37] While the music that is being shared was presumably copied from a copyrighted CD at some point, this is not apparent in the file-sharing process.[38] In peer-to-peer sharing, files stored on computers belonging to individuals are shared directly with other individuals; they move fluidly from person to person like any other form of data.[39] And like John Doe, who was aware, at some basic level, that he was "misusing" electric light technology, file-sharers are aware, at some level, that the music they receive and distribute was probably copied from a copyrighted, commercial CD. And yet they do not see what they are doing as "wrong."[40]

File-sharers offer various explanations for this, such as blaming the recording industry for high prices.[41] But the real explanation may lie not in logic but in the evolving disconnect between technology and law. To us, the notion of holding John Doe liable for "misusing" electric light technology is absurd because we all "know" electricity is "out there" for us to "use"; we have difficulty even accepting the idea that Doe "used" electricity in his theft. Something similar may be going

---

34    See *id.*
35    See John P. Strohm, Comment, "Writings in the Margin (of Error): The Authorship Status of Sound Recordings under United States Copyright Law," *Cumberland Law Review 34* (2003–2004), 127, 132.
36    See *id.*
37    See "File sharing," *Wikipedia*, http://en.wikipedia.org/wiki/File_sharing.
38    See *id.*
39    See *id.*
40    See Perlman, "Why File-Sharing Doesn't Feel Like Stealing."
41    See *id.*

on with file-sharing: Thanks to a transitional technology (personal computer technology), music files are "out there" in some generalized, anonymous fashion waiting for us to download them. Those who are familiar with computer technology and the online environment give no more thought to downloading music than our hypothetical John Doe did about taking advantage of the streetlights. The technology erases the context in which copyright laws originally applied—the deliberate "use" of technology to make tangible, physical copies of sound recordings in violation of the law—and thereby erodes the effectiveness of those laws.

We "know" the result in the John Doe example is wrong, but we find it difficult to articulate why it is wrong. (Many of us, anyway, are probably more ambivalent about file-sharing, so we will concentrate on the Doe hypothetical for the remainder of this discussion.) What is the difference between "using" a telephone to harass someone and Doe's "using" streetlights to rob Smith? In both, a technology is "used" to facilitate the infliction of a proscribed "harm," the commission of a crime.[42] The perpetrator's focus in telephone harassment is not on "using" telephone technology; it is on harassing the victim. The telephone plays a minor, facilitative role in the commission of this offense, just as the streetlights do in the commission of Doe's offense. We are comfortable with the context-specific rules that apply to telephone harassment but find context-specific rules targeting the "misuse" of electric light technology absurd and unreasonable.

The explanation for why we react so differently to what seem to be analogous situations lies in our relationship with the respective technologies. As we saw earlier, telephones are transitional technologies; when we make a call, we are aware that we are "using" a technology, but that fact recedes into our consciousness as we focus on the process of communicating.[43] Telephones are a transitional technology because while we do not fully "interact" with them, we tend to take them for granted; when "using" a phone we do not focus on the mechanical process involved in that "use" in the same way we do when we operate a motor vehicle. Telephone technology is moving into the background of our awareness but is not yet invisible. Electricity is, as we saw earlier, in a class by itself; we do not "interact" with it (and probably never will), but it is invisible.[44] We are, at best, minimally aware we

---

[42]  See Chapter 3.
[43]  See Chapter 5.
[44]  See Chapter 5.

are "using" electricity when we read by lamplight, work on a computer, or play music on our iPod.[45]

That explains the difference in our reaction to the scenarios noted above: We are comfortable with the telephone harassment scenario even though we tend to take telephones for granted because we know harassers deliberately "use" telephones to conceal their identities.[46] Conceptually, therefore, we can accept laws that criminalize telephone harassment because these laws target a focused "misuse" of the technology. We cannot accept the hypothesized "misuse" of electric light laws because we realize, intuitively, that people do not consciously "use" electric light; the "use" intentionality that is present in the telephone harassment scenario is absent in the Doe scenario.

We may be able to accept that someone who deliberately chooses to "use" a telephone to harass his victim thereby enters the empirical context in which telephone "misuse" rules apply and can reasonably be held liable for violating those rules. But we cannot accept that such rules can or ever should apply to electricity; for us, the break between "use of electricity" and "nonuse of electricity" is nonsensical. Electricity is such an integral, and invisible, part of our lives that our "use" of it blurs into whatever activity we happen to be engaged in at a particular time. As the beginning of this chapter noted, the technology dissolves into the behavior. We can therefore accept that Doe violated the rules that prohibit robbery because robbery was his goal, his intention; but we cannot accept that he violated our hypothetical "misuse" of electric light rules because we simply cannot accept that he "used" electricity.

This brings us back to the "smart," ambient technologies described in Chapter 6, which will be even more problematic in this regard than electricity. How can we possibly say someone "uses" the technology in an "aware home," a "smart office" or a "U-city"? As the products of twentieth century technology, we may be self-conscious when we first experience an intelligent, interactive environment; we will not be accustomed to "letting the home (or office) handle it," at least not at first. We will become accustomed to that, just as our ancestors became accustomed to electricity; and those who have grown up in the period during which that technology is being implemented will no doubt take it for granted in the

---

same way as, but probably to a greater extent than, we take electricity for granted.[47] (I still have to "use" electricity because it is a passive technology; "smart," ambient technologies will be active, and so will relieve me of that responsibility.[48])

We have been assuming only "smart," ambient *environmental* technologies. The analysis becomes more complex when we consider the cyborg alternative— embedded *individual* technologies.[49] If I have a wireless electronic interface implanted in my brain that I activate with my brain waves, with my thoughts, am I "using" technology or have I "become" technology? How could we possibly employ context-specific "user" rules to control what I do with my implant? Now imagine a fusion of the two types of evolving technologies: My brain implant lets me "interact" with "smart," ambient environmental technologies. They, in turn, react to my movements, my habits, and my thoughts by preparing food (home), by adjusting the ambient temperature (home and office), by scheduling a meeting with people I need to see face-to-face (office), by monitoring my health and making medical appointments for me (home), by adjusting traffic signals as I walk down the street (environmental), and in hundreds of other ways.[50] The fused technologies let me "interact" with people and/or devices located around the world, summon an elevator, and operate my car. And I take it all for granted in much the same way as we take electricity or the operation of our home heating and air conditioning system for granted; I "know," at some level, that the systems are there and are operating at my behest and for my benefit, but I am conscious of them only when they malfunction.[51]

As we move from "using" technology to "interacting" with technology, the efficacy of use context-specific rules to control the "misuse" of technology continues to erode and ultimately vanishes. Continuing to rely on this strategy in an era of "smart," ambient technology would be analogous to applying twentieth century traffic rules devised to control the behavior of individual humans to a twenty-first-century automated highway system. We must, therefore, devise a new approach.

The next section takes up that task. In so doing, it addresses an issue that has been neglected so far: Precisely how *can* "smart," ambient technologies be "misused"?

---

[47] See Chapter 5.
[48] See Chapter 6.
[49] See Chapter 6.
[50] See Chapter 6.
[51] See Chapter 6.

## Law

Context-specific rules that are designed to control the "misuse" of a technology misconstrue the nature of "misuse." They do this because, as is explained later in this section, they are the product of an historical error: They derive from the historically viable premise that the implementation of technologies is carried out by specialists who operate in a distinct empirical context; as we saw earlier, context-specific rules were originally, therefore, intended to minimize the negative consequences that attend the defective implementation of a technology by controlling how the specialists, the "users" of a technology, implement it.[52]

This is a logical, practicable strategy when specialists implement technology.[53] Because specialists "use" a technology in a distinct empirical context, it is reasonable to conflate "use" and "technology" in rules that seek to control their implementation of that technology. The rules' only concern is with the implementation of the technology; the conduct element of these rules ("use") is significant only insofar as it impacts upon how the specialists—the "users"—implement a technology. So, as we saw in Chapter 2, the rules designed to control the defective implementation of the technologies responsible for commercial air travel (a) are directed exclusively at the specialists who implement the various technologies and (b) are directed at them only insofar as, and as long as, they implement those technologies.

As we saw in Chapter 3, this strategy was devised to control the defective implementation of technology and was later extrapolated to encompass the improper implementation ("misuse") of certain preconsumer and consumer technologies. The extrapolation was predicated on the premise that though specialists did not implement these technologies, they were implemented in a distinct empirical context; the context became one's "use" of a particular technology, such as a bicycle or, later, an automobile.[54] A secondary premise supporting these rules was the assumption that those who "used" such a technology assumed a distinct status analogous to that of the specialists to whom context-specific rules had historically applied; one's assumption of this status supported the enforcement of context-specific rules designed to control the "misuse" of the technology.[55] Early extrapolations of

---

52   See Chapters 2 & 3.
53   See Chapters 3 & 4.
54   See Chapters 4 & 5.
55   See Chapters 4 & 5.

this strategy were concerned more with the defective implementation of technology than with improper implementation or "misuse"; bicycle rules and early automobile rules were primarily designed to ensure that the new vehicles were not operated in a way that posed a safety hazard for pedestrians or those riding in carriages or on horseback.[56]

Defective implementation rules are intended, and designed, solely to ensure the integrity of that process. They are therefore "about" a technology. Unlike other rules, defective implementation rules are not rules of general application; they usually apply only to the specialists who implement a technology.[57] Defective implementation rules can apply to civilians instead of, or in addition to specialists, when the implementation of a technology migrates in whole or in part outside the realm of specialization; they will, though, apply only to the extent society has an interest in controlling the role civilians play in implementing a particular technology. Societies therefore adopted rules to control civilian implementation of motor vehicle technology but made no effort to control civilian implementation of photography.[58] Societies have an interest in controlling civilian implementation of motor vehicle technology because the defective implementation of this technology threatens peoples' limbs, lives, and property; societies have no interest in controlling civilian implementation of photography because the defective implementation of this technology by civilians "harms" no one but the photographer (and, perhaps, those with whom she shares her work).

As we saw earlier, defective implementation is a systemic concern; societies are inherently interested in seeing that certain technologies are implemented as effectively as possible. This is always true for tool and machine technologies because of the role these technologies play in supporting critical infrastructures,and it can be true for some consumer technologies. The rise of consumer technologies, for example, resulted in the development of product liability law, which holds manufacturers liable for their role in the defective implementation of consumer technologies and thereby protects us from exploding toasters and other hazards.[59]

---

56  See Chapters 4 & 5.

57  See Chapter 4.

58  See Chapters 4 & 5.

59  See Donald G. Gifford, "Public Nuisance As A Mass Products Liability Tort," *University of Cincinnati Law Review, 71* (2003): 741, 744. Certain consumer technologies can evolve to the point that they, too, become an integral part of a society's critical infrastructures. We have already seen this happen with telephone technology and the Internet. See Chapter 5.

"Misuse" is a very different phenomenon and a relatively recent phenomenon.[60] As we saw in Chapters 3 and 4, "misuse" is not a concern as long as the implementation of technology is in the hands of specialists. There are two reasons for this. One is the mental state involved in the problematic implementation of a technology. As we saw in Chapter 3, defective implementation is the product of inadvertence, while "misuse" is the product of intent, specifically, an intent to inflict "harm" on persons or property. "Misuse" has simply never been a problem when the implementation of technology is reserved for specialists, possibly because the selection and training processes involved in producing specialists eliminates those who would "misuse" the technology if given the opportunity. The presumptive effects of these processes are enhanced by another factor—the other reason why "misuse" is not a concern when implementation is reserved for specialists.

Evolved tool technologies and machine technologies are complex technologies; as such, their implementation involves collaborative effort and a division of labor among many people. It would, as a result, be extraordinarily difficult, if not impossible, for one of the specialists involved in the implementation of a complex technology to achieve its "misuse." So although it is not inconceivable that a specialist might *want* to "misuse" the technology she helps to implement, the fact that her contribution is only a segment in a complex process is very likely to inhibit her ability to act on that desire.

If, for example, a commercial airline pilot wanted to highjack a Boeing 737 and fly it to Colombia to join the drug trade, she would find it very difficult, if not impossible, to do so because she controls only a small part of the process involved in air transportation. The same is true of a worker on an automobile assembly line: He might want to use the machinery on the line for some improper purpose, such as constructing an untraceable vehicle, but would for all practical purposes never be able to do so. Neither the pilot nor the assembly-line worker can exercise enough autonomous control over the technology in question to be able to misuse it.

Neither of the factors that constrain "misuse" by specialists applies when the implementation of technology is in the hands of civilians.[61] As we saw earlier, until the twentieth century, specialists implemented most technologies; even if civilians "used" aspects of a technology (by, say, "using" rail transportation), they did not exercise sufficient control over a technology to be able to

---

[60]   See Chapter 3.
[61]   See Chapters 3–5.

"misuse" it.[62] While a few pre-twentieth-century technologies were implemented—in whole or in part—by civilians, the risk of negative consequences resulting from the "misuse" of those technologies was so slight societies made no effort to address it.[63]

"Misuse" became a problem with the rise of consumer technologies, because non-specialists implement them ; civilian "use" is their sole purpose.[64] Telephone technology was the first consumer technology to be "misused" in ways that required a societal response.[65] As Chapter 5 explained, at the beginning of the last century, states began to adopt laws that criminalized the "misuse" of a telephone to make obscene (or harassing) calls;[66] the laws targeted a new phenomenon—the "misuse" of what was becoming a consumer technology.

Societies cannot ignore "misuse" because it has negative consequences for a society's ability to maintain essential functions and internal order.[67] "Misuse" has this in common with defective implementation, but the two differ in the genesis and effects of the negative consequences they produce.[68]

The negative consequences of "misuse" are of particular concern to a society for two reasons: One is that the consequences themselves may be as serious as, or more serious than, those caused by defective implementation. If a digital cable company does a poor job of providing the services it offers (defective implementation), its customers will be inconvenienced by problems with their television and Internet and access; if a hacker deliberately uses the company's Internet connections to access a credit card company's customer database and steal identities ("misuse"), those identities were stolen suffer a "harm" of greater magnitude—individually and collectively—than the cable customers who were merely inconvenienced by the cable company's incompetence.[69] It follows, therefore, that since societies seek to control negative consequences resulting from the implementation of technologies, they will be at

---

[62]  See Chapters 3–5.

[63]  See Chapter 4.

[64]  See Chapter 5.

[65]  See Chapter 5.

[66]  In the discussion that follows, we will combine obscene calls and harassing calls into one phenomenon: harassing calls. Although this is done for the sake of simplicity, it also arguably reflects reality, since obscene calls are generally made to harass.

[67]  See Chapter 3.

[68]  See Chapter 3.

[69]  There may be defective implementation in both aspects of this scenario: If the hacker also "hacked" the cable company, i.e., obtained access to its services without being one of its customers, we could have

least as concerned about the second aspect of this scenario ("misuse") as they will about the first (defective implementation).

The hacker scenario also illustrates the other reason why "misuse" is of particular concern to societies. As Chapter 3 explained, when someone "misuses" a technology they *deliberately* employ it for a negative ("harmful") purpose; more precisely, they *mean* to "use" the technology "against" someone or something, to "use" it to "harm" them. In the scenario above, the hacker intentionally "uses" the cable company's technology "against" the credit card company and its customers. This is a negative consequence of a very distinct type; it is not a "systemic" defect, it is a challenge to social order.[70]

Societies must maintain internal order if they, and their citizens, are to survive.[71] Social order is not a given; it is a construct, the product of rules societies adopt and enforce.[72] These rules are directed at individual conduct (acts or omissions) because we can only seek to control the outward manifestation of one's thoughts and desires.[73] "Civil" rules—including the context-specific rules societies use to control the defective implementation of technologies—ensure that the processes and systems on which a society relies for its survival function with the requisite level of efficiency.[74] Other rules operate at a more primitive level; these "criminal" rules are designed to control the extent to which members of a society prey upon—"harm"—each other.[75]

---

defective implementation of the technology that was intended to prevent this from happening. We will assume the hacker was a customer, and therefore will not consider this defective implementation issue.

The other potential defective implementation scenario arises with regard to the credit card company; its implementation of the technology it used to secure its credit card database may, or may not, have been defective. The hacker may have been able to access the credit card company's database because its security technology was not being effectively implemented; or its implementation may have been effective, in terms of what it was designed to do, but the hacker simply bypassed or otherwise evaded the security technology.

The fact that either or both companies implemented its security technology in a defective manner is, however, irrelevant to the issue of the hacker's criminal liability for "misusing" technology. Defective implementation may provide the occasion for criminal conduct ("misuse"), but it cannot provide an excuse for such conduct. See Susan W. Brenner, "Toward a Criminal Law for Cyberspace: Distributed Security," *Boston University Journal of Science & Technology Law 10* (2004): 1, 102–104.

[70]  See Chapter 3.

[71]  See Brenner, *Toward a Criminal Law for Cyberspace*, 6–64.

[72]  See *id.*

[73]  See Wayne R. LaFave, *1 Substantive Criminal Law § 6.1(b)*, 2nd ed. (St. Paul, MN: West, 2006). See also Brenner, *Toward a Criminal Law for Cyberspace*, 6–64.

[74]  See *Id.*

[75]  See *id.*, 44.

This brings us back to "misuse" and the hacker scenario set out above: Societies must control the "misuse" of technology because "misuse" is a type of criminal conduct.[76] Societies have recognized this, at some level, since "misuse" began to be a problem; the telephone harassment laws noted above, for example, were criminal rules, not the civil, regulatory rules societies employ to control the defective implementation of technologies. This is appropriate because unlike defective implementation rules, "misuse" rules are not "about" technology; they are, like all criminal rules, "about" inflicting "harm" on persons or property.[77] But while societies have imposed criminal sanctions for "misuse," they have not approached "misuse" as what it really is: merely a type of criminal conduct.

Instead, they transpose the approach they utilize for defective implementation to the "misuse" context. The result is that the "misuse" rules societies adopt are "use" rules rather than criminal rules; they target the "use" of a specific technology to inflict "harm," instead of focusing on the "harm" itself. The "misuse" rules therefore become "about" a technology, just as defective implementation rules are (properly) "about" a technology.

So instead of approaching "misuse" as problematic behavior (like rape or murder, say), societies adopt context-specific rules that treat "use" and "technology" as if they are of equal importance in controlling "misuse."[78] As we saw in Chapter 5, state legislators responded to the "misuse" of telephone technology by adopting "use"-of-a-telephone-to-harass rules. These rules focused as much on the technology as on the ultimate result: harassment. They therefore did not encompass "using" other technologies to harass someone; when the Internet came into general use, states responded to the gap in their law by adding "use"-of-a-computer-to-harass rules[79] and thereby continued along the path of technologically specific "misuse" rules. If we were to continue with this approach, we might ultimately have "use"-of-an-intelligent-refrigerator-to-harass" rules.[80]

---

[76]   See Chapter 3.

[77]   See Chapter 3.

[78]   They are of equal importance in controlling defective implementation because the sole concern is with the technology. They are not of equal importance in controlling improper implementation because a technology plays a minor role in improper implementation; as was explained earlier in the text, it becomes the instrument someone uses to achieve a particular negative result—the infliction of a "harm."

[79]   Some states consequently have both "computer harassment" and "telephone harassment" statutes. See Ga. Code Ann. §§ 16-11-39.1 & 16-5-90; W. Va. Code §§ 61-3C-14A & 61-8-6.

[80]   See Chapter 6.

This bring us back to an issue raised earlier: By misconstruing "misuse," the law-makers who adopt criminal rules targeting "misuse" transform the rules from what they *should* be—result rules—into what they should *not* be—method rules.[81] As we saw earlier, criminal rules are used to control the extent to which the members of a society inflict various types of "harm" upon each other.[82] The rules therefore target the infliction of specific, societally intolerable "harms" such as injuring or killing someone, taking their property without permission, damaging their property, or undermining the administration of justice.[83] Because their purpose is to limit the infliction of "harms," criminal rules properly focus on the result (infliction of "harm), not on the method (how one goes about inflicting "harm").[84]

Like the telephone "misuse" rules noted above, criminal rules targeting the "misuse" of technology increasingly tend to focus on the method, not the result. As we saw in Chapter 5, our persistence in this regard has certain disadvantages: One is that it produces overlapping rules (e.g., rules outlawing theft, rules outlawing the "misuse" of computers to commit theft and rules outlawing the theft of computers). Another is that this approach produces rules that are transient, and therefore unstable  We began with "use"-of-a-telephone-to-harass rules and then added "use"-of-a-computer-to-harass rules. This leaves us, at the moment, with rules that may or may not overlap, that is, if one "uses" a computer to access a telephone line and "uses" that connection to harass another, is this "use"-of-a-telephone-to-harass, "use"-of-a-computer-to-harass, or both? Yet another disadvantage of this approach is that as technologies converge and the distinction between a "telephone" and a "computer" erodes, it may take us back to where we began: with a "harm" (harassment by an as-yet unimplemented technology) that is still not proscribed by existing law.[85] Finally, as we saw earlier in this chapter, the focus on method becomes increasingly untenable as our "use" of technology ceases to be a segmented, compartmentalized part of our lives and becomes an integral, invisible part of our daily routine.

---

[81] See Susan W. Brenner, "Is There Such a Thing as Virtual Crime?", 4 *California Criminal Law Review 4* (2001): 1, http://www.boalt.org/CCLR/v4/v4brenner.htm.

[82] See Chapter 3. Historically, human societies have used criminal rules directed at their own citizens to maintain order within a society, and have relied on military forces to maintain external order, i.e., to fend off threats from other societies or organized groups. See Brenner, "Toward a Criminal Law for Cyberspace," 42–45.

[83] See Brenner, "Is There Such a Thing as Virtual Crime?".

[84] See Brenner, "Toward a Criminal Law for Cyberspace," 42–45; Brenner, "Is There Such a Thing as Virtual Crime?".

[85] See Chris Oakes, "Single Gadget Weaves Phone, Internet and Media Services," *International Herald Tribune* (July 25, 2005), http://www.iht.com/articles/2005/07/24/business/wireless25.php.

Our persistence in using context-specific rules to target "misuse" perpetuates an error that occurred long ago. When "misuse" began to appear, societies reacted (as societies often do) with an *ad hoc* solution: extrapolating the strategy they employed for defective implementation to "misuse." We (modern societies) inherited the practice of relying on this extrapolation to control "misuse" and so we do not question its suitability. Indeed, it seems the practice may actually have become more influential by giving rise to a derivative empirical assumption: the legislators who are responsible[86] for "misuse" laws may have come to assume that a "misuse" of a particular technology inflicts a *sui generis* "harm" that is necessarily addressed by a new, technologically specific criminal prohibition.[87] If that is true, and if this assumption is valid, it would mean that the rules we have criticized for being "method" rules are really "result" rules, that is, each proscribes the infliction of a distinct, unique "harm." (And that would mean that the critique I have offered of the law's current approach to "misuse" rules is misguided and erroneous.)

We will assume for the purposes of analysis that this is indeed true so we can examine the validity of the underlying assumption. To do that, we need to divide "misuse" into two categories: (a) "misusing" a technology to inflict "harm" in a way that has not heretofore been possible (new crime) and (b) "misusing" a technology to inflict a "harm" that has been proscribed by criminal rules in a way that has not heretofore been possible (old crime, new method).

## New Crime

Logically, the first category seems to offer the strongest case for the validity of the postulated assumption because it posits a necessary linkage between a particular technology and the infliction of a unique, as-yet unaddressed "harm." If such linkages actually exist, then the rules adopted to control the infliction of the "harms" they produce will necessarily be "about" the technology involved; if the linkages do not exist, then the rules should, as we saw earlier, focus on the "harm" not on the technology.

---

[86]   In the United States, anyway, criminal rules are the product of legislative, rather than judicial, action. See LaFave, *1 Substantive Criminal Law § 2.1.*

[87]   Although it imports the rationale for the adoption of criminal rules, i.e., the infliction of "harm," the assumption derives from the strategy we use for defective implementation. This is apparent in its focus on the "use" of "technology" to inflict the "harm."

We will analyze the existence of this posited linkage by examining two real-world scenarios: (a) the situation early-twentieth-century legislators confronted when citizens began to become the targets of harassing telephone calls; and (b) the situation late-twentieth-century legislators confronted when websites began to become the targets of Distributed Denial of Service (DDoS) attacks.[88] Both scenarios involve the "misuse" of technologies to inflict unique, as-yet unaddressed "harms."

## Phone Harassment

A century ago, harassing calls were not a crime, primarily because harassment was not a crime at common law and had not been outlawed by statute.[89] A secondary factor contributing to the lack of criminalization was the novelty of the technology, which had as yet gone unaddressed by criminal law. Confronted with activity that inflicted an acknowledged but as yet unproscribed "harm," legislators had to adopt a new criminal rule. They could have done this in either of two ways: They could have, but did not, criminalize harassment; they could have, and did, criminalize "use"-of-a-telephone-to-harass. State legislators chose the second option because they focused on the "use" of a specific technology not on the peculiar "harm" being inflicted.[90]

In their defense, they may have assumed this *was* the "harm." That is, because law had not yet found it necessary to address the "harm" of harassment, they may well have assumed that harassment was unique to the telephone, that is, that it would be carried out—if at all—by telephone, and only by telephone. Given their historical vantage point, it would probably have been reasonable for them to assume this.

---

[88]  See "Denial-of-service attack," *Wikipedia*, http://en.wikipedia.org/wiki/Denial_of_service; DDoS attack "causes a loss of service to users . . . by consuming the bandwidth of the victim network or overloading the computational resources of the victim system." In a Distributed Denial of Service (DDoS) attack, the attacker uses a series of compromised personal computers which he or she controls remotely.

[89]  See Chapter 5.

As we saw in Chapter 5, harassment was not a crime at common law, but using words to provoke another was considered a type of assault. See LaFave, 2 Substantive Criminal Law § 16.3(b). See also *Commonwealth v. Bittenger*, 25 Pa. D. & C.3d 627, 628–629, 1982 WL 534 *2 (Pa.Com.Pl. 1982); *State v. Hazen*, 160 Kan. 733, 738, 165 P.2d 234, 238 (Kan. 1946). Using obscene language was a crime at common law, but the criminalization of obscene language derived from a concern about blasphemy rather than a desire to prevent the use of such language to harass or annoy someone. See IV William Blackstone, *Commentaries on the Law of England*, facsimile of 1st ed. 1765–1769 (Chicago: University of Chicago Press, 1979), 61.

[90]  See Chapter 5.

As we saw earlier, technology was only beginning to infiltrate "civilian" life; the telephone was among the first (if not the first) consumer technologies.[91] Since the telephone-harassment legislators' experience with technology was consequently very limited, they had no reason to believe that (a) other technologies would emerge and (b) some of these technologies would also be used to harass. Or, to phrase it differently, they had no reason to know that the telephone did not play a distinct, unique role in the infliction of the "harm" at issue (harassment) but was, instead, merely a method—one particular method—that could be employed to inflict the "harm." Looking back, we can see that the better course would have been to focus solely on the "harm" and criminalize harassment;[92] this would have eliminated the problems we noted earlier, such as the need for later legislatures to deal with harassment by computer (and, perhaps, for future legislatures to deal with harassment by other technologies).

We must conclude, then, that the assumption postulated above is not valid for telephone harassment and, by extension, is not valid for other varieties of technically mediated harassment, such as online harassment. While the emergent phenomenon of harassment required the adoption of a new criminal rule, the technology used to harass is not an integral part of the "harm" inflicted by harassment. Technology seems to have created the occasion for harassment to emerge as a type of socially intolerable activity, but it is only the method that is used to achieve an unacceptable result.

We now turn to a much more recent, but equally problematic "harm": DDoS attacks.[93]

## DDoS Attacks

A DDoS ("Distributed Denial of Service") attack is intended "to make a computer resource unavailable to its intended users. Typically the targets are . . . web

---

[91]  See Chapter 5.

[92]  See, *e.g.*, Haw. Rev. Stat. Ann. § 711-1106(1) (outlawing harassment).

[93]  See note 88. In recent years, DDoS attacks have been coupled with extortion demands; a common scenario is for an attacker to shut down traffic to an online casino and demand the payment of extortion money for letting the casino go back online. See, e.g., "Gambling Sites, This Is a Holdup," *Business Week* (August 9, 2004), http://www.businessweek.com/magazine/content/04_32/b3895106_mz063.htm. This type of attack presents far fewer legal issues than does a "pure" DDoS attack because it can always be prosecuted as extortion.

servers, the attack aiming to cause the hosted web pages to be unavailable on the Internet."[94] In the simpler, older DoS ("Denial of Service") attack, the attack comes from a single source; in the more evolved DDoS attack, it comes from "multiple compromised systems," each of which the attacker controls.[95] The DDoS attack overwhelms the targeted system: floods its "bandwidth or resources" until the website effectively goes offline and becomes unavailable to potential visitors.[96] Several years ago, for example, the Gibson Research Corporation's website was shut down by a DDoS attack launched by thirteen-year-old hacker.[97] Because the Gibson Research Corporation uses the website to market and sell the computer security software it produces, the attack "harmed" its ability to do business (and also, perhaps, somewhat undermined its credibility).[98]

The public became aware of DDoS attacks in 2000, when a series of attacks "left some of the Web's most high-profile sites staggering under . . . tens of thousands of bogus messages."[99] The attacks targeted Amazon.com, eBay, and CNN, among others, and caused hundreds of millions of dollars in losses; since then, DDoS attacks have only increased in frequency and sophistication.[100]

As noted above, a DDoS attack overwhelms the resources of the target website, making it inaccessible to would-be visitors and effectively taking it offline. DDoS attacks are a "misuse" of technology; the attacker "misuses" computer hardware and software to mount and sustain the attack, which "harms" the victim.[101] When a DDoS attack takes a commercial site offline, the company is "harmed" because it loses actual revenue, revenue opportunities and opportunities for

---

[94]  See "Denial-of-service attack," *Wikipedia*.

[95]  See *id.* For more on the techniques used in a DDoS attack, see Dave Dittrich, "Distributed Denial of Service (DDoS) Attacks/tools," http://staff.washington.edu/dittrich/misc/ddos/.

[96]  See "Denial-of-service attack," *Wikipedia*.

[97]  See Steve Gibson, "The Strange Tale of the Denial of Service Attacks Against GRC.com," http://www.grc.com/dos/grcdos.htm.

[98]  See *id.*

[99]  "Cyber-attacks Batter Web Heavyweights," CNN.com (February 9, 2000), http://archives.cnn.com/2000/TECH/computing/02/09/cyber.attacks.01/.

[100]  See *id.*; D. Ian Hopper, "'Mafiaboy' Faces up to Three Years in Prison,'" CNN.com (April 19, 2000), http://archives.cnn.com/2000/TECH/computing/04/19/dos.charges/. See also Dan Ilett, "Expert: Online Extortion Growing More Common," *CNET News* (October 4, 2004), http://news.com.com/Expert%3A+Online+extortion+growing+more+common/2100-7349_3-5403162.html; "Botnet," *Wikipedia*, http://en.wikipedia.org/wiki/Botnet.

[101]  See "Denial of Service Attack (DoS)," *Symantec*, http://securityresponse.symantec.com/avcenter/venc/data/dos.attack.html (denial of service software).

advertising and public relations. The same holds for attacks that target nonprofit sites maintained by government agencies, educational institutions, charities, religious institutions, or other groups; agency and educational sites cannot provide services, and charities and other groups lose opportunities to solicit financial and other support. There is also a "harm" if an attack shuts down a personal website an elderly gentleman uses to share information about his grandchildren and hobby; he has paid whatever fees are necessary to allow him to create the website and has the right to have it remain online, undisturbed.

DDoS attacks, therefore, clearly inflict "harm," though the precise type of "harm" can vary somewhat, depending on the target of the attack. But as they undeniably inflict "harm," DDoS attacks are not criminal, in traditional terms. The attacker shuts down a website but takes nothing so he commits neither theft nor extortion; the website is "interrupted" but not "damaged" or "destroyed," so we cannot construe his activity as damaging or destroying property, nor is it vandalism.[102] One could argue that a DDoS attack is analogous to false imprisonment because it effects a restraint on someone's "liberty," but the analogy fails because it does so indirectly; the object of the attack is a website, not a person.[103]

For our purposes, DDoS attacks are a contemporary analogue of the telephone harassment that emerged at the beginning of the last century. Although a DDos attack does not inflict the same "harm" as telephone harassment, it does inflict a new *type* of "harm," a "harm" criminal law has never before had to address. This presented late-twentieth-century legislators with precisely the same questions their counterparts had to deal with roughly ninety years before: What type of rule should we adopt in an effort to control the infliction of this "harm"? Is the assumption postulated above valid? Does the "misuse" of this particular technology inflict a *sui generis* harm that justifies our adopting a technologically specific criminal rule? Or is this (like telephone harassment) merely an instance in which new technology is the mutable method that is currently being "used" to inflict what is (or, more precisely, will become) a generic "harm"?

---

[102]   See Brenner, "Is There Such a Thing as Virtual Crime?", 1. A "pure" DDoS attack cannot be prosecuted under what we might call first-tier computer crime statutes, i.e., laws adopted to address gaining illegal access to a computer system and using such access to alter data or otherwise damage the system. Because the DDoS attacker carries out the attack from "outside" the system, there is no access and therefore no violation, even under these provisions.

[103]   See *id.*

DDoS attacks are a useful analytical tool because we do not have the benefit of hindsight to help us answer these questions. We must do so ourselves (with, as we will see in a moment, a little help from what legislators have already done). Logically, the first step is to identify the "harm"—the legal "harm"—resulting from a DDoS attack; once we do that, we can then analyze the significance of the role technology plays in inflicting that "harm."

(The DDoS "harms" noted above are true "harms," and they are factual "harms," which means they tend to be idiosyncratic. Criminal rules that target the inflic-tion of "harm"—by whatever means—cannot be idiosyncratic, if only because one of their essential functions is to provide clear guidelines as to what is, and is not, forbidden.[104] Battery is a good example; criminal rules defining "battery" as an offense essentially outlaw the "unlawful application of force to another."[105] The offense encompasses the infliction of bodily injury of basically any level of sever-ity and by any method that would qualify as a use of "force," for example, the use of bullets, knives, "sticks, stones, feet or fists."[106] But though the offense of battery can be *predicated* on the actual infliction of a variety of idiosyncratic factual "harms," the rule we have adopted to discourage the infliction of this type of "harm" is structured around a legal concept, a categorical, legal "harm."[107])

In identifying the legal "harm" caused by a DDoS attack, we need not start from scratch; some states and the federal system have adopted rules that criminalize such attacks. We can begin by consulting these provisions to see what they can tell us about the legal "harm" we need to address in criminalizing DDoS attacks.

Most of the states that have addressed this issue define the legal "harm" caused by a DDoS attack as denying computer services to those who are authorized to "use" the computer/computer system that is attacked.[108] Pennsylvania defines it more narrowly, that is, as impeding or denying "the access of information or initiation

---

[104] See Chapter 3.

[105] See LaFave, Substantive Criminal Law § 16.2 (2005).

[106] See *id.*

[107] See Jerome Hall, *General Principles of Criminal Law* (Indianapolis, IN: Bobbs-Merrill, 1960), 24.

[108] See Ariz. Rev. Stat. Ann. § 13-2316(A)(4); Ark. Code Ann. § 5-41-203(a)(1); Cal. Penal Code § 502(c)(5); Conn. Gen. Stat. Ann. § 53a-251(d); 11 Del. Code Ann. § 934; Fla. Stat. Ann. § 815.06(1)(b); La. Stat. Ann. § 14:73.4(A); Miss. Code Ann. § 97-45-5(1)(a); Ver. Ann. Missouri Stat. § 569.099(1)(2); Nev. Rev. Stat. § 205.477(1); N.H. Rev. Stat. § 638:17(III); N.J. Stat. Ann. § 2C:20-25(A)(b); N.C. Gen. Stat. Ann. § 14-456; Oh. Rev. Code § 2913.81(A); 21 Okla. Stat. Ann. § 1953(6); W. Va. Code § 61-3C-8; Wy. Stat. § 6-3-504(a)(ii).

or completion of any sale or transaction by users" of the system that is attacked.[109] The applicable federal statute treats a DDoS attack as inflicting the same type of "harm" as a computer virus that is, as "damaging" a computer.[110] The federal statute defines "damage," *inter alia*, as impairing "the availability of data, a program, a system, or information."[111] The state and federal statutes are all context specific; like the telephone harassment provisions, these statutes focus on the technology involved and specifically define "computer crimes" and criminalize attacks on a "computer" or "computer system."

Is the characterization of the legal "harm" resulting from a DDoS attack used in these statutes accurate? It is if we limit our analysis to the specific problem at hand: DDoS attacks. We understand DDoS attacks, we have experienced DDoS attacks, and the statutes noted above are our very literal response to such attacks. But is it likely that the core "harm" a DDoS attack inflicts is inevitably and exclusively the product of current computer technology? Or is it reasonable to assume that other, more evolved versions of computer or derived technologies may someday be used to inflict the core "harm" we associate with a DDoS attack? (This, of course, is what happened with the "harm" that began as telephone harassment.)

Because we cannot forecast the future, the only way we can hope to answer these questions is to determine if there are any extant real-world analogues of a DDoS attack; we said earlier that DDoS attacks themselves are something new in our experience, but perhaps if we parse the "harm" associated with a DDoS attack we can identify analogous (but not identical) "harms" that are inflicted by methods other than computer technology. The utility of this approach is that it focuses on what societies are really concerned about—"harmful" human behavior—instead of on the instruments employed in such behavior.

If we find there are real-world analogues of a DDoS attack, then the "harm" such an attack inflicts is clearly not a unique product of computer technology and should not, therefore, become the focus of a context-specific, technologically specific rule. If we find no real-world analogues of a DDoS attack, we may have to assume the "harm" such an attack inflicts is *sui generis*, at least for now. Even if we reach that conclusion, however, adopting context-specific rules predicated on the

---

[109]    18 Pa. Cons. Stat. Ann. § 7612(a).
[110]    18 U.S. Code § 1030(a)(5)(A)(i).
[111]    18 U.S. Code § 1030(e)(8).

"misuse" of computer technology is still not the best approach for controlling the infliction of this *"harm"*; we may want to structure these rules more generally so they anticipate the possibility that people can devise new ways to inflict this particular "harm."

Harassment, for example, was not *really* a new phenomenon; people certainly engaged in harassment prior to the implementation of telephone technology, and the severity and incidence of the "harm" did not justify a special criminal rule. The reason it did not justify such a rule was that until telephone technology was implemented on a wide scale, the only way one could harass another person in real-time was by doing so face-to-face.[112] Harassing someone face-to-face may have been emotionally satisfying for the harasser, but it also increased the risks he face: The victim (or a friend or a family member) might retaliate physically (which is no doubt why the common law only criminalized harassment when it was likely to provoke a physical confrontation),[113] the harassment might erode the perpetrator's standing in the community, or being identified as a harasser might have other negative consequences potential harassers did not wish to incur.

Telephone technology changed all this. It made harassment more attractive, and more common, by letting someone harass another in real-time but do so remotely and anonymously, which reduced the risks of identification and/or retaliation by the victim.[114] Telephone technology simply created new opportunities for the infliction of what had been an uncommon "harm."

If we examine the DDoS statutes summarized above, it becomes clear that the core "harm" each addresses is really a problem of access, in this instance of access to a computer system and the "data, program, or information" it provides. When we examine a DDoS attack from this perspective, we see that it really inflicts two distinct "harms:" One is that the person or entity which seeks, via a website, to

---

[112] It has, for centuries, been possible to harass someone in writing, via the post. This was obviously not a significant problem, though, because it did not produce rules that were designed to control the infliction of this "harm" (mail harassment rules). The reason for this probably the lesser degree of satisfaction the harasser derives from not being able to inflict the "harm" directly, in real-time. The harasser who relied on the post would have no way of knowing *if* his victim actually read his harassing missive or, if he she did, *when* she read it, and *when* the "harm" was inflicted.

[113] See Chapter 5.

[114] See Brenner, "Toward a Criminal Law for Cyberspace," 49–75 (effect of computer technology on criminal activity). See also Brenner, "Toward A Criminal Law for Cyberspace: Product Liability and Other Issues," 2.

provide access to data or information is denied the opportunity to do so because the site is effectively taken offline. The other "harm" is that those who would like to access the data or information on the attacked are denied the opportunity to do so, again because the site is effectively taken offline.

We could, as noted earlier, analogize the "harm" to the *operator* of the website to false imprisonment because the site is in a sense "imprisoned." Law has long criminalized false imprisonment, which it defines as intentionally "restrain[ing] another unlawfully so as to interfere substantially with his liberty."[115] As we also noted earlier, however, false imprisonment does not really apply here because it requires a *substantial* interference with someone's freedom of movement and freedom of action.[116] Because it derives from the more serious offense of kidnapping, false imprisonment assumes the victim has been "confined" in a place ("in a bounded area") and has consequently lost the capacity for independent, volitional action.[117] That is really not the "harm" at issue in a DDoS attack; as we noted earlier, the attack focuses on a thing—a website, usually—rather than a person.[118] The website operator's ability to provide access to the website has been curtailed, the operator himself or herself (or itself) otherwise still retains the capacity for free, unfettered action.

The same holds to an even greater extent for the other victims of a DDoS attack, the people who would like to access data or information on the compromised site but are denied the ability to do so. We can at least entertain the notion of analogizing the site operator-DDoS-victim to a "real" victim of false imprisonment because the site operator, like the "real" victim, suffers a type of confinement, in that the site operator has lost the ability to interact with the outside world via the compromised site. Though this analogy is inadequate to justify equating the "harm" a DDoS attack inflicts on the operator of the attacked site with the "harm" inflicted on the victim of "real" false imprisonment,[119] it has some factual basis, some logic

---

[115]   American Law Institute, Model Penal Code § 212.3. See also 2 LaFave, Substantive Criminal Law § 18.3; common law criminalized false imprisonment.

[116]   *Id.*

[117]   See *id.* See also *Black's Law Dictionary*, 8th ed., "False imprisonment" (St. Paul, Minn.: Thomson/West, 2004).

[118]   See Brenner, "Is There Such a Thing as Virtual Crime?", http://www.boalt.org/CCLR/v4/v4brenner.htm.

[119]   The scenario is analogous, as I have explained elsewhere, to two other online "harms:" the "harm" inflicted by hacking and the "harm" inflicted by aggravated hacking (or cracking). As I explain in "Is There Such a Thing as Virtual Crime?", it is possible to analogize the "harm" inflicted by hacking to the "harm" inflicted by criminal trespass, a venerable common law crime. See Brenner, id., 1. It is also possible to analogize the

to it. The "harm" a DDoS attack inflicts on would-be visitors to the compromised site is conceptually very different; like the victims of false imprisonment and the site operator victim of the DDoS attack, they, too, are "denied" something. But their freedom of movement in the real- and/or virtual world is in no way compromised by the attack; the "harm" they suffer is the inability (often the transient inability) to access data or information available on a specific site. They are, in effect, denied *entry* to the site, rather than being denied the opportunity to *leave* the site (or, in the instance of "real" false imprisonment, to leave the place of confinement).

The "harm" both victims (website operator and would-be website visitor) suffer is really a denial—a denial—of "access." The ability to seek, and to gain, access to a website (or other place) is a component of the "liberty" one loses in false imprisonment, but it is a much narrower, much more focused "harm." The "loss" of access, in either sense implicates, very different interests than does the "loss" of liberty that occurs when one is falsely imprisoned (e.g., taken captive); the "harm" in false imprisonment is one person's depriving another of volitional control over their life, for at least some period of time. The "harm" consequently implicates fundamental issues of human dignity and self-determination, along with some concern for the perpetrator's use of violence in effecting and/or maintaining the imprisonment. The "harm" involved in a DDoS attack goes not to liberty, not to human dignity and the capacity for individual self-determination, but, as we saw earlier, to "access."

The "loss" of access the respective victims suffer is actually a loss of opportunity: a loss of the opportunity to provide access (site operator) and a loss of the opportunity to seek access (would-be visitors). Since the inflicted "harm" in both instances centers on "access," the logical conclusion is that any criminal rule ("misuse" rule) implemented to discourage the infliction of this "harm" should be predicated on the concept of "access." Before we go any further, then, we need to define this concept. For the purposes of analysis (and for the sake of simplicity), we will use the definition that already appears in a number of computer crime statutes. These statutes define "access," in the computer context, as "to instruct,

---

"harm" inflicted by aggravated hacking (cracking) to the "harm" inflicted by real-world burglary, another venerable common law crime. See id. In both instances, however, the analogy is too weak to bring the infliction of the online "harm" within the definition of the traditional, real-world crime. The better approach, therefore, is to define a new crime encompassing the infliction of each type of online "harm."

communicate with, store data in, retrieve data from or otherwise make use of any resources of a computer, computer system, or network."[120]

If we translate this definition into the real-world context, the analogue is denying someone access to a place and to the services it provides; websites are, after all, the cyber version of real-world "places," and they do provide services in the form of data, commercial transactions, and other interactions. Although there are no criminal rules that address denying or impeding access to a place, as such,[121] the phenomenon of denying access is not entirely unknown in the real world.

It has arisen, for example, in anti-abortion protests in which demonstrators mass to block or impede women's access to an abortion clinic and the services it provides.[122] The First Amendment protects such demonstrations and therefore prohibits criminalizing the acts of massing outside clinics or other places to express one's views on a particular issue.[123] The Supreme Court has, however, upheld rules,—noncriminal rules—that are designed to preserve the right of access to an abortion clinic.[124]

The activities of anti-abortion and other protestors are, however, an imperfect analogy for the "harm" caused by a DDoS attack because the only purpose of a DDoS attack *is* to inflict "harm," that is, to deny the opportunity to provide or to gain access. The "harm" caused by the protestors' activities is an incident of their primary purpose (which is usually lawful in itself), but it is not their only goal. The real-world protestor analogy is useful, though, because it draws our attention to two propositions relevant to the issue under consideration.

One is that as things currently stand with DDoS attacks, we have (as we had with telephone harassment) technologically specific criminal rules which target a "harm" that *can* transcend the use of a specific technology (computer

---

[120]   See Ariz. Rev. Code § 13-2301(E)(1); Idaho Code § 18-2201(1); Kansas Stat. Ann. § 21-3755(a)(1); N.J. Stat. Ann. § 2C:20-23(a); W. Va. Code § 61-3C-3(a).

[121]   There are statutes that criminalize "unlawful assembly," but they are concerned with preventing riots, not with denying "access." See Alaska Stat. § 12.60.180 ("unlawful or riotous assembly").

[122]   See *Madsen v. Women's Health Center, Inc.*, 512 U.S. 753, 757–759 (1994).

[123]   See *id.*, 773–776. See also *NAACP v. Claiborne Hardware Co.*, 458 U.S. 886, 917 (1982).

[124]   See Madsen v. Women's Health Center, Inc., 770–771.

technology).[125] It seems likely that here, as with telephone harassment, we have a "harm" which *can* be inflicted in the real world but is not because its infliction in that context is fraught with difficulties and/or consequences that discourage its occurrence, except in unusual situations such as the abortion protests.

The second, derivative proposition goes not to the "harm" that is inflicted by denying "access" (of whatever type) but to the "harm's" emerging in a new guise as a distinct threat to social order. Here, as with harassment, a new technology created new opportunities for inflicting what had been an extant but uncommon "harm." Real-world denial of access has been of little concern to the law because of the physical difficulties involved in inflicting the "harm."

To deny others access to a facility in the real world, I need a group of individuals who are willing to physically block access to that facility for whatever period of time I (we) deem adequate. It is at least within the realm of possibility that I can recruit such a group when the denial of real-world access supports a political or social issue they care about. It is unlikely, to say the least, that I could recruit such a group to block access to a facility for my own amusement or out of a desire to exact personal "revenge" on the owner or operator of the facility. Lacking a higher motive, my potential recruits would no doubt be disinclined to participate unless I paid them (which could be quite problematic). And even if I could summon the resources to hire a group to block access to a physical facility, they might well hesitate for fear they would be sued, be embarrassed publicly (which could have negative consequences for their employment and private life) or even be charged with unlawful assembly. (As was noted earlier, there are state statutes that criminalize "unlawful assembly," but they do so to discourage the "harm" of rioting, not the "harm" of denying access.)[126]

Here, as with harassment, computer technology eliminates these disincentives and difficulties and makes it possible for me, acting alone, to launch a DDoS attack for revenge or for caprice—because I am bored or because I want to experiment

---

[125]   Denying access has been criminalized in at least one other context: A few state statutes criminalize denying access in the context of disrupting funeral services. See Ala. Code § 13A-11-17(a)(2) (crime to block access to the facility being used for a funeral service); Vernon's Texas Penal Code § 42.055(a)(3)(C) (same); Wis. Stat. Ann. § 947.011(2)(a)(2). These statutes, however, are more about disrupting a funeral than they are about guaranteeing access to a particular facility, a particular place.

[126]   See Alaska Stat. § 12.60.180 ("unlawful or riotous assembly"); Cal. Penal Code § 726 (same); Ky. Rev. Stat. Ann. § 525.050 (same).

with the DDoS technology. This suggests that as technology continues to evolve, we will see the emergence of new ways of inflicting the "harm" of denying access (and, no doubt, new ways to inflict other extant but still inchoate "harms").

We know access will only assume an increasing importance in an era of "smart," ambient technology.[127] Today's DDoS attacks aggravate potential visitors to websites and prevent the operators of those sites from supplying the data or services they provide for profit, for the social good or for self-realization. These "harms" are real, not trivial, but they pale in comparison to the "harms" future attacks might inflict. Tomorrow's versions of DDoS attacks could imprison people in their homes or offices, cause massive traffic accidents and even inflict serious, targeted physical injury by interfering with the proper functioning of brain or other physiological implants.[128] (The implants we described in Chapter 6 are all trivial—experiments with a new technology. If people begin to depend on implanted technology, its failure to function could have serious consequences for their physical and/or mental health.)

It is, unfortunately, only reasonable to assume that some individuals will find the idea of denying access to those technologies engaging, even absent a desire to use the denial for other criminal purposes. (DDoS attacks began as experiments with computer technology, what we might call "recreational" DDoS attacks. They have since evolved into something more sinister; organized crime and other professional criminals now use DDoS attacks to commit extortion and financially motivated crimes.[129])

It is also reasonable to assume that the techniques they will use to deny access—and the technologies that provide that access—will bear little if any resemblance to the "computers" we rely on today. For us, computers are boxes: desktops, laptops, handhelds, servers. The boxes may be networked, but they are, and we still approach them as, a free-standing device with specific, idiosyncratic uses. As we saw in Chapter 6, "smart," ambient technology will eliminate the boxes and embed some future iterations of computer technology into our environment (and

---

[127]   See Chapter 6.

[128]   See Chapter 6.

[129]   See Jaikumar Vijayan, "E-Business Sites Hit with Attacks, Extortion Threats," *Info World* (September 24, 2004), http://www.infoworld.com/article/04/09/24/HNattax_1.html?INCIDENT%20RESPONSE; Jack M. Germain, "Global Extortion: Online Gambling and Organized Hacking," *Tech News World* (March 23, 2004), http://www.technewsworld.com/story/33171.html.

ourselves);as the boxes disappear, the concept of denying access to "a computer" becomes untenable.[130]

Assume, say, that in ten years one of my law students holds a grudge against me for the C- she got in my Criminal Law class. To get back at me, she exploits the "smart," ambient technologies that have been implemented by then to shut down the heating in my "aware" home on a cold, January night. Has she denied me access, either, to "a computer" or to "computer services"? One conceptual problem with characterizing this as a denial of access indistinguishable from that inflicted by a DDoS attack is that while my "aware" home and the heating system it oversees both rely on an evolved version of computer technology, they are far, far from being the "box" computers we know today. Another conceptual problem with characterizing this as a DDoS-style denial of access derives from the nature of my relationship with these technologies; as we saw in Chapter 6, I do not "use" them in the way I "use" today's "box" computers. Instead, I "interact" with them because the "aware" home, at least, is not only ambient technology, it is also intelligent.

Assume another scenario. Assume that, ten or fifteen years from now Jane Doe's former, disgruntled boyfriend exploits the "smart," ambient technologies that are then in general use to disable her automated motor vehicle as she is on her way to work, leaving her stranded on a cold, January day. Has he denied her access to "a computer" or to "computer services"?

Here, again, we are dealing, not with contemporary "box" computer technology, but with "smart," ambient technology —complex, evolved computer technologies that are functionally intertwined with a myriad of other technologies and that are autonomous, at least to some extent. Many of these technologies (my "aware" home) will be both an "entity" (artificially intelligent) and a "they" (part of many interlinked "entities"). Jane and I have both suffered a detriment (a "harm") by being denied access to "something." From our vantage point, however, the "something" we have lost is not (as with a DDoS attack) the opportunity to use our own efforts to gain or provide access to a "box" computer or computer network composed of linked "box" computers.

---

[130] The technology will presumably be predicated on evolved versions of our computer technology, but that does not mean it will be "a computer." A dial-up modem, for example, uses a telephone line to connect a computer to the Internet, but it most definitely is not "a telephone." See "Modem," *Wikipedia*, http://en.wikipedia.org/wiki/Modem.

We have "lost" something else, something that may, though, be analogous to the opportunity "loss" inflicted by a DDoS attack. If we characterize the "loss" as a "loss" of services (services of my "aware" home and her automated, presumably "aware" vehicle) then our "loss" is credibly analogous to the "harm" inflicted by a DDoS attack. Because the services are automated, the interference with my heat and Jane's vehicle both implicate (at least in an attenuated sense) our respective ability—our opportunities—to "access" a sixth- or seventh-generation version of contemporary computer technology.

We reach the same conclusion if we alternatively characterize the "loss" Jane and I respectively suffer as an interruption in our relationship with an intelligent entity (my "aware" home or Jane's intelligent vehicle) because the actual "harm" resulting from the interruption of each relationship is a specific, focused loss of commercial services. These relationships are "service" relationships; the only purpose my "aware" home and Jane's intelligent vehicle have is to "serve" us.

And we can conceptualize the "loss" one suffers in a DDoS attack as a loss of service, though not the sophisticated, personalized services that are involved in these hypotheticals. In a DDoS attack, the attacked site clearly suffers a loss of service in that it "loses" the ability to utilize the Internet services (access) for which it is paying. And the same is true, albeit to a lesser extent, of the potential visitors to the blocked site; they have not entirely lost the "use" of the Internet services for which they are paying, but they have "lost" a portion, an aspect, of those services in that they cannot access a particular website.

There is, however, at least one conceptual difference between a DDoS attack and the events hypothesized above. In the attacks on my "aware" home and on Jane's intelligent vehicle, the technology does not play the central role it plays in contemporary DDoS attacks. DDoS attacks are "about" denying access to computer technology, not interfering with access to heat and transportation. We have the core "harm" of denying someone something to which they are lawfully entitled, but the "harm" takes a different and potentially more serious form.

Imagine, for example, that Jane's former boyfriend intentionally disables her automated vehicle as it is traveling in a high-speed lane on an automated highway. While the highway would presumably be programmed to deal with situations such as this, it is still possible that disabling her vehicle could cause Jane physical injury. Or assume that instead of shutting down my heat my former, disaffected student locks me out of my bank accounts and voids my credit cards so I have no access to funds. While this might not be life threatening in the short run, it would be certainly be inconvenient.

This brings us back to the first proposition: the logical and empirical inadequacy of utilizing context-specific laws to address the core, legal "harm" inflicted by denying access to (evolved and unevolved) computer services. Some would argue that DDoS statutes such as those described earlier are sufficient to deal with denial of access "harms" for the foreseeable future. They could point out that the implementation of "smart," ambient technology is not imminent, so the issues outlined above are not likely to arise for some time. And that is true; "smart," ambient technologies are, as we saw in Chapter 6, being developed and are already being implemented selectively, but it will be some years before they even begin to become the dominant technology.

The problem with the argument postulated above is that the "harm" associated with DDoS attacks will not remain where it is. As we saw earlier, even though they are now being exploited for extortion, DDoS attacks still target only the technology, as such; DDoS extortion succeeds because the operator of a website pays to have the attack stop, usually so the site's commercial customers can continue to access it and thereby ensure the operator's revenue stream. It is already apparent, however, that the attacks can evolve and expand the "harms" they inflict. A conventional DDoS attack targets the technology by shutting down access to a website. Denying access may be the only "harm" the DDoS perpetrator seeks to inflict (which was true in the early days of DDoS attacks), or it may be coupled with another, consequential "harm"—exploiting the site shut down to extort money from the site owner.

A recent case from California illustrates how even a contemporary-style DDoS attack could be used to inflict "harms" of much greater severity. Christopher Maxwell and two associates created a botnet—a network of compromised civilian computers—and used it to install adware on people's computers without their permission.[131] Their purpose was to receive the money the adware companies

---

[131] See U.S. Department of Justice, Press Release: California Man Pleads Guilty in "Botnet" Attack That Impacted Seattle Hospital and Defense Department (May 4, 2000), http://www.usdoj.gov/criminal/cybercrime/maxwellPlea.htm:

In simple terms, a botnet is created when a computer hacker executes a program over the world wide web that seeks out computers with a security weakness it can exploit. The program will then infect the computer with malicious code so that it becomes essentially a robot drone for the hacker (also known as a

paid them for installing their product on as many computers as possible.[132] Unfortunately, without ever intending to do so Maxwell and his associates launched a DDoS attack that targeted a hospital:

> As the botnet searched for additional computers to compromise, it infected the computer network at Northwest Hospital in north Seattle. The increase in computer traffic as the botnet scanned the system interrupted normal hospital computer communications. These disruptions affected the hospital's systems in numerous ways: doors to the operating rooms did not open, pagers did not work and computers in the intensive care unit shut down.[133]

Because the DDoS attack was an unanticipated, unintended by-product of the botnet's intended activities, the hospital's backup systems were not disabled, so it was able to maintain an adequate level of patient care.[134] This probably would not be true if someone —a terrorist or a very disturbed person—were to intentionally launch a DDoS attack at a hospital for the *purpose* of shutting down its computer systems and inflicting physical "harm" (even death) on its patients. If this were the perpetrator's goal, he would no doubt ensure that the backup systems were compromised, as well. Here we have a intermediate scenario, one that falls somewhere between conventional DDoS attacks (for experimentation or for profit) and the evolved DDoS attacks on my hypothetical "aware" home and Jane's hypothetical automated vehicle.

This example should illustrate the pitfalls involved in relying on context-specific "misuse" rules that focus primarily, if not exclusively, on technology. In the scenario hypothesized above, the perpetrator does "misuse" computer technology to shut down the computer systems at the hospital; we therefore have the "harm" inflicted by a DDoS attack, that is, a denial of access to computers and a computer network. But that is only a small part of the actual "harm" the perpetrator has inflicted. He did not *merely* cause the hospital to suffer the "harm" of losing computer access; instead, he used the denial of access—the DDoS attack—to inflict physical injury and death on those being treated in the hospital.

---

"botherder") controlling the botnet. The computer is ordered to connect to the communications channel where the botherder issues commands. Botnets can range in size from just a few computers to tens of thousands of computers doing the bidding of the botherder.

[132] See *id.*

[133] See *id.*

[134] See *id.*

How should the law deal with this situation? It is obviously a DDoS case, but it is also more than that. The issue is how we should deal with the "more than that" aspect of the case. Do we need to devise specific laws that criminalize the "misuse" of computer technology to cause death and physical injury? Do we, in other words, need to focus on the fact that this perpetrator used computer technology (instead of a bomb) to cause injury and death? Is there any logical reason to link the perpetrator's use of technology (a DDoS attack) with the nontechnological "harm" he inflicted? Or should we simply treat his infliction of the nontechnological "harm" as assault and murder?

As this and the other examples given above should demonstrate, technology is not our true concern; our true concern is with human behaviors and the "harms" they can inflict. As we saw earlier in this chapter and in Chapter 5, rules predicated on "misusing" a particular technology to inflict "harm" are limited in scope and are therefore likely to become inadequate and/or obsolete. We can deal with both problems by revising and updating the rules, but there is a better way to approach "misuses" of technology. We need to discard our reliance on context-specific rules and the strategy from which they derive. We need to quit focusing on the "misuse" of a "technology" and focus on what criminal rules should address: the infliction of socially intolerable "harms" (by whatever means). This shift in strategy resolves the practical issues generated by the increasingly accelerated pace of technological innovation; if early twentieth century legislators had criminalized harassment (by whatever means), use-of-a-computer-to-harass rules would have not been needed.

## *"Harm"*

This shift in strategy also resolves the conceptual issue we examined earlier: the increasing untenability of assuming that we "use" technology. Our "misuse" rules are not "technology" rules at all; their real concern is not technology, but the human infliction of socially intolerable "harms." Technology is merely a method, a vehicle we can use to inflict "harm." The practice of incorporating the "use" (or "misuse") of technology into the rules we use to control the infliction of socially intolerable "harms" is the product of an historical error; lawmakers confronting the application of technology to inflict more-or-less novel "harms" reacted with an *ad hoc* solution, an extrapolation of the strategy they were already using to control defective implementation. In so doing, they erroneously assumed there *was* a logical, inevitable linkage between the "harm" and the technology at issue;

this was an understandable assumption given their relative inexperience with technology, but we must not continue their error.

How, then, should we approach the DDoS scenarios set out above? In each, we have the infliction of "harm" in new and varied ways, ways that will certainly be repeated unless we take steps to discourage others from following in our respective perpetrators' footsteps. The scenarios therefore raise a critical issue, one we should always consider when new technologies are utilized to inflict what seem to be "new harms": Do we *need* new rules—new laws—to deal with the various "harms" inflicted in the hypotheticals given above?

As we saw earlier, basic DDoS attacks themselves required the adoption of new law because they inflict "harm" of a type and in a way that was not possible prior to the development and widespread implementation of computer technology. But we now have rules criminalizing DDoS attacks; we can use these rules to prosecute the perpetrator in each of the hypotheticals for launching a DDoS attack and inflicting the "harm" caused by such an attack. The criminal DDoS statutes described earlier—especially the federal DDoS statute—would encompass the conduct at issue in all of our hypotheticals, even the "evolved" ones dealing with my "aware" home and Jane's automated vehicle.

Is that enough? Do we need additional laws to address the incremental "harms" that are inflicted when a DDoS attack targets newer, more complex technology? These questions arise for the "evolved" technology hypotheticals involving my "aware" home and Jane's automated vehicle. We will assume, for the purposes of analysis, that these attacks involve the "misuse" of computer technology that is far more sophisticated than that currently in use. The technology is therefore different, and that means the structure and process of the DDoS attack is different, as well. The logic of the attack is different, as well. A contemporary DDoS attack shuts down a website posted on the Internet; the site therefore targets a "public" area and, in a sense, occurs in a "public" place. The DDoS-style attacks on my "aware" home and on Jane's automated vehicle both target "private" areas, and the attack on my home, at least, seems to occur in a "private" place. Does any of that matter? Do any of those incontestable empirical differences warrant the adoption of new criminal rules to deal with instances such as these?

The answer to those questions lies not in the incidents of the attacks—the nature of the technology employed, the "public"-"private" conceptualization of the arenas where the attack occurred—but in the "harms" they inflict. If the only "harm" inflicted on Jane and on me is a denial of service (vehicle service and home service), then the "harm" is indistinguishable from the "harm" at issue in a contemporary DDoS attack. We might need to tweak the language of our existing DDoS statute to ensure they encompass the actual mechanics of these evolved attacks, but adopting new laws that somehow encompass the technical circumstances involved in the attacks is not needed.

This should be our guiding principle in deciding whether we need to adopt new laws to address innovation in the "use" of technologies to inflict "harm." The dispositive question is, "Does this inflict a `harm' that has not been addressed by our criminal law?" The answer for all the hypotheticals given above is, "no." The hospital attacker can be prosecuted for (a) the DDoS attack, (b) assault (if patients are injured as a result of the attack), and (c) murder (if any patients die because of the attack). The same answer would apply if Jane or I were injured or killed as a result of the respective attacks on her vehicle and my home.

## New Method

Method rules, as we saw earlier, target the infliction of categorical "harms" by particular means, which usually involve technology. Telephone harassment rules are an example of method rules that targeted an as-yet unproscribed "harm." But method rules can also target already-proscribed "harms." As we saw earlier in this chapter, "computer method" rules that target already-proscribed "harms" are quite common, and are still being adopted. We now need to decide if method rules are an appropriate way to deal with either type of "harm."

The analysis given in the section above will determine the advisability of using a method rule to address a particular unproscribed "harm." Criminal law will obviously need to adopt a rule designed to discourage the infliction of this new "harm"; the issue to be resolved is not the need to adopt *a* rule, but whether the rule that is adopted should be predicated on (a) the method (the technology) that is employed to inflict the "harm" or (b) only on the "harm." If the "harm" is severable from the method—as with harassment—then the rule should focus only on the "harm," for reasons noted in the section above. If the "harm" is intrinsically bound up with the technology—as seems to be true for DDoS attacks—then the rule should focus on the method as well as on the "harm." (It would presumably be very difficult, not to mention counterproductive, to disentangle the "harm" and the method.) As we saw in the previous section, "harm" rules should be the norm; method rules should be the exception.

What about using method rules to target already-proscribed "harms"? Can there be any justification for this, because the "harm" has already been addressed by proscriptive criminal rules? Logically, there are two possible justifications for adopting method rules that target already-proscribed "harms," only one of which can be valid.

We begin with the one that can be valid. New method rules targeting already-proscribed "harms" are valid when two conditions are met: (a) the existing rules are *necessarily* method rules, that is, it is simply not possible to adopt a general, nonmethod rule that targets the core "harm" at issue; and (b) the existing rules do not adequately address the "harm" being inflicted. The second condition exists when a change in circumstances—such as the implementation of new technology—results in the "harm's" being inflicted in ways that are simply not encompassed by the existing method rules.

The general federal statutes outlawing fraud can be construed as an example of this: Section 1341 of title 18 of the U.S. Code makes it a federal crime to use the mails to commit fraud; section 1343 of the same title makes it a crime to use wire, radio or television communications in interstate or foreign commerce to commit fraud. Section 1030(a)(4) of title 18 of the U.S. Code criminalizes the use of a "protected computer" to commit fraud; a "protected computer" isa computer used by the federal government or in interstate or foreign commerce.[135]

One can argue that § 1030(a)(4) is redundant because it reaches conduct that has already been criminalized by § 1343. If someone used a computer with dial-up or wired cable modem access to the Internet to commit fraud, the signal would travel in interstate commerce via "wires" and could therefore be prosecuted as wire fraud under § 1343.[136] The § 1030(a)(4) offense is redundant in this scenario but there are occasions when § 1343 could *not* be used to prosecute the use of a computer to commit fraud: (a) arguably, at least, when the signal traveled wirelessly; and (b) when the perpetrator used a computer that was not linked to the Internet

---

[135]   See 18 U.S. Code § 1030(e)(4)(A)-(B). It also encompasses computers used by a financial institution or by the U.S. government. See 18 U.S. Code § 1030(e)(4)(A).

[136]   See *United States v. Schreier*, 908 F.2d 645, 646 (10th Cir. 1990), *cert. denied*, 498 U.S. 1069 (1991).

to commit fraud.[137] The wireless scenario is probably self-evident, but I should probably give an example of the other possibility. A perpetrator could, for example, employ a computer that was not linked to the Internet to create false documents—falsified deeds, say—and then use them to defraud someone out of money. Though it is not linked to the Internet, the computer our perpetrator uses would qualify as a "protected computer" as long as it has even a relatively minor impact on interstate commerce; the owner's buying computer supplies from companies in other states might suffice.

We have established that § 1030(a)(4) is not totally redundant, but why, you may ask, it is necessary to have three separate method prohibitions for fraud? The answer lies, at least in part,[138] in the nature of the federal power to criminalize: "Federal criminal jurisdiction is limited by federalism concerns; states retain primary criminal jurisdiction in our system."[139] Use of the mails is the jurisdictional predicate justifying § 1341; the use of wire communications in interstate commerce is the jurisdictional predicate justifying § 1343; and the use of a computer in interstate commerce is the jurisdictional predicate justifying § 1030(a)(4).[140] It seems, then, that this particular configuration of method rules is valid given the jurisdictional constraints Congress operates under in adopting federal criminal provisions.[141] (More precisely, it seems this configuration is valid unless and until the use of wired and/or wireless communications and the use of computers becomes inextricably intertwined.)

We see similar configurations of method rules in state statures,[142] but they are more the product of history than jurisdictional constraints. American states are

---

[137] See *United States v. Butler*, 16 Fed. Appx. 99, 100 (4th Cir. 2001). Section 1343 is not redundant because it reaches the use of instrumentalities other than computers to commit fraud.

[138] History is another reason. The mail fraud statute dates back to 1872, long before people were using telephones to communicate. The wire fraud statute was added to the federal criminal code "in 1952 as an extension of the Mail Fraud statute to a newer form of communication." Peter J. Henning, "Federalism and the Federal Prosecution of State and Local Corruption," *Kentucky Law Review 92* (2003–2004), 75, 135n.229. The computer crime provision was added to the federal code in 1984. See Ryan P. Wallace, Adam M. Lusthaus, and Jong Hwan (Justin) Kwan, "Computer Crimes," *American Criminal Law Review 42* (2005): 223, 228.

[139] *United States v. Prentiss*, 206 F.3d 960, 967 (10th Cir. 2000).

[140] See Ryan Y. Blumel, "Mail and Wire Fraud," *American Criminal Law Review 42* (2005): 677, 680–681; Eric J. Bakewell, Michelle Koldaro, and Jennifer M. Tjia, "Computer Crimes," *American Criminal Law Review 38* (2001): 481, 492.

[141] It would seem prudent to combine the wire fraud and computer fraud provisions into a single fraud-other-than-by-mail provision.

[142] See 11 Del. Code § 913 (insurance fraud); 11 Del. Code § 913A (health care fraud); 11 Del. Code § 916 (home improvement fraud); 11 Del. Code § 2738 (computer fraud).

effectively presumed to have criminal jurisdiction, at least as long as the crime or an element of the crime occurred in their territory.[143] Absent jurisdictional or other constraints dictating the utilization of "method" rules, the "harms" these configurations target can more properly be addressed by collapsing the redundant provisions of discrete criminal statutes into an omnibus provision targeting the core "harm."

The second justification for method rules targeting already-proscribed "harms" is that because of its specificity, the existing rule does not encompass the version of the "harm" that results from utilizing a new technology. Theft is a classic example of this. Historically, theft was defined as the unauthorized appropriation of tangible property.[144] Theft of tangible property is a zero-sum event; the possession and use of the property passes wholly from Owner to Thief.[145] This zero-sum conception of theft encompasses the use of a computer to steal funds (by, say, initiating a wire transfer from Owner's bank to an account controlled by Thief) because the possession and use of the funds shifts entirely from Owner to Thief.

But the zero-sum conception of theft cannot encompass the use of a computer to "steal" data by copying it.[146] Copying data is "theft" in that the Thief gains something he did not have and is not lawfully entitled to have, but it is not a zero-sum transaction.[147] It deprives Owner of the *exclusive* possession and use of the data, but the possession and use of the data does not shift entirely from Owner to Thief; Thief has a copy of the data, but so does the Owner. In one sense, Owner has not "lost" anything because she still has the data; in another sense, however, Owner *has* lost something because she has lost the exclusive right to control, access and otherwise use the data.

States responded to this gap in their law in one of two ways: (a) by modifying the existing theft law so that it encompassed non-zero-sum theft (copying data);[148]

---

[143]  See *The Report of the ABA Task Force on the Federalization of Criminal Law* (Washington, DC: American Bar Association, 1998).

[144]  See Minn. Stat. Ann. § 609.52. See also 2 LaFave, Substantive Criminal Law § 19.4.

[145]  See Brenner, "Is There Such a Thing as Virtual Crime?", 1.

[146]  See *id.*

[147]  See *id.*

[148]  See West's Ann. Md. Code §§ 7-101(i)(2)(xiv) & 7-104.

or (b) by adopting a separate, "computer theft" rule.[149] As we saw earlier in this section, the only justification for adopting an additive method rule is the unavoidable specificity of the existing, necessary method rule. When, as is the case with theft rules, the excessive specificity of the existing rule is the product of nothing more than historical accident, the second alternative—adopting a supplemental method rule—is not valid.

## Summary

Over a century ago, societies began relying on an extrapolation of the approach they employ to control the defective implementation of technologies to address a very different phenomenon: the utilization ("misuse") of technology to inflict "harm" of varying types. This was an *ad hoc* solution to a perceived new problem—the assumption that "misusing" technology to inflict "harm" was a distinct type of antisocial behavior, one that required the adoption of new, context-specific "misuse" rules to keep it within acceptable bounds.

This solution is inapposite insofar as it focuses on technology instead of on the real concern: the infliction of "harm." As we have seen in this chapter and elsewhere, defective implementation rules are properly "about" technology, but rules targeting the intentional infliction of socially intolerable "harms" are "about" the harms not "about" the implements that are employed to inflict "harm."

The inappropriateness of this approach has begun to become apparent over the last decade or two, primarily due to the obvious proliferation of "misuse" laws. As we shall see in the next chapter, this increase prompted some to call for a new approach, one based on "harm" rules not on "technology" rules. As we shall also see in the next chapter, the calls for a new approach have fallen on deaf ears probably because we tend to cling to practices to which we have grown accustomed.

As we saw in this chapter, we simply will not be able to continue do this as our relationship with technology shifts from one of "use" to one of "interaction." Chapter 8 summarizes the implications this shift will have for the way we approach "misuse" rules, which are the primary focus of this book.

---

[149] See Minn. Stat. Ann. § 609.89 (computer theft). See also Cal. Penal Code § 502(c)(2). Rhode Island's computer theft statute is peculiar; it makes it a crime to take computer data with the intent to permanently deprive the owner of its possession and use, which seems to defeat the purpose of criminalizing "computer theft." See R.I. Gen. Laws § 11-52-4.

# Beyond "Misuse"

Before we proceed to Chapter 8, however, it is important to reiterate one point I have already made and raise an issue I have not yet addressed. The point I have made is that "misuse" rules are the primary, indeed, excusive, focus of this book. In Chapter 2, I explained why the analysis concentrates almost exclusively on the problem of "misuse." I will not repeat that explanation here, but I would like to note an issue I have not raised before: Although this book is exclusively about criminal ("misuse") rules, the analysis it presents will apply with equal force to any area of substantive civil law which is primarily concerned with channeling human behavior into certain, desired paths. This would include, for example, tort law and family law.

The issue I have not yet addressed goes to the other great division in law, the substantive versus procedural division. In Chapter 2, I explained how substantive civil and criminal law differ; basically, substantive law defines "rights" and "wrongs." We have seen in some detail how criminal law defines various "wrongs," each of which involved the infliction of some type of "harm." Civil law does that to some extent, notably in tort law, which allows someone to obtain civil damages from a person who has injured them "by accident," that is, negligently or recklessly. Unlike criminal law, however, tends to be purely proscriptive, civil law is also prescriptive; civil substantive laws also give people "rights." "Rights" are affirmative interests that can be enforced against others; when I bought my house, for example, I acquired the "right" (the property "right") to do certain things with it and to bar other people from doing things to it without my permission.

Procedural law is very different. Civil procedural law prescribes, essentially, how people can go about asserting and defending claims that "rights" have been violated. So civil trial rules specify how Jane Doe goes about initiating a legal action against a person who is alleged to have violated one of her "rights." Procedural criminal rules specify how the government goes about initiating a prosecution of someone who is alleged to have violated a criminal rule by inflicting a proscribed "harm" on someone.

There is, however, another huge category of criminal procedural rules. These are the rules that govern what government agents (law enforcement) can and cannot do in investigating crimes. In the United States, there is a vast complex of these rules at the federal level and there are correlate constellations of investigative criminal procedure rules in each and every state. They specify, for example, what government agents must do to be able to tap my telephone calls or obtain the contents of my emails; they also, as most everyone knows, specify what government agents must do in order to be able to enter my home and search it for evidence of crime. We have not considered how technology influences these rules, even though it has an obvious, and profound, influence; a hundred and fifty years ago, for example, government agents would not have known what it meant to "wiretap" a telephone conversation or to obtain "copies of emails." Now they do both routinely.

The same phenomenon we have analyzed in the context of substantive criminal rules ("misuse" rules) has affected procedural criminal rules. Over the last half century, these investigative rules have become increasingly technologically specific. The federal rules governing wiretaps and access to emails, for example, were adopted in the 1960s, were updated in the mid-1980s to encompass then-existing computer technology and have not been significantly updated or revised since; they are consequently out of date in large part. They assume technology that is no longer "used" and do not encompass technologies that are now routinely "used" in our society. Like the substantive "misuse" rules we have analyzed in detail, these procedural rules very much focus on technology. Because they are context-specific rules, that is, because they assume technology that was new and influential years ago, these rules cannot encompass the evolving technologies we examined in Chapter 6. But "smart," ambient technologies will have (indeed, are already having) a major influence on how law enforcement agents go about conducting their investigations.

The approach I argue for in this book can—and, I submit, should—apply with equal force to procedural rules such as these. Instead of focusing on technology, the rules that specific what government agents can/must do in the course of investigating crime should be predicated on a variant of the "harm"—inflicting behavior that is the proper predicate for criminal ("misuse") rules. Criminal procedural rules also need to focus on preventing the infliction of a type of "harm," though it is typically a different type of "harm" than that involved in substantive criminal rules. In this context, the "harms" to be prevented are things like unjustifiable law enforcement invasion of individuals' privacy or of their interest in the secure possession and "use" of their property. If use this as the conceptual premise of our criminal procedural rules, they will be far more flexible than rules based on specific technology; they will also be far less likely to become antiquated than rules based on technology.

A detailed description of how the approach I advocate for "misuse" rules can be applied in these and other legal contexts is quite beyond the scope or ambitions of this book. My goal, here, is simply to emphasize that while criminal rules are an obvious, and immediate, candidate for the implementation of this strategy, they are certainly not the only context in which it would prove advantageous.

.

# CHAPTER 8

# Implications

*. . . the global legislatosaurus. . . .*[1]

The value of the strategy outlined in the last chapter may seem obvious, but it apparently is not. For one thing, although some argue for eliminating our reliance on context-specific rules to control the "misuse" of technologies, others disagree.[2] For another, societies continue along the path of adopting context-specific rules to control emerging "misuses" of various technologies without ever analyzing whether this is (a) necessary and/or (b) advisable.

Forecasting the intertwined future of law, technology, and human behavior is a tricky proposition. We can reasonably assume—absent some extraordinary event such as Earth's colliding with an asteroid—that in the not-very-distant future technology of the type described in Chapter 6 will become an increasingly influential yet subtle force in our lives. We can also reasonably assume—subject to the same caveat—that technology will become far more complex (and far more intelligent) than it is today and that this will open up new possibilities for "misuse." And we can assume with complete assurance that criminals and would-be criminals will take advantage of these possibilities; as we saw in Chapter 2, criminals tend to be among the first adopters of new technologies.[3]

---

[1]  Charles Stross, *Accelerando* (New York: Ace, 2005), 122.

[2]  This debate centers around the advisability of adopting "technologically neutral" (vs. "technologically specific") laws. Compare Richard W. Downing, "Shoring Up the Weakest Link: What Lawmakers Around the World Need to Consider in Developing Comprehensive Laws to Combat Cybercrime," *Columbia Journal of Transnational Law 43* (2005): 705, 716–717, arguing for technologically neutral law; with Ellen S. Podgor, "Cybercrime: National, Transnational or International," *Wayne Law Review 50* (2004): 97, 101–102 (arguing for technologically specific law). See also Lionel Bentley, "Copyright and the Victorian Internet: Telegraphic Property Laws in Colonial Australia," *Loyola of Los Angeles Law Review 38* (2004), 71, 176: "the drive for 'technologically neutral' laws . . . comes . . . with the danger of bringing perfectly acceptable social practices into the realm of law . . . and unnecessarily juridifying life worlds."

[3]  See David Ronfeldt and John Arquilla, *What Next for Networks and Netwar?* in *Networks and Netwars: The Future of Terror, Crime and Militancy*, ed. John Arquilla and David Ronfeldt (Santa Monica, Calif.: RAND, 2001), 311, 313; available at http:// www.rand.org/publications/MR/MR1382.

To imagine how "smart," ambient technology will be "misused" is difficult for us because the context is so alien to us. If this book were being written in the 1950s, it would assume mainframe technology (only) and would consequently analyze how to control "misuse" by programmers and others with face-to-face access to mainframe computers. We are in a similar situation with regard to "smart," ambient technology; we know enough to understand the kinds of things it is *intended* to do but not enough to be able to forecast with any precision how it can, and will, be "misused."

We can, however, focus on the constant in "misuse": Human behavior resulting in the infliction of "harm." It is possible that—at some in the future—artificial, machine intelligences will evolve to the point at which they, too, can engage in "misuse." That the so-far parallel evolution of human and machine intelligences will fuse at some point to produce cyborgs and even creatures that are more machine than human is possible.[4] Many believe these scenarios are not only possible, but likely.[5] We have not specifically addressed the possibility of enhanced-human or nonhuman "misuse" of technology for two reasons. One is that, however likely it is that these scenarios will come to pass, that almost certainly will not happen in the near future; other-than-purely-human "misuse" is, therefore, not a matter of immediately pressing concern for lawmakers and, therefore, for this analysis.

The other reason is that the biological or other nature of the entities that are engaging in "misuse" may very well be irrelevant to the articulation of "misuse" rules. The core goal of "misuse" rules is to control socially intolerable behavior by intelligent beings; arguably, anyway, the methods we rely on to realize this goal (proscriptive rules coupled with sanctions) should apply with equal efficacy to enhanced human or even nonhuman intelligences.[6] It is certainly possible that the system of sanctions we have devised to deal with "regular" human malfeasance may not be as effective in combating "misuse" by enhanced human or nonhuman intelligences. On the other hand the loss of one's liberty or the loss of one's existence should be as effective in discouraging "misuse" by enhanced humans or nonhumans as they are for humans.

---

[4]  See Chapter 6.

[5]  See Ray Kurzweil, *The Singularity is Near* (New York: Viking 2005). See also "2005 BT Technology Timeline" (August, 2005), http://www.btplc.com/Innovation/News/timeline/TechnologyTimeline.pdf.

[6]  See Chapter 3.

We have several millennia's experience with the human capacity to inflict "harm" of varying types. Therefore, it is reasonable to assume that whatever methods humans, enhanced humans, and/or post-human intelligences employ for this purpose, the "harms" will remain relatively stable, that is, that our successors will continue to inflict the same general types of "harm" we have already encountered. Humans, at least, will continue to injure each other, damage others' property and attack the social order in more specific ways, all out of varying types and degrees of passion. Passion may or may not remain a purely human characteristic. Even if it does, we can assume that humans, enhanced humans and even nonhuman intelligences will, quite rationally, continue to appropriate others' property and take other measures to enrich themselves in impermissible ways.

Most of the cybercrime, indeed, most of the "misuse" of technology we have so far experienced, is merely old wine in new bottles—old crimes being committed by new methods. This is not to say that new types of "misuse" are not possible; DDoS attacks are, as we saw in Chapter 7, a new type of "misuse." But as we also saw in Chapter 7, we can apply the approach we have long used to deal with conventional, real-world-based "misuse" to more sophisticated technological iterations.

And yet, as we have seen, our legislative responses to these mostly conventional "misuses" of computer technology tend to overlook this—tend to ignore the behavioral constant in the "misuse" (the "harm") and focus on the technology. This is probably because our experience with technology, especially the "misuse" of technology, is still very much in its infancy. Technology still dazzles us; we therefore respond to what we see as "novel" and ignore the constant, the "harm."

Chapter 7 essentially assumed that for the most part there are no new "harms," that all we have is old wine in new bottles. This state of affairs may or may not persist. We may ultimately see the evolution of intricate new technologies the "misuse" of which does result in the infliction of a truly *sui generis* "harm."[7] As noted above, however, the approach I have outlined should be able to encompass that possibility, whatever form it takes. My argument is that we should predicate "misuse" rules on "harms," rather than on technology; this does *not* mean we should predicate "misuse" rules *only* on already-identified "harms." The goal is to pursue a parsimonious, flexible approach to the rules we use to control

---

[7]    See Chapter 7.

the "misuse" of technologies; such an approach allows, as it has in the past, for proscribing "harms" we have not previously encountered or have encountered but have not found significant enough to warrant a criminal rule. The approach I outline, which is simply a continuation of an approach that has worked in the past, gives us the flexibility to adapt to what is really new ("new harm"), instead of what seems to be new (use-of-new-method-to-inflict-old-"harm").

We must not be hypnotized by technology. We must analyze specific "misuses" in a dispassionate manner, always asking how significant the technology's contribution to the "harm" really is. And we must always keep in mind that "misuse" of technology rules are criminal rules and that criminal rules are about people in whatever guise, not about devices or systems or implants.

# Index

## A

access, denying, 167–170, 168n125
air travel, commercial, 11, 11n18, 97, 113n170,
    150, 152
Ambient Agoras, 124n6
ambient intelligence, 10n16, 126, 126n16,
    141n17–142n17
ambient technologies. *see* "smart" technologies
Apple Computer, Inc., 106, 106n140
ARPANET, 107, 108
AT&T, 92, 92n77
automobile technology, 77–91
    defective implementation laws, 82–85, 82n29, 88
    defective implementation laws, enforcing, 84–85,
        84n38
    driver's license laws, 82–85, 82n29
    European law, 80n22, 81n24
    history of, 78–79
    "misuse" laws, 87–90, 89n61, 111n167, 119, 144–145
    pervasiveness of, 79, 93
    public welfare offenses, 85–86
    rules as based on bicycle rules, 82, 82n28
    safety laws for, 80–82, 80nn22–23
    "smart", 1–2, 140–141, 141n15
    societal impact of, 79–80
    "use" laws, 82–84
    "using", 114
    vehicular homicide, 87–88, 89–90, 89n61, 118n198
    *vs.* telephone technology, 93–94, 100
autonomic computing, 126n16
"aware home", 140, 142

## B

Babbage, Charles, 105, 105n130
Bell, Alexander Graham, 91
Berners-Lee, Tim, 107
bicycle technology, 34–46
    bicycle traps, 36n50
    criminal fines, 36n49
    criminal law and, 44–46, 44n83
    early "harm" laws, 35–40, 35n49–36n49, 36n50

early "use" laws, 40–41, 43–44
implementation of, 35
influence of, 34, 34n43
"misuse" and, 44
modern "harm" laws, 39, 39n71–40n71
operator's license for, 82n31–83n31
origins of, 34n44–34n45
pervasiveness of, 34–35, 36, 37
professionals and, 65n170
theft of, 44, 44n83
*vs.* photography technology, 64–65
botnet, 172n131–173n131
"box" computer technology, 120, 170
bridge technology, electricity as, 74
Britain, telephone harassment law in,
    98n105–99n105
broadcast media technology, 100–104
    audience passivity and, 103–104
    as based on older modes of communication, 101
    beginnings of, 100n110–101n110
    defective implementation of, 104, 104n127
    "use" *vs.* "using", 103–104
    *vs.* telephone technology, 101
*Burger v. State,* 45n84

## C

capital punishment, 8
censorship, 53–54, 53n118
cinema technology, 100n110–101n110, 102
*City of Geneva v. Geneva Telephone Co.,* 59n142
civil law
    procedural, 181
    sanctions under, 8, 20
    *vs.* criminal law, 7–8, 20, 154, 181
Code of Hammurabi, 18n18
Commodore Business Machines, 106
common law
    rules of the road under, 38
    on telephone harassment, 99n105
    on watching and besetting, 99n105
*Commonwealth v. Kneeland,* 54n122
communication technologies, as not machine, 27